MOM'S HOUSE / DAD'S HOUSE

MOM'S / DAD'S HOUSE / HOUSE

Making Shared Custody Work

Isolina Ricci, M.A., L.M.F.C., Ph.D.

COLLIER BOOKS
Macmillan Publishing Company
New York

COLLIER MACMILLAN PUBLISHERS
London

Macmillan Publishing Company
866 Third Avenue, New York, N.Y. 10022
Collier Macmillan Canada, Inc.

Library of Congress Cataloging in Publication Data
Ricci, Isolina.
    Mom's house, dad's house.
    Bibliography: p.
    Includes index.
    1. Joint custody of children—United States.
I. Title.
[HQ777.5.R53   1982]   306.8′9   82-4494
ISBN 0-02-077710-8   AACR2

First Collier Books Edition 1982

10

Mom's House/Dad's House is also published in a hardcover edition by Macmillan Publishing Company.

Macmillan books are available at special discounts for bulk purchases for sales promotions, premiums, fund-raising, or educational use. For details, contact:

>   Special Sales Director
>   Macmillan Publishing Company
>   866 Third Avenue
>   New York, N.Y. 10022

Designed by Jack Meserole

Printed in the United States of America

This book is dedicated to my students, my clients, my open family of relatives and friends, my children's other family, and most especially to those in my own family—Cindy, Eric, Beth, Andrew, and Amy.

Contents

Preface

This book is a practical and systematic guide for parents which shows them how to build two homes for their children after divorce, even when the parents are not on friendly terms with each other. This approach, which I developed and refined over eight years as an educator and child and family therapist, goes beyond the concept of legal custody to a new way of reorganizing family life after divorce. It can be used by families with all types of custody and living arrangements and does not require that parents change their present divisions of time, authority, or responsibility.

The "two-home" approach means that, whenever possible, (1) each natural parent has at least *some* share in the parenting (hence, "shared custody"), (2) that each parent has an independent and meaningful relationship with the children no matter how the children's time is divided, (3) that children have a right to be out of the middle of their parents' disagreements, and (4) that each parent has a right to an independent life without interference from the other parent. The first two chapters will describe these principles, how they can work for you even if the other parent is uncooperative, and how you can best use this book.

The remaining fourteen chapters and eight appendices show, in practical, step-by-step ways, how parents have established two homes. They are a compilation of those aids parents found most effective and useful—checklists, self-surveys, descriptions, guidelines, sample agreements, examples of what other parents have done and how to design your own approach, drawing a little from one concept, a little more from another. The subjects covered in these chapters run the course from how to relate to your former mate to guidelines for negotiating your own agreement and to the dangers that recur two and three years after the divorce. A new vocabulary is offered which encourages parents to take a more positive view of life to replace the "broken home" view. The parent-to-parent interaction, for example, is not expected to be especially cordial or even cooperative, but it should be workable. Since it is a way of transacting necessary parenting business, I have coined the term "working relationship" for a process that allows parents to communicate, make plans, and control their feelings. While the two-home approach may not work for all parents, or be unsuitable or unwise for others, this "emotional divorce" which takes children out of the middle is something all divorced people should get for themselves regardless of whether or not they decide to make two homes for the children.

This two-home approach began in the early 1970s in community classes and groups for parents. It quickly grew into a permanent component of a continuing series of educational programs I developed at UCLA Extension, and the first Single Parent Program at Family Services, Santa Monica. From there, it spread to other West Coast universities and community colleges, and by 1975 courses were offered for social workers, attorneys, psychologists, and teachers. Since then, many parents and professionals have incorporated the concepts of the two-home approach into their personal and professional lives. In turn, their reports after months or years of use provide a continual basis for evaluating the effectiveness and usefulness of the techniques, frameworks, and concepts. Consistently, these people expressed a need for a clear, easy-to-read-and-use resource book that compiled the various aids. They wanted it for themselves, and to give to their older children, to friends, relatives, and to the professionals working with them.

I have tried to maintain a balance between mothers and fathers, parents in majority residence and those with minority time, without ignoring the importance of their differences. To protect the privacy of clients, students, and colleagues who have shared their experiences with me, all names, places, and identifying circumstances have been changed. Moreover, to allow readers to compare themselves with these parents, the examples in the book reflect representative composites of many personal experiences rather than isolated case histories.

The pages that follow are short on theory and long on practicalities. For those readers who wish more technical information, the Notes at the back of the book provides references and additional commentary.

The practical methods found on the pages that follow are not set in concrete. Rather they continue to evolve and adapt to changes in customs, behavior, and custody laws that surround the modern world of families and interpersonal relationships.

Mom's House, Dad's House remains a process—which you can take and make your own.

ISOLINA RICCI

Stanford, California

Acknowledgments

I am grateful to the many parents, children, colleagues, friends, and members of my immediate and open families who have contributed to this book. A number of these people are given specific mention in the Notes; still others left unmentioned know of my gratitude.

My appreciation to those who encouraged my work in the 1960s with families under stress, especially Marianne Wholman and Elizabeth Jones at Pacific Oaks College and my compatriots in the Christian Family Movement. A special thanks to Sallie O'Neill and George Esposito who provided me with the opportunity to develop the first programs for single parents at UCLA Extension and at Family Services, Santa Monica. I am much indebted to Lorraine Sanchez, Stuart Warner, Art Herman, and George Holland, the core leaders for the early parent workshops, for their ideas, experience, compassion, and enthusiasm; to Hugh McIssac and Meyer Elkin, present and past directors of the Conciliation Court of the Superior Court of Los Angeles County, for their encouragement; to Dr. Anne Steinmann for her continuing interest; and to Peter Getzoff, Jennifer Presley, Ellen Chaffee, Anna Nurenberger, Ann Metcalf, Beth Firstman, and Ron Ricci for their support, comments, and criticisms; and to my parents and my children for their understanding and patience.

A special thanks to Lois Clements and Margie Bresnahan for their unfailing good cheer and editorial perspective during the initial stages of this project, and to Sheila Vogel for her expert production of the final manuscript.

MOM'S HOUSE / DAD'S HOUSE

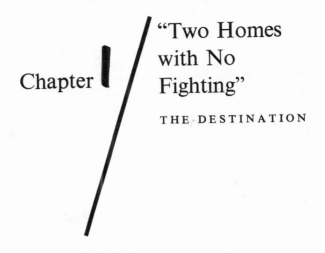

Chapter 1

"Two Homes with No Fighting"

THE DESTINATION

"Where do you live?" the middle-aged businessman asked the nine-year-old girl sitting next to him on the plane.

"I live with my dad in Oregon and my mom in California."

"I mean, where do you live?"

"I live with my dad in the summers and my mom during schooltime."

"I understand, honey," he said, "but where is your *real* home?"

The little girl looked as puzzled as her seatmate. Then she explained: "I have *two* real homes. My mom's house and my dad's house."

The businessman and the youngster spoke from widely separated views of the reality of life for parents and children after divorce. The man saw every divorce producing a "broken home" in which only one parent remains a real parent, while the other becomes an outsider or at best an interested spectator. He could conceive of only one home for any child, run by one parental authority.

The child, on the other hand, had seen her original home divide like a living cell into two complete new families. She seemed to be a loved and happy member of each. Her home wasn't broken—it had divided and multiplied. Her mother and father developed a way of raising her that seems highly unorthodox to most outsiders. Each parent felt that he or she was heading a family, even though, as further conversation disclosed, only one had remarried. The two homes under separate parental authorities gave the child time with each parent and the security of the agreement between her natural parents.

Given any voice in the matter, younger children will almost always choose the newer two-home alternative over the traditional one-home settlement with one parent consigned to the sidelines. The children I've worked with inevitably go straight to the heart of the issue, even when parents are caught in tunnel vision of a "real home." When they "visit" their noncustodial parent, they stake out territory. They leave behind books, shoes, pajamas, toothbrushes, homework. The kids are wisely, perhaps unconsciously, carving out their own place. They are saying, "I am your child. My things belong here, too. Don't forget me when I'm gone. This is my home, too." They shy away from words like "visit my Dad." Instead they say they're going to "be with my Dad" or "live with my Dad this summer." And for good reasons: outsiders visit; families live together.

Children, after they are convinced that they can't have both parents living together under one roof, will settle for both parents, separated, but still functioning as parents and families. One youngster, when asked what he saw as the ideal life for a child of divorced and/or remarried parents, put it simply: "two homes with no fighting."

This book is all about how to build this new family life, "two homes without fighting." The approaches described in this book have been developed over a period of eight years of working with parents and professionals. They have helped many parents achieve what they want—independent lives which include their children. Children have been given what they want—both parents, two homes, and less strife. What appears on these pages goes well beyond the traditional concept of child custody; it is a redefinition of family life, how to organize it, strengthen it, and keep it in Mom's house and Dad's house.

In order to follow the guidelines suggested here, neither parent is required to take on or to give up sole child custody. Although some parents with two-home arrangements keep traditional child custody/visitation arrangements, many choose the joint child custody arrangements which are just now gaining legal favor. Some parents have a fifty/fifty time-split between the homes, others an eighty/twenty or even a ninety/ten division. Some live but a few blocks apart, others are separated by thousands of miles. No one family is exactly like another.

Regardless of their differences, many parents have used the methods described in this book to learn how to stake out their own territory, set up their own standards, make their own agreements, and stay out of each other's hair. They have acquired the skills that allow them to wave a slow but definite good-bye to their old marriage, start a new parenting relationship, make a new life, and *keep the kids out of the middle.*

Parents have adapted the two-home approach to just about every conceivable circumstance—to former spouses who were friendly, angry, vindictive, possessive, dropouts; to those living down the street or across the continent; to those who had remarried, who were single, or who were in living-together arrangements. Even parents who were completely alone engineered unique cooperative "parenting" relationships with close friends or relatives.

The two-home approach can even function with a minimum of communication between you and the other parent. You do not have to love your former mate any more than you have to love your druggist in order to get a prescription filled. What you do need is a working relationship to help you carry out one of the most important jobs anyone ever undertakes —rearing your children.

How the Two-Home Approach Began

In the early 1970s I began my first seminars and classes in a southern California community. As a counselor, my intent was to share some of my research on families, support networks, and how the stress from divorce could be eased by people helping people. My focus at that time was on single mothers and their need to meet with others in the same boat—the search for new reference points and new friends. The reaction I got during the first few months of classes showed clearly that ending a marriage and reorganizing family life was a far more complicated phenomenon than I ever would have guessed.

The first and most obvious realization was that fathers—with and without custody—were just as important to children's post-divorce adjustment as were mothers. Furthermore, the needs of parents without custody were just as poignant and acute as those of parents with custody. The courses then were immediately expanded to include both parents regardless of their legal custody status, so as to provide both parents with a forum and a way to explore new ideas.

The second realization followed quickly: The traditional approach to custody just wasn't working. Countless girls and boys were left with "responsibility mommies" and "recreation director daddies" or worse, with overburdened mothers and dropout fathers. This approach didn't strengthen family life, it weakened it. The child's life was reduced by one parent; the custodial parent's responsibilities were doubled; the other parent was reduced to the status of a paying visitor. Such a lopsided arrangement bred distrust, resentment, and acrimony between the parents that did not diminish when one of them remarried.

A further discovery was that divorce precipitated a confrontation with many traditional values and beliefs, especially those that defined the best interests of children and dictated what made for a fit parent, a real family, and a good home. Fathers and mothers spoke up in anguish and in anger to tell of their frustration, their sense of powerlessness, and their search for new standards. There were feelings of failure, of shame, of resentment. Because people had been raised to believe that divorce meant failure and destruction of the family, they felt that a one-parent home was automatically a second-class way to raise children. The parent with custody was viewed as heading an "incomplete" family and the parent without custody didn't have a family at all!

Finally, there is the fact that even when the parents and the court decided on a good and fair custody arrangement, the settlement alone meant little if the parents didn't know how to put it into practice. A first-class legal agreement is at best a good piece of surgery. It cuts asunder one relationship (husband-wife) and applies stitches to another (parent-child). But a court award can't prepare parents for the *process* of ending a marriage and continuing their parenting any more than it prepared them for beginning marriage. What many parents found was that surgery could be a success, but the patient could die in the postoperative confusion. Parents needed to know how to make agreements work in daily life.

Of course, not all legal agreements are first-class, nor are they all arrived at justly. Most people have seen divorcing acquaintances engaged in a tug-of-war over their children. The battling "exes" who drag themselves and their children through court confrontations may make good dramatic material, but in truth they are a small percentage of the couples who divorce. About nine out of ten couples reach out-of-court agreements —sometimes alone, sometimes with a mediator or a counselor, most often through their attorneys. Although the underlying issues of custody and visitation lie at the heart of many difficulties for parents, the overwhelming majority of them will not take their dissatisfactions into the courtroom. They either can't be bothered, don't have the money, or just don't want to take the risk of making things worse. There has been little in the legal system that has introduced the idea of two homes or reinforced *both* parents for being closely involved with their children.* So, parents looking to the law for help are not likely to find it.

One father, after learning about two-home arrangements, said in hurt and anger, "Nobody told me three years ago that I could have this when I was going through a divorce. They all told me—the judge, attorneys, and friends—that I had to give my wife sole custody, I had to take limited visitation. They all said there was no other way. Now I've lost three years."

These realizations—that both parents are equally important, that the traditional custody arrangements could be destructive, that stigma and bias against divorced families demoralized their efforts, and that the legal process was only a part of the problem—led to a greater understanding of

---

* A pioneering California child custody law, in effect since January 1, 1980, expects that, whenever possible, a child should have close and continuing contact with *both* parents.

the two-to-three-year family reorganization process. From this understanding, the two-home approach was born.

The Principles for a Good Divorce and Two Real Families

Over the first three years of workshops and private counseling sessions, the "how" of the family reorganization process took shape. Certain patterns emerged which revealed natural yet powerful processes marked by recognizable stages. The "good divorce" was not a mystery. It yielded to systematic training and practice, much like driving a car on different kinds of roads in different traffic conditions. First a person has to learn how to drive, then with practice comes experience and expertise. The basic ingredients of a good divorce are things most parents can learn. Education and practice are the keys.

The first basic principles to emerge were:

· Each parent had a home, a family.
· Each child had two homes, two families.

Based on these two principles, the "second-home" parents learned to ignore the implications of being "visitors" and began to set up real homes with their own routines. The "first-home" parents began to relax, to feel less strained, less guilty. Both parents were encouraged to reject the myths about "broken homes," about being "second-class" families, and to move toward updating their language and their meaning of family. Both parents were offered guidelines to help them understand the impact which the end of the marriage had on their feelings and their bodies; they were encouraged to be respectful if not sensitive to the other parent. The final pattern to identify, however, was the most difficult to attain—how parents could retreat from their former relationship as mates while at the same time develop a civil working relationship regarding their roles as parents. Once this breakthrough happened and a working model tested true, the next path to new legal arrangements and to a clearer definition of parents' roles and communications with one another was found.

We all had our concerns, of course, and as might be expected, the most serious were about the children. We all questioned: "Would children be confused when there were two homes?" "Didn't children need one home base alone?" "What about the possibility of increased contact (or agitation) with a former spouse whom one would rather keep in the background?" The answer as to whether or not the children needed a single home base with only one authority came quickly. Every day most children demonstrate their ability to adapt to different authorities, different family rules. After all, they follow different rules at school, in their organized sports, in their neighborhood games, at camp. They live every moment of their lives in a fast-paced pluralistic world, where rules change with settings. They learn that at one house they get carrot sticks for snacks, while at another ice cream or cookies. One dad plays baseball with the kids, and another yells at them to shut up. Differences are the norm. Two-home parents found that the system usually worked as long as they adopted a principle of noninterference and kept children out of their personal problems. Furthermore, when the second-home parent began to act like a real parent again, children visibly relaxed.

Over the past few years, new research findings have begun to identify the important factors that lessen the impact of divorce: children who do best after their parents' separation are those whose parents make them feel loved and wanted in each home, who keep the children away from the parents' disagreements and bad feelings, who allow the children independent relationships with each of them. It seems, in short, that children do best when parents learn how to separate their roles as parents from their roles as former mates and lovers. As a result, the children are free to love them both without a conflict of loyalty, to have access to them both without fear of losing either. These same factors have long been part of the commonsense two-home approach.*

Briefly stated, what we have learned so far suggests a new family bill of rights and principles.

A New Family Bill of Rights

1. Each child has the right to an independent and meaningful relationship with each parent.
2. Each child has the right to be free from listening to or being part of parents' personal battles. Neither parent uses the child as a go-between or uses the time spent with the other parent as a threat or bargaining chip.
3. Each parent has the right and responsibility to contribute to the raising of his or her child.
4. Each parent has the right, during time spent with the children, to follow his or her own standards, beliefs, or style of child-raising without unreasonable interference from the other parent.
5. Each parent has the right to his or her own private life and territory.
6. Each parent and child have the right to call themselves families, no matter how the children's time is divided.

* See Notes for research references.

Principles of Two-Home Parenting

· When parents divorce, they divorce each other not their children.
· The parents' parenting functions can be systematically disentangled from their personal differences.
· Both mother and father pledge themselves to finish what they started —raising their children.
· Each parent can develop a personal style and method of child-rearing with minimal interference from the other parent. Each style may differ from one they would have framed jointly, but both can still be first-class parenting.
· Two real homes with no fighting does not happen overnight. It takes work, sweat, and tears. But it's worth the effort!

Two homes come in many shapes and styles. No one set of families will shape its associations like any other. Times change. Circumstances change. Parents move, remarry, get new jobs. Children grow into teenagers. A working relationship has its ups and downs, its good times and bad times; the essential fact about it is that, given time and effort, it usually works.

Parents settled into two homes do, of course, make mistakes. Their old feelings sometimes get the best of them. They may not like each other much, but they can now work together. As a result, they and their children put down the burdens of active strife and take up the tools that build the future. The children now have two homes: Each parent has one home, an independent private life and a stronger hand with the children during the times they are living together.

When the children no longer have to be parties to or be affected by their parents' wrangling and their inability to separate their relations with the children from their adult disagreements, the kids often breathe sighs of relief and scamper out of the middle. They get back to the totally absorbing business of growing up.

How to Use This Book

I strongly urge all of you who read this book—parents, children, friends, and relatives—to read the whole book from cover to cover before making any changes or decisions in your own situation. Each chapter has an important message, like a piece of a picture puzzle. Many of the parents and professionals who have used one or more of the methods in this book have convinced me that, although using just a few pieces of the puzzle is often useful, because they are just a few pieces the overall picture can remain obscure or even misunderstood. You may not need all the pieces to get the outline of the picture, but you do need to know which pieces you are leaving out and why. This may be especially useful after a year or two.

If you are in the process of ending your marriage now, pay special attention to the overall guides offered in Chapters 2, 3, and 4 and the more specific guides in Chapters 6 through 13. Most people who have used the methods given here have found that the rapid changes they went through during their first two years of separation were eased over and over again by reviewing certain basic principles and guidelines. After a few years, people report that what they once felt was elementary became more and more profound as their lives unfolded and certain methods took on new value and increased usefulness.

The information which follows emphasizes the order and direction of events—not the good or the bad. Furthermore, much information is given in easy-to-use checklists, self-surveys, frameworks, and guides. Parents have complicated, often stressful lives with little time or energy for theory and polemics. They consistently ask for practical information that will help them place their own experience in perspective and give them a sense of direction and purpose. Parents can make better choices once they identify their alternatives.

Timing may be important to the usefulness of this book. A person deep in regret and hurt about a marriage may not have the heart to read much during this period, but may return to the book several months later when faced with a myriad of decisions about house, children, money, and relating to the other parent.

The information here is for you, the reader. Expand it, revise it, ignore it. Even your disagreements with an idea can sharpen your own point of view and produce additional alternatives. If some parts do not feel good this month, try them next month or next year. The purpose of the book is to offer you more alternatives and information on how to make these different choices work for you. The final and best judge of what will be best for you and your children is—and will continue to be—you.

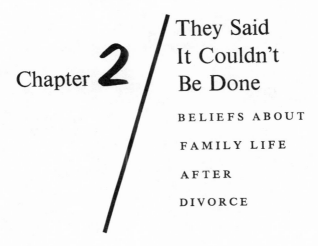

Chapter **2**

They Said It Couldn't Be Done

BELIEFS ABOUT

FAMILY LIFE

AFTER

DIVORCE

"It can't work," said a psychiatrist, when he heard about training parents to develop a working relationship after divorce. "If couples couldn't get along when they were married, they aren't going to get along after divorce." An attorney in the group nodded in agreement.

When I went on to describe my years of experience with couples who had learned how to build a working relationship as parents, the psychiatrist's concluding comment was: "If those couples can apply that kind of effort to their divorce, they should have done it for their marriage. They should never have split up in the first place."

As you move to explore the two-home concept, you are probably going to come up against some very common beliefs such as the one just quoted—that parents cannot get along after they separate, and that if by some miracle they do accomplish this feat, their divorce probably could have been avoided. This belief, like many others, is deeply rooted in our myths about families and what they ought to be. You are likely to meet these common roadblocks, be tempted to play a few games yourself, and run headlong into a trap or two. These roadblocks can be powerful deterrents to the development of a working relationship and to the actual emotional "divorce." While later chapters will describe how you can avoid these common problems, this chapter will outline some of the guises in which these temptations might appear.

Stumbling Blocks for Families

Prove the Divorce Was Necessary: Need for a Reason "Why"

During a weekend workshop, one of the first discussions parents have among themselves concerns the reactions of friends, family, and professionals to the couples' separation or divorce. Commonly, parents report both support and divisiveness. One father, for example, described a commitment he and the children's mother had made to keep their parenting functions separate from their anger with one another, only to have her family interfere and push her hard for an all-out battle. "The children's mother and I felt good about our working relationship, but her parents were outraged. They think that I should have nothing to do with the kids, that I'm a bastard for not being the son-in-law they had expected, and that the farther away I am from her and the kids the better. Their disapproval of me is hard on her. She needs their support and understanding, yet she feels she has to agree with them about me." This couple didn't hold the old beliefs about divorce, but people close to them wanted clear evidence that the divorce was unavoidable.

Countless times I have heard people say you need a strong reason for going through the trauma of divorce. "It's a powerful experience that changes your life and if you are going to put yourself and your kids through it, the reasons had better be damned good ones. Otherwise, when the going gets tough, you ask yourself 'was it worth it?' You have to find support for your view that either what you left was so bad, or what you have now is so good that you can safely say 'yes, it was worth it.' It's much easier if you say 'I had no choice.' "

The temptation to play dirty, to play "blame games" with the other parent or your children can be high. Most people give in to this temptation during the first year of divorce, but it shouldn't become a way of life. The search for reasons why marriage has ended is a natural response to a needed reassessment, but seeking reasons to place blame is an occupational hazard. When blaming becomes too strong, it can put a monkey wrench in both your "emotional divorce" and in a working relationship with the other parent.

Blame Games

Playing with what happened in the marriage, with who left who as a rallying point, usually brings in the element of failure.

The blame games come in many disguises, but boiled down they say things like: "The only thing wrong with me (or the marriage) was you." The continual reminder that divorce means failure, and failure means someone is to blame, is deeply embedded in our society. Few people escape without asking, and being asked, one or all of the following questions:

- Who's to blame for the failure of the marriage? *Somebody* failed as a man or woman.
- Who's to blame for ruining the kid's homelife? *Somebody* is causing them a lot of pain.
- Who's to blame for hurting the kid's grandparents? *Somebody* is causing them a lot of pain.
- Who's to blame for destroying the American Dream? *Somebody* is breaking the backbone of society.

"Failure feels terrible" said one gentle-looking man in his twenties. "You don't want to carry that around with you if you can help it. You blame the other guy and you feel better. Or you blame yourself and you feel even worse." The third alternative, blaming no one, is a difficult stance to take against the force of popular opinion.

A hidden hook on which to hang the "reasons" for a divorce is that both of you can find enough circumstantial evidence in the past to support your blame. Surprisingly enough, the strength of these negative feelings can provide a continuing attachment between any separating couple. In Chapters 7 and 8, and elsewhere throughout the book, you will read more about the force of these old ties. Most people feel hurt, angry, guilty, or vindictive during parts of the divorce process. Such feelings are natural, but they also mean that you are not yet emotionally disentangled from your former mate.

Competition is as essential to blame games as chips are to poker. When Dad zips around in a sports car with the children's young gym teacher, Mom, to dramatize the contrast, stays home submerging herself in household chores and bemoaning the problems of her new job. She calls him an irresponsible playboy; he sees her as a killjoy drudge. Mom wins the morality stakes; he has the fun. Both say: "See what I had to put up with?" Each watches the other after separation to see how he or she will turn out now. An extension of this thinking is the proclamation that "the only thing wrong with the kids was *you.*" Still-married parents play these "your child/my child" games too, but the potential damage to everyone is multiplied during divorce.

Behind these emotional and social roadblocks, parents have small companions. Children can't pack their bags, say: "See you when you've worked it out," and walk out into the streets. Children know they need adults to survive. Their instincts will lead them to secure the basic necessities of life. They may not have to take sides to survive physically, but too often they are expected to prove their loyalty or love to one or the other parent. Then they conclude that they must line up with one parent or the other to survive emotionally.

Children can play their own alternative to blame games—manipulating the adults around them. Sometimes they carry messages, losing bits or introducing changes along the way, to make things turn out the way they wish things were. Even when children never attempt to manipulate their parents, they may blame themselves for their parents' hostilities, and for other unhappy outcomes of the parental division. It's important to remember that if you insist on adult blame games you run the risk of placing your children in the center of the table.

The All-or-Nothing Traps

The all-or-nothing traps look at life after divorce in extremes. The following is an all-too-common example of how lack of knowledge about post-divorce behavior by children and parents can lead parents to expect the worst and eventually get it. "The kids are so rotten when they come home from a weekend with their father, it takes me two days to settle them down," said a mother of four. "Sometimes I wish he were in Alaska or Australia. Then I wouldn't have to put up with this stuff from the kids." The father's version was: "I got to thinking, 'What's the use? My influence is worthless anyway.' She's got all the authority, now that she has sole custody. Anything I do with the kids will just be wiped away after they return home. Besides, how can a man be a father without a woman, a regular house, or a yard?"

Both these people are reporting garden-variety complaints of the newly divorced parent. Some simple remedies could straighten the situation out but few people have access to this kind of information. In their frustrated search for a reason, both parents reach the conclusion that the other parent is at fault. Then they fall into the all-or-nothing trap; "do it right or don't do it at all." The parent with custody takes on the double burden of being father and mother, and the parent without custody feels parenting can't be done at all without the necessary equipment of house, spouse and yard. Distrust and resentment grow until a turning point is reached.

Perhaps Mom, in desperation, tells the children that if they don't stop their bad behavior when they return from their father's place they won't be able to see him at all. Or maybe Dad gets a chance to take a weekend vacation for the first time in three years. Secretly relieved that he won't have to face his dilemma once more, he cancels his time with the kids. The stage is set for a widening rift. Eventually Dad fades away from active involvement with the children. He can't stand the pain anymore. Mom thinks good riddance. But eventually she wishes for his parental involvement, as the real effects on the children of the loss of their father become more visible.

Some day, after Dad remarries, he may try again to reenter the children's lives, often by attempting to obtain full custody. Again, we see an all-or-nothing view of parenting after divorce, rather than a reasonable, measured approach to a middle ground.

Parents who insist on playing blame games give credence to the stereotype of the continually battling "exes." A warring couple is found at one end of the all-or-nothing scale that provides only two models for parents after their marriage ends. The battling "exes" at one extreme are made up of one parent with sole custody and the other parent angrily looking on. The parents' acrimony and distrust cause them to act like spiteful, irrational children. According to this stereotype, the divorced parents are supposed to hold grudges against each other for the rest of their lives, with their children severely hurt in the cross fire. Their only recourse is repeated court battles, or for one parent eventually to retreat from it all and to drop out.

The other extreme is occupied by the couple who have managed a "perfect divorce." They cooperate cordially in evenly divided times between homes—three days, four days, or one week at a time. No hostility, no mistakes and no hard feelings. The children seem to express no pain, no objections. This "ideal" model, while comforting to contemplate, is hardly attainable for most families.

Most divorcing parents fall somewhere between these two extremes. Parents weary of hostilities and threats of legal action say that there has to be a better way. Those who heartily dislike each other look at the "perfect" model and protest, "We'd never be able to do that."

One particularly devastating outcome of the all-or-nothing mentality is the *one-home, one-authority trap*. Parents beginning new family patterns must recognize that a powerful legacy of their earlier ideal family vision no longer works. The undivided Mother-Father front—which allows for no difference of opinion, no division of authority—may no longer exist. According to the myth of the united front, when parents living in one home disagree about something concerned with guiding or disciplining the children, one must give way and step back to support the other view which thereafter dominates. Children, so the theory goes, should not be confused with two points of view.

When parents no longer live together under one roof, the one-home, one-authority trap is well and truly triggered. Instead of seeking out some middle ground of compromise, separating parents can trap themselves in old one-authority binds, insisting that one parent's view triumph over the other's.

· In court, one parent retains all the authority (sole custody) while the other (often against his or her will and best judgment) is forced to take an ineffectual and frustrating minor role.

· Out of court, parents disagree openly, expecting their children to choose one of them over the other. "This is a two-party system," said one father, "where children are expected to register with either Mom or Dad."

As a result, many parents without custody fight for custody themselves or in time drop out, arguing: "Why pay that other parent money to keep my children away from me?" Or: "Why try to maintain a relationship with my kids when my influence is negligible and erased the minute I drop them at that other doorstep?"

There is no room in the one-home, one-authority trap for parents to disagree, to be apart, or for the children to maintain independent relationships with each parent, even though such a separate bond between parent and child is a healthy development in both married *and* single families! This ability for parent and child to develop individual relationships without the interference of another family member allows the entire family to respect personal differences. Such relationships can offer opportunities to build character and individual judgment. But this separate relationship with a parent is not part of the one-home, one-authority view, nor, in the minds of some family experts and family courts, does it lend itself to a healthy developmental environment for a child.

You Have a Family

The power of opinion and the need for acceptance are strong in any culture, and our Western world proves no exception. Beliefs about a good parent, a good family, even a good divorce spring from the people around us as well as from our personal experience and philosophy. If a person's beliefs about what makes a real family or a real parent have been defined solely by the structure of marriage, a good deal of unhappiness can come about when that marriage ends. By updating your view of your family—especially by separating out the notion of marriage from the notion of family—you can be well on your way.

What is a family to you? Take a moment to think of (and write down if that helps you) all the ideas that come to mind when you hear or see the word *family*. Pay attention to one particular question: Which dominates? The family you grew up in, the one you've been raising lately, or perhaps even some Hollywood image you've never seen in real life? When you say *family* right now, what do you mean?

If your first answer, regardless of custody or marital status, is "the kids and me," you're on the right track. Grown-ups and children as a nucleus are the basic ingredients of every form of family visible in this country today. The total amount of time spent together is not even the most important characteristic of a family, but the caring for one another is.

Forget about marriage for the moment. Marriage may have begun a family but it doesn't continue it. Nor does divorce end it. When the marriage ends, the family does not break, does not magically disappear. It can instead, like the family of the girl on the airplane in Chapter 1, divide and multiply into separate healthy organisms. Family members come in many combinations of old and young, male and female. And in addition to living together, the family members also feel important to one another. What does family mean to you today? What did it mean when you first married?

For most of us, the original dream of family went something like this: "Marry and live happily ever after. Grow old together. Watch the kids grow up, leave home, make their own homes, and come back visiting with wonderful grandchildren."

I know I thought that if I worked conscientiously as a wife and mother, I could later begin to relax. I might devote some of my time to a career, begin to do things family demands had kept me from trying. I would have earned time for myself and time to be with my husband. The satisfaction of a good marriage, successful children, and financial security lay just ahead. Divorce was something that happened to other people.

Many parents have told me of the American Dreams they once had. While they had their own variations and hopes, their dreams and mine shared certain common elements:

- The intimate relationship between the husband and wife and how we saw and filled those roles
- The relationship between the parent and the child
- The shared residence—that one home
- The shared family culture, the "old family feeling," its own distinctive reflection of religious and ethnic heritage, preferences, and immediate surroundings
- The way the parents shared their responsibility and authority with the children—preferably the "united front"

A number of parents report that they attempt soon after divorce to live up to as many of their original married standards as possible, but they are uneasy and say that something doesn't feel right about this.

Their uneasiness stems from their need to update old standards to fit their new realities. When a marriage ends, the family can retain all of the ideal elements, but arranged somewhat differently. The parents still have a residence but they parent alone. Their children now have two residences. The parents still have their roles as parents, but are now parenting separately. The family customs can be maintained or revised by each parent in his or her own home. The major changes are that first, the relationship between the man and woman has shifted from being both lovers and parents to the single focus of being parents; and second, that the united front of shared responsibility and authority has to be revised into a new and workable form.

The First Big Step: Separate Marriage from Family

We know at bottom that being lovers and married people calls forth a different part of us than does being parents. Married or divorced, we function differently in our roles as lovers and as parents. You can be parents and separate individual adults at the same time, just as you can be engineers, lawyers, teachers, nurses, salespeople—and lovers, friends, sons, daughters, and parents. The end of the marriage bond does not mean the destruction of your bond in parenting. This truth is one of those you might write on your mirror and look at when you put on your makeup or shave.

The legal divorce is just one part of the ending. It is as if there are four divorces to obtain—the legal one, the one from intimate love, the one from hurt and anger, and the one from competition between one another. Learning how to separate your roles and functions as a parent from those of a former lover usually brings about all these divorces.

Luckily, the principles that lead to this emotional and practical disentanglement at the same time also provide a solid foundation for a working relationship with the other parent, take children out of the middle, and set the tone for your own independent life.

The Extra Push: Commitment

Most parents have a spill-over of hard feelings they wade through during the first part of their separation. How might they give themselves a goal to work for, some standard to follow?

Some parents meet the problem of such hard feelings head-on. They make a vow to keep their personal feelings separate from their roles as parents. Dozens of times, I have heard people say: "No matter what we feel about each other, we will try to keep our parent-to-parent relations as wholesome and clean as possible." This heroic goal, difficult as it may be to reach, is still a good one to keep in mind. In many areas we must deal with difficult persons or problems we'd rather avoid—the store clerk with an irascible customer, the lawyer with an obnoxious opponent. As one father put it, "Once you accept the fact that you have to deal with that other parent, life seems to get easier."

Change in Custody Laws

As the 1980s begin, both the definitions and patterns of parental rights and responsibilities are changing rapidly. The very word *custody* is now subject to disfavor, recalling the selling and trading of human beings, a practice that went out with slavery. The historical view of children as property has continued in the same language which is used about houses, cars, and other possessions that accumulated during the marriage. Custody has meant possession and authority.

"How can you have custody of someone you love?" asked one parent tearfully. He, like so many who trusted the law to provide some structure during his bewildering divorce, had discovered how ill-equipped some courts have been to guide sensitive domestic policies.

In some states, custody laws are changing rapidly, the concept of joint custody no longer reserved to the highly educated or the very rich. In such regions, mediation, counseling, and negotiations are replacing the older adversarial models.* But, in many states, the traditional one-home, one-visitor process continues supreme, allowing for few modifications through traditional channels. Parents must resort to private mediation or negotiation, or risk the judgment of a one-home, one-authority point of view.

The Best Interest of the Family

In some tragic but easily definable situations, one parent must assume all the rights and authority over a child's ongoing life. When one parent is subject to long disabling illness, has a long history of abuse or other criminal behavior, children must be assigned to one home quickly, and often permanently. But such dramatic conditions are not typical for most divorcing couples who are law-abiding, competent parents. These parents are simply ending their marriages. They are not ill, handicapped, or breaking a law. They need different standards and procedures for the resolution of family disputes. They should not be lumped into the same mold with parents subject to extreme problems.

Many loving sincere parents would have willingly attempted to share child-rearing responsibilities and joys if:

1. They had some good examples to follow of a reasonable middle ground;

---

* The first post-divorce counseling services were offered in 1974 at the Los Angeles Conciliation Court of the Superior Court of Los Angeles County under the direction of Meyer Elkin. Since that time, other conciliation or family courts have followed this example.

2. They knew that it was an approved way to raise children;
3. Some community organization or practice had supported them in their efforts;
4. Laws had made it possible, even desirable, for them to work out agreements tailored to their individual situation;
5. They had an opportunity to learn how it could be done.

The New Pioneers

Even before the current upsurge of dissolving marriages and reorganizing homes, families weathered various kinds of reconstruction. In the United States, colonists and pioneers who moved westward over mountains, rivers, and deserts suffered enormous losses in wars, natural disasters, and epidemics. Those who survived carried on and raised their children under the most adverse conditions, alone if necessary, or with help from assorted family members, friends, and neighbors. The crucial quality in these families was the strength that came from shared experience and conquered obstacles.

When family survival demanded, frontier men and women could set aside rigid ideas about men's work and women's work. The father of two girl toddlers didn't let them starve because he wouldn't cook their meals after their mother died. A woman who had spent years hacking a homestead out of the wilderness with her husband and children wasn't going to give up and go home to Mother in Buffalo after her husband's death—not if she could help it.

Families composed of "significant others" have ranged all the way from groups led by grandparents, godmothers, and older sisters and brothers taking on the task of raising orphaned children to "Sourdough" Charlie bringing his cousin's ten-year-old son across the prairies. These nontraditional families didn't see themselves—and were not labeled—as deviant or unacceptable any more than Dad and two kids who live together during holidays and summers need to be so labeled today. All these clusters share the key elements of a family: a bond of love and experience between adult and child, a shared residence, family traditions, customs, and pride. All are families.

Today's parents can use the same pioneering kinds of courage and ingenuity as they reorganize their family life. By learning to separate spousal and parental roles, they can maintain pride in themselves as parents and heads of families. And by incorporating the essential qualities of family closeness and caring into the reorganized family, they can make the transition from the family-that-was to the family-that-is with grace and hope.

When children believe—because their parents believe—*that they have two intact homes where they belong and are wanted,* everyone gains the security of continuity as well as a sense of the parents' commitment to their parental roles. The definition of a family must, as is true in the search for so many other meanings and values, come from within. If parents think they have a family, they have one.

One mother put her experiences in this new two-home world this way: "Yes, people tell me it can't work, but I ask them what alternative they can suggest. All they have to offer me is isolation in one home or destructive attitudes that lead only to more hurt for all of us. The two-home approach may not work for some. It may be out of reach for some who want to try for it. But I think it's the best show in town when you're shopping for something good for you and your kids."

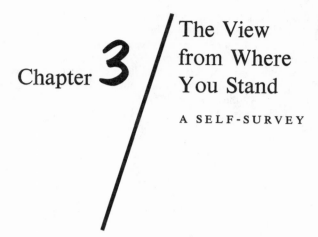

Chapter **3**

The View from Where You Stand

A SELF-SURVEY

The questionnaire that follows is a learning tool. Some people find it helps them to measure their current behaviors and attitudes; some people use it to project into the future; others see it as a way to get a handle on the past. Each of the seven sections introduces an important aspect of parenting and parent-to-parent interaction. Each question touches on an issue often found to be important in developing a two-home pattern.

Parents going through this major reorganization of their lives need to take inventory from time to time. As you yourself answer the questions on this survey, you will probably not only learn about your own strengths and sore points, but also get a glimpse of the new ways other parents are reacting in similar situations.

It has been my experience that parents appreciate having examples so that they can compare their individual family's needs with those of others. Therefore, I have pulled together some typical family characteristics and combined them into composite case studies so you can see some of the many different ways the survey has been used. Each person in these examples represents a common type of family experience.

Look for the differences in the ways these parent-types differ from each other in their expectations about what the survey will do for them, about how they wish to use their answers and about what their motivations for taking the survey are. Compare your own situation to each of theirs. How are you like them? How are you different? This process will help you prepare for answering the questions in your own way and for your own purposes. Since each family experience is unique, you may find questions that you feel have been left out and questions that do not apply to you. The uses and interpretations of this survey are many and varied; you must keep in mind that you are the best judge of your own situation and how you choose to use this questionnaire.

Immediately following the case studies is a summary of the way these representative parents answered the questions. Once you have given your answers, you can compare your responses with these typical ones.

Typical Case Studies

Eileen has had a joint custody arrangement with her children's father for more than five years. For four of those years, the two parents shared times with the children, costs, and responsibilities equally. Over the last year, however, Eileen's new job required her to move three hundred miles away. Time with her children has been reduced to vacations and holidays. Although she has had a good working relationship with the children's father, she has felt a strain that she can't yet put her finger on. She's using the survey as a learning device and as a self-test.

Tom is a "visiting" parent who lives about 45 minutes by car away from his only daughter. He pays for half of his daughter's expenses, according to a highly specific agreement that outlines his rights and responsibilities. Now, two years after his divorce, he feels "halfhearted" about his daughter's school and other activities. The questionnaire, he hopes, may pinpoint some hot spots of either dissatisfaction or possibility for change.

Ed is still married and living (uneasily) with his wife and three children. The first four sections of the questionnaire do not apply to his circumstances even though they do give him ideas about possible arrangements for the future. Ed could have answered the first four sections from his fantasies about legalities, distances, sharing expenses and time, but he chose instead simply to read them for his information. He then answered sections E, F, and G based on present dynamics in relation to his wife and his children. The behavior and attitudes he perceives today could quite possibly carry over into separation and divorce. He sees the self-survey as a learning tool.

Dennis has been separated from his wife for about a year and a half, but they have not yet filed for divorce. Two children under the age of ten live most of the time with his wife. Dennis and the children's mother have an unusually structured post-separation relationship with bewildering consequences for Dennis, who seeks some kind of closure on their marital status. Right now he fears the effect on his wife's emotional stability if they get legally divorced. He will use this questionnaire for self-assessment and for self-teaching.

Marie has sole custody of her son and has had no contact with the child's father for more than a year. She took the survey for two purposes—as a self-teaching exercise, and to gain insight into her resentments and feelings about desertion and divorce. She could answer the questionnaire depending on her memory of their interaction when Jim was still in the picture and/or as she perceives the situation today. She chose to take the self-survey as if it were two years ago, remembering what it was like when her former spouse was accessible.

When these parents finished the questionnaire this is what their scores looked like:

	Eileen	Tom	Ed	Dennis	Marie	Working Score
SECTION A Legal Agreements	7	6	—	—	2	5+
SECTION B Sharing	11	10	—	12	3	—
SECTION C Distances	4	8	—	10	5	—
SECTION D Schedules	45	38	—	36	17	31+
SECTION E Children	21	16	11	20	9	25+
SECTION F Feelings	69	53	37	51	27	55+
SECTION G Finances	88	68	70	43	6	80+

Now, before you dive in to take the survey yourself, take a few minutes to decide what perspective is best for you. If you are now out of touch with your child's other parent, you may want to answer as Marie has, by looking back at a time when you were still communicating. If you are not yet separated from your spouse, like Ed, you may want to write an "as if" scenario in your answers, to look at your fantasies about the way things might turn out.

Remember, the questionnaire can help you chart your status at a given point on your own time scale. You can retake it again next week, next month, or next year and use it in a different way each time.

If you are not now ready to assess your situation in this way, or for some other reason you do not want to take the survey, read the questions and summary answers the representative parents gave. Doing so can help put the material in the rest of this book in perspective.

Where Do You Stand? A Self-Survey

Most of the questions on this questionnaire are based on some form of a five-point rating scale. Work at the questions at your own speed. If you feel uncomfortable at any point, stop and put the survey aside until you are ready to go on. Remember, no answers are "right" or "wrong"; some simply record facts, others reveal opinions or feelings. If the five-point scale doesn't suit your needs, make up one of your own. If an important issue has been left out, write it in your own words at the space that says "Other."

Use the score sheet on page 33 to record your answers. Be sure to put down the date.

Now, before you start, rate your emotional climate from "great" (5) to "awful" (1) and circle the appropriate number on the score sheet.

Refer back to this score sheet often as you use this book. Any time you feel like tackling any one or all sections again, make a fresh score sheet and record your answers before looking back to the first results. These score sheets can be your own personal inventory.

How to Interpret Your Scores

The first thing you do is to add up the score for each section and record these section totals on the score sheet. In general, the higher the score on each section, the closer a parent seems to be to a strong working relationship. It is very rare, of course, for anyone to attain a perfect score with all 5s; in fact, if your score is like that, it may be a good idea for you to take some time to reconsider your assessment. This is not the time for rose-colored glasses; it is time for a clear and realistic look at your own situation.

So, if a perfect score is not expected, then just what do I mean by a high score? I have discovered over many years of counseling parents that certain behaviors and attitudes often precede or accompany a successful working relationship between parents. A high score by both parents reflects this fortunate situation, often revealing a good deal of mutual respect that has transferred into a working relationship between the parents and an independent relationship between each parent and child. These scores are listed on your score sheet next to the appropriate section of the survey. (Two sections, B and C, are exceptions and will be explained later.) Beside each section I have also listed chapters in this book which deal with the particular issues presented in that section of the questionnaire.

It is very important to remember that the "working scores" are interpretive only. If your score falls below that level, it doesn't mean you can't

SECTION A   *Legal Agreements*

What kinds of words are used in your legal agreement about custody? How specifically are the arrangements spelled out? When you answer these questions, try to put aside the way things actually work and focus *only* on what the papers say.

	Score	Not Applicable
1. What does your legal agreement say about custody? Circle the *one* score that comes closest to your agreement.		
a. Joint physical custody, where authority, responsibility, and perhaps time are shared equally	5	NA
b. Joint custody, where authority and responsibility are shared nearly equally but residence is primarily with one parent	4	NA
c. Joint "legal" custody where authority and responsibility are shared unequally, child lives the majority of the time with one parent	3	NA
d. Sole custody is awarded to one parent ("custody shall be with the mother/father") with *specific* authorities, responsibilities, and visitation rights to the other parent ("visitation rights shall be on Thursdays and every other weekend, beginning on . . .")	2	NA
e. Sole custody is awarded to one parent and "reasonable visitation rights" to the other parent. No specifics are itemized	1	NA
f. Other	—	
2. How specific is your legal agreement about such things as holidays, authority, time, responsibilities? *Circle one score.*		
a. Highly specific	5	NA
b. Specific	4	NA
c. Combination	3	NA
d. General	2	NA
e. Vague	1	NA
f. Other		

TOTAL, Section A _____

SECTION B   How Do You and the Other Parent Now Share Costs, Responsibilities and Time?

For this set of questions, use the last twelve months as a guide. Give yourself a 5 if you think you share about 60 percent of the costs, etc. Give yourself a 1 if you think there is little or no sharing. Circle *one* score for each question.

	SCORES					
	50–50%	65–35%	75–25%	85–15%	95–5% (or less)	Not Applicable
3. How are the children's costs divided between you and the other parent?	5	4	3	2	1	NA
4. How are authority and responsibilities shared or divided between you in areas such as education, health, religious activities, and so forth?	5	4	3	2	1	NA
5. How much time does your child spend with the "second-home" parent compared with the "first-home" parent? (Add overall times together to estimate an annual percentage.)	5	4	3	2	1	NA

TOTAL, Section B _____

or don't have a working relationship. Instead it points to something that would merit more of your attention and possibly some thoughtful changes. Some parents who eventually reach their goal of two homes at first have low scores in many sections, especially newly separated parents. Scores usually change as attitudes and behaviors change. When it takes time to get into a situation, it usually takes time and effort to get out of it.

In addition, pay close attention to the 0s, 1s, and 2s you marked. These questions indicate "hot spots"—issues or feelings that could flare up and cause trouble. By looking at the specific questions that earned these low scores, and by learning about the way they fit into the overall picture, you can get an idea on where you stand.

If you have found that a very high percentage of your answers falls into the "not applicable" or the "other" category, then some of the interpretations that follow may not make sense in your own situation. But

SECTION C   How Far Apart Do You and the Other Parent Live?

Can the children bike from one home to the other or do they take a bus or a car? Do you live so far from one another that travel between one home and the other is a major expenditure of time and money? The closer the homes are, the higher the score; the farther they are, the lower the score. Circle *one* score for each question.

	SCORES				
	Car or Bus Necessary		Car, Plane Necessary		
Walking, Biking Distance	2 hrs. or less	2+ hrs.	200+ miles	1000+ miles	Not Applicable
6. How far apart do you and the other parent live from one another? 5	4	3	2	1	NA

	COSTS PER TRIP				Not
Negligible	Reasonable	High	Very High	Prohibitive	Applicable
7. Is the cost of transportation between homes a major budget consideration? 5	4	3	2	1	NA

8. Other (write in)

TOTAL, Section C _____

take a minute to read them anyway. They provide an interesting framework for looking at situations. Where only an occasional "NA" (Not Applicable) shows up on your score sheet, you may find your overall scores are still within the range I've outlined for a "working score" or "hot spots." For each "other" category you have identified, I recommend that you make up your own five-point scale. Make 5 equal a satisfying cooperative answer and 1 its opposite. Any 1s and 2s will help you identify your own unique "hot spots." The following sections will help you interpret your scores.

SECTION A   Legal Agreement

A specific agreement that allows both parents to know what they can expect often, but not always, helps build a working relationship. As par-

SECTION D *Schedules*

In this section shift to a time frame of the past two months. Of course, if your children are at one home for blocks of time, such as summers and holidays only, you may want to answer the question from the point of view of the entire past year. Pick the time frame that works best for you.

Circle the *one* score for each question that best describes your situation.

SCORES

	Regularly	Often	Sometimes	Rarely	Never	Not Applicable
9. Do you and the other parent have a schedule regarding times the children are with each of you?	5	4	3	2	1	NA
10. Is it a written schedule?	5	4	3	2	1	NA
11. Do the children stay overnight with the second-home parent (or parent without custody)?	5	4	3	2	1	NA
12. How often do the children eat meals with the second-home parent?	5	4	3	2	1	NA
13. When the second-home parent cancels plans, are substitute plans set up by that parent within a short period of time?	5	4	3	2	1	NA
14. When the second-home parent doesn't show up or cancels a planned time with the children, is there an important reason?	5	4	3	2	1	NA
15. When the first-home parent cancels plans, are substitute plans made by that parent within a short period of time?	5	4	3	2	1	NA
16. When the first-home parent doesn't show up or follow through with plans made with the "second-home" parent, is there an important reason?	5	4	3	2	1	NA
17. When scheduled plans are changed on the other parent's time, has that parent been asked for advice or permission?	5	4	3	2	1	NA
18. Other (write in)						

TOTAL, Section D _____

SECTION E   *The Children*

This section can be answered by all parents, separated or not. Think about your own situation. For these questions, "Almost Always" equals 1 and "Almost Never" equals 5.

Circle the *one* score for each question that best describes your situation.

SCORES

	Regu-larly	Often	Some-times	Rare-ly	Never	Not Appli-cable
19. Do the children talk about the other parent to you?	1	2	3	4	5	NA
20. When the children talk about the other parent, do you talk with them for more than a few minutes?	1	2	3	4	5	NA
21. Do the children seem upset, fearful, or anxious when they return from being with the other parent?	1	2	3	4	5	NA
22. Do you ever fear for the children's emotional or physical safety with the other parent?	1	2	3	4	5	NA
23. Do you ever fear losing custody or contact with the children because of your former mate's resentments or vindictiveness?	1	2	3	4	5	NA
24. Do you ever fear losing influence or contact with your children because of other circumstances?	1	2	3	4	5	NA
25. Do you feel uncomfortable with any differences in values that you and the other parent may have?	1	2	3	4	5	NA
26. Do you feel uncomfortable with how any differences in values between you and the other parent may affect your children?	1	2	3	4	5	NA
27. Other (write in)						

TOTAL, Section E _____

SECTION F   *Feelings*

Try to answer each question based on your circumstances over the last twelve months. These questions focus on your relationship to your former spouse and how you see the children's other parent as a parent. Circle the *one* score for each question that expresses your belief or feeling.

SCORES

	Al-most Al-ways	Usu-ally	Some-times	Rare-ly	Never	Not Appli-cable
28. Are you in control when you talk to the other parent?	5	4	3	2	1	NA
29. Do you think the other parent is sensitive to the children's needs?	5	4	3	2	1	NA
30. Do you and the other parent agree on basic values for your children?	5	4	3	2	1	NA
31. Do you and the other parent agree on ways to discipline your children?	5	4	3	2	1	NA
32. Do you think that your children have a good relationship with the other parent?	5	4	3	2	1	NA
33. Do you feel the other parent respects your parenting style?	5	4	3	2	1	NA
34. Looking back over the past six weeks, would you say the two of you have been getting along well?	5	4	3	2	1	NA
35. Looking back over the past year, would you say you two have been getting along well?	5	4	3	2	1	NA
36. Can you trust the other parent to follow through on what he/she has promised or agreed to regarding dates, times, arrangements with the children?	5	4	3	2	1	NA

SECTION F   *Feelings (Cont.)*

SCORES

	Almost Always	Usually	Sometimes	Rarely	Never	Not Applicable
37. Can you trust the other parent to inform you of major events in the child's life when the child is with the other parent, such as major illnesses, difficulty in school?	5	4	3	2	1	NA
38. Are you generally comfortable with the way you and the other parent make your arrangements for times with the children?	5	4	3	2	1	NA
39. Do you think the other parent usually respects your territory, your home, and your privacy?	5	4	3	2	1	NA
40. Can you count on the other parent to be flexible regarding changes in plans or circumstances?	5	4	3	2	1	NA
41. Are you satisfied with your legal arrangements with custody, visitation, responsibilities, and rights?	5	4	3	2	1	NA
42. Would most of your relatives and friends agree with the concepts of a two-home situation? (Or if you have one already, do they support it?)	5	4	3	2	1	NA
43. Do you think that most of your former spouse's friends and relatives agree with the concepts of a two-home situation? (Or if you have one already, do they support it?)	5	4	3	2	1	NA
44. Other (write in)						

TOTAL, Section F _____

SECTION G *Your Financial Relationship*

Look carefully at the different problems listed below concerning payment of stipulated support amounts. If you have had any of these problems during the last year, circle 0 for *yes*. If the problem does not apply to you, circle 5 for *no*.

PAYMENTS

Have child support payments varied in any way from the agreed amount, method, or time of payment? Circle *one* score for each question.

	SCORES Yes	No	Not Applicable
45. Past due payments	0	5	NA
46. Amount paid less than agreed	0	5	NA
47. General discontent	0	5	NA
48. Irregular payments	0	5	NA
49. Disagreement over money use	0	5	NA
50. Other problems	0	5	NA
51. Other (write in)	0	5	NA

LEGAL ACTION

Have you or the other parent ever taken legal action involving the payment, amount, or nonpayment of child support? Circle *one* score *only*.

		SCORE
52.	(a) Yes	0
	(b) Threatened, but did not go to court	10
	(c) No	25
	(d) Not applicable	NA
	(e) Other	(Give your own score)

CHILD SUPPORT AND SEEING THE CHILDREN

Has child support or visitation been withheld for any reason? Circle *one* score *only*.

		SCORE
53.	(a) Yes, support held back because visitation denied	0
	(b) Yes, visitation denied because child support held back	0
	(c) Yes, I feel this is a necessary control I have over other parent	0
	(d) No, I wanted to do this but I have not	6
	(e) No, but I would do this if I thought it would work	6
	(f) No, I would not do this	10
	(g) Not applicable	NA
	(h) Other	(Give your own score)

SECTION G   *Your Financial Relationship (Cont.)*

INSURANCE, FIXED COSTS, FEES

Do you run into trouble over certain bills? Circle *one* score *only*.

	SCORE	Not Appli-cable
54. (a) Yes, he/she doesn't follow legal agreement	0	NA
(b) Yes, he/she doesn't pay amounts in-formally agreed to	5	NA
(c) Yes, he/she agreed to pay certain bills, but does so irregularly or irresponsibly	7	NA
(d) Yes, disagreement as to who promised to pay what, but bills get paid	15	NA
(e) No, such problems get worked out	20	NA
(f) Rarely, no major problems	20	NA
(g) Not applicable	NA	NA
(h) Other	(Give your own score)	

TRUST IN OTHER PARENT

When it comes to money, how much do you trust the other parent? Circle *one* score *only*.

	SCORE
55. (a) Much trust	15
(b) Trust	13
(c) Some trust	8
(d) Little or no trust	0
(e) Not applicable	NA
(f) Other	(Give your own score)

TOTAL, Section G _____

ents develop a working relationship, they sometimes ignore the legal arrangements. But they have that agreement to fall back on in rough periods. A specific legal agreement does help parents to separate their parenting from their mating relationship. A high score here usually promotes progress toward a two-home arrangement.

SECTION B   *Sharing*

How you share costs, responsibilities, and time can vary from 10 percent to 50 percent in a good working relationship. Some parents have their children during one year, with some 15 percent of time spent with the

SCORE SHEET

Date: ———————

		Great	Pretty Good	OK	Not so Good	Awful
My current emotional level:		5	4	3	2	1

		Section Total	"Working Scores"*	Relevant Chapters
SECTION A	**Legal Agreements** (Questions 1 and 2)		5+	11, 12
SECTION B	**Sharing** (Questions 3–5)		—	10, 11, 12
SECTION C	**Distances** (Questions 6–8)		—	10, 13, 15
SECTION D	**Schedule** (Questions 9–18)		31+	9, 10, 11, 12, 14, 16
SECTION E	**The Children** (Questions 19–27)		25+	5, 7, 8, 9, 10, 13
SECTION F	**Feelings** (Questions 28–44)		50+	2, 5, 6, 7, 15, 16
SECTION G	**Finances** (Questions 45–55)		80+	11, 12

* How to adjust your working score when "other" or "not applicable" answers are added or subtracted is discussed later.

other parent, and then switch for the next year. Others divide time like Eileen or Tom. There is usually some important connection, however, between a very low total score and the amount of effort the "first-home" parent has to put out to get the other parent reinvolved and/or the effort a "second-home" parent expends to be a parent. The lower the score, the more work the parents may have to do initially. However, no particular score can be easily identified as the best working score.

SECTION C   *Distances*

The distance between the two homes also is a simple but important section. The farther apart you live, the more expensive and time-consuming travel will be. A high score on this makes two homes logistically far easier. A low score means (1) time and money may be big factors; and (2) specific two-home parenting needs a solid, well-thought-out plan. As in Section B, there is no special score. Good working relationships can be built even when distances are great.

SECTION D   *Schedules*

This section is a self-survey of skill and attitude, a measure of what goes on between the parents and how changes are made. Any score above 31 means you're heading in the right direction. A score below that level means parents need to communicate better. Once two-home techniques are digested and put to work, scores in this section often change dramatically.

SECTION E   *Children*

This is a very important section; your answers here identify special "hot spots." The reasons behind the answers must be sought and dealt with. Any combination of scores under 25 is a signal of work to do—work explained in later chapters. If your scores are 25 or over, you are probably in good shape. Give special thought to any individual score that is a 2 or a 1.

SECTION F   *Feelings*

Any score here over 50 offers excellent hopes for an immediate two-home future. As you develop more effective techniques of communication and make finer distinctions between your role as a parent and your relation to your former spouse, scores usually go up. Even if two or three items stay the same, an increase in understanding and techniques usually leads to higher scores on others. For example, you may never agree with the other parent on discipline for your children, but you may increase your mutual respect for one another's right to a different point of view and different behavior with the children. Pay attention to your "hot spots."

The emotions of divorce and the underlying principles of a working relationship go hand in hand in the determination of scores in Sections C, D, E, F. Increased communication and two-home skills can raise scores here.

SECTION G   *Finances*

The lower your score in this section on finances, the less trust you have in the other parent and the less you can leave up to chance or to your imagination. Sometimes parents, like Marie, have extraordinarily low scores during big squabbles over child support amounts and payments, or conflicts that lead to court actions. One parent may have withheld payments while the other withheld visitation, and bills and fees were left hanging while the battle went on. These experiences erode trust and can easily bring scores down to zero.

Summing Up

Some parents ask how they can use this self-survey to know what their chances are of negotiating their own two-home arrangement without a third party or respective attorneys. There is no one answer to this question because your scores represent your private assessment only. You cannot speak for the other parent. Even if you have a strong "working score" the other parent may not. But before you rush over to the other parent's home with a copy of this survey, or attempt to negotiate a joint-custody or two-home arrangement by yourself, please:

1. Read the rest of this book before you act. Later chapters discuss the elements of private negotiations and the use of this survey in detail.

2. Recognize that the other parent may not have the same feelings or see things the same way you do. This holds true even if he or she takes the survey and also has a strong working score. Two high scores indicate success, they don't promise it.

3. If you are in a hurry to negotiate a joint-custody or two-home arrangement, find a trained mediator or counselor to act as a third party from the beginning; it can save you time, money, and anguish in the long run. Don't try to negotiate alone if either of you has low scores.

Use this self-survey to see where you stand today. Take the time to put some of the methods given in this book into practice—several months is not an uncommon length of time for a trial period—and then take the survey again. Look at your second score. If your scores are still low across the board, something is missing. You may need more practice, a different approach, even a different survey. It could also mean that the timing for shared parenting is off for now.* If your scores have gone up, however, you are on the right track.

After you have read the book, know where you stand, and feel comfortable with your working score, you may want to consider the method some parents follow. They both take the self-survey, then they get together and compare their scores, isolating their "hot spots" and their strengths. Some parents feel confident enough to do this alone, others use a counselor as a third party. Identical scores are not at all necessary, but knowing what the problems are often helps mutual understanding. Sometimes they

---

* When the other parent is uncooperative or out of the picture, you would probably do better sharing the parenting with relatives or friends. Following chapters will show how this can be done.

do this to work out a legal agreement, often they do it just to understand their working relationship better.

Sometimes, taking the survey changes people's attitudes. A father, reviewing his scores about his former wife, realizes he can't trust her to inform him of major events and other important issues about the children. He now has a clearer understanding of his problem with her and what he wants to change. A mother, looking at the total time the father spent with their child and considering the steadfast manner in which he honored each cancellation with an immediate substitution time, might find herself retracting some of her complaints that he "never takes any responsibility for our daughter."

Taking a questionnaire such as this can bring up a lot of feelings. Some people are curious and excited about their discoveries, others angered or saddened by their memories or present circumstances. People have many understandable reactions and some of them are not easy to bear. But take heart, the next chapter can help to put these feelings into perspective, for it shows the actual steps people can take when moving from one home to two.

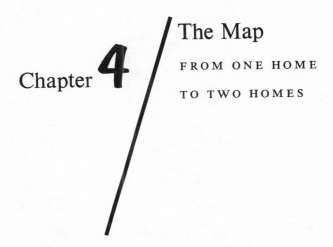

Chapter 4

The Map

FROM ONE HOME
TO TWO HOMES

Few people embark on a major journey without a good map to advise them of the major landmarks and roadblocks. But ending a marriage, reorganizing a family, and setting up a new life is often done in just such a blind fashion. "A year and a half ago," said one petite mother of two teenage daughters, "nothing was *new*. Now nothing is *familiar,* and everything is new. There's got to be some order, some direction to this chaos!" There are no package tours for this unfamiliar terrain, but adults and children alike need to know what's up ahead.

This chapter decribes the stages of transition from one home to two. To illustrate what happens, a diagram called "From One Home to Two Homes" was developed for parents to use. Like a map, it shows the major landmarks, the rough roads, the smooth spots, and the points of interest. It can be used to mark progress, and as a way to remember that the crooked places will straighten out. Others have gone through this; you can too.

Remember that this framework is to be used as a guide, not a gospel. Each person's experience is unique, as is the pace through the transition. You and the other parent may or may not be in the same place, feeling the same way at the same time. Sometimes the person who has advanced to a calm emotional stage is baited by a volatile partner in an earlier phase, and soon the two are out of control, fighting as if they were still married. A family's progress through each period is not like going from first grade to sixth; and everyone, young and old, seems to follow different zigzag patterns: sometimes two steps forward, three back, four forward, one back,

ONE HOME   *Family History 1*

STAGE ONE	**The American Dream Home** Two-parent household (trust and respect intact)	
STAGE TWO	**The Problem Home** Two-parent household (trouble, discord)	
STAGE THREE	**The Dividing Home** Two-parent household (severe difficulties)	
STAGE FOUR	**The Divided Home** Separation	

TWO HOMES   *Family History 2*

STAGE FIVE	**Mom's House, Dad's House** Off-the-Wall: Two one-parent households (troubled but separate working order established)	
STAGE SIX	**Mom's House, Dad's House** The Reshaping Process Settles Down: Two one-parent households ("I've survived! I'm coping.")	
STAGE SEVEN	**Mom's House, Dad's House** From Coping to Creating: Two one-parent households	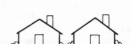

and so on. This is natural. Despite the different tempos, you can be on the way to a calmer, more rewarding existence, an updated normal life.

Children also go through these stages, but at different speeds. Some do not express their true feelings about the divorce, but hold back or deny strong emotions for months, sometimes years. Other children may move slowly, often clinging to the hope that some day their parents will reunite.

Let's begin with marriage and what happens as it moves toward separation. These familiar stages are the same ones that spawn the "can't-work" stories and our beliefs about single parenting and remarriage described in the previous chapters.

From One Home to Two Homes

ONE HOME   *Family History 1*

STAGE ONE   *The American Dream Home*

Two-parent household
(trust and respect intact)

Most people begin their family history with Mom, Dad, and the children under one roof. Some see this stage as the American Dream come true. If the marriage is solid, there is love, respect, and trust. Dad has a job with the county; Mom works parttime in an insurance office. Twelve-year-old Johnny is in middle school, and nine-year-old Suzie in the elementary grades. They all enjoy backpacking, belong to a church and bowling league, and visit back and forth with relatives. They feel the economic pressures of inflation and worry about the headline stories in the news. But they feel that they can make it. When Dad gets a raise, he and Mom plan to take a second honeymoon trip. This is a stable home.

STAGE TWO   *The Problem Home*

Two-parent household
(trouble, discord)

Dad has been working late frequently and Mom's acting unhappy. Before school one morning, Suzie found Mom asleep on the den couch. Some type of problem troubles Mom and Dad, but no one talks about it.

Even in the happiest of marriages, families disagree in either open fighting or private arguments. Many couples resolve their differences and return to Stage One with the enrichment of a successful resolution of their problems. Love is renewed, and trust and respect deepened as a result of their special rhythm of ups and downs.

However, if trouble in the home carries over a long period, the trust and respect so necessary to intimate relationships begins to wear thin, and tension rises to uncomfortable levels. Sometimes this erosion is gradual, hardly noticeable, until something points it out—overlong working hours, an extramarital affair, repeated illnesses.

If the discontent is not resolved, the uneasiness deepens and a return to Stage One becomes less and less likely. Marriage counseling may begin. Perhaps there is talk of separate vacations or even of a trial separation.

STAGE THREE   *The Dividing Home*

Two-parent household
(severe difficulties)

When the difficulties seem to be irreconcilable, the marriage has entered Stage Three. Parents may worry, weep more, and argue. All too often trust and respect are replaced by distrust and disrespect, and the household shows signs of dividing. Mom cries a lot, and Dad loses his temper, especially at Suzie who is very like her mother. Relatives on both sides may be included in blow-by-blow descriptions of Dad's wandering eye or Mom's extravagance. Johnny, now a teenager, either ignores what's happening or has unexpected temper tantrums, while Suzie's asthma increases as a physical reaction to the family's emotional pain. Perhaps a long vacation without the children or marriage counseling can bring back the important trust and respect, and everybody can return to Stage Two and then One for a happy continuation of the first family history.

But the longer a family remains in Stage Three, the more difficult the road back. The discord and tension can be intense. Sadness and the fear of divorce, with all its implications, add to the building stress. Mom and Dad ask: "Should we separate or should we stay together?" Long-term indecisions can be very damaging because the stress level remains too high for too long a time. Some families bounce back and forth between stages two and three for years, unwilling or unable to end the marriage or make it work.

Ordinarily, when a couple cannot rebuild their relationship, a decision period eventually begins. In this case, Mom can sleep only two or three hours a night, Dad lives on coffee and cigarettes, Suzie's home with severe asthma, and Johnny's never home at all. The family is deep into the pain of deciding about the future. Even though the home is not yet visibly divided, it is pulling apart.

STAGE FOUR   *The Divided Home*

Separation

The physical separation has finally happened. Mom and the children remain in the original family home, while Dad sets up another temporary residence. They want to build two homes for the children, but at this stage everyone feels the psychological and physiological shock that comes with this new and strange reality. No matter how much preparation has been made for the separation, a sense of numbness (and sometimes relief) sets in. Sometimes day-to-day functioning seems impossible or continues at only marginal levels. This dysfunctional reaction is common but dangerous, as people are especially accident-prone in both this and the next stage.

Luckily this stage is finite, lasting one hour, one day, or one month—no longer than it takes Mom and Dad to set up two *distinct working routines in their two residences*. The question is not how satisfying these arrangements may be, but how functional. Basic survival is a vital issue. If you can get through a day at the office, get home again, and feed yourself, there is a sense of order—perhaps makeshift and insecure, but workable. You may be sad, angry, depressed, or troubled, but if you are functioning you are not broken. You have moved on to the next level where some reality has penetrated the numbness and shock. The hard work of reorganization begins in earnest.

These four stages, beginning with the first family and ending with the dividing home, are familiar. Now is the time to depart from the known and begin to explore the lesser-known stages of family life *after* the separation.

The first marriage and family has produced Family History 1. The next set of steps shows the beginning of Family History 2.

TWO HOMES   *Family History 2*

STAGE FIVE   *Mom's House, Dad's House*

The Unsettled Period—Off-the-Wall:

Two one-parent households
(troubled but separate
working order established)
(six months–two years)

Stage Five begins a new family history—two new households. Mom's house and Dad's house. This stage can be the most difficult and the longest-lasting, with the first months a time of crisis.

A deluge of changes demand attention in these two new homes. Everything can be affected: income, jobs, personal habits, friendships, routines, and a sense of security and of self. The stress mounts as the question of survival in the midst of this upheaval continues to loom. Everyone knows ending a marriage costs, but until the bills pile up, few realize how severe the economic pinch can be. Feelings are raw, sometimes out of control. Mom and Dad are remorseful one minute and unexpectedly distrustful and angry with one another the next. Dad says he feels like he's on a roller coaster. He even goes through a period of bargaining with Mom, hoping he can patch up the marriage. Because of the many ways people act out of character during this time, this stage was nicknamed "off-the-wall."

The jobs to do are many: learn how to cope with stress; evaluate the past and air strong feelings; separate the old roles of lovers from the new roles of parents living separately; make a series of important decisions about who will live where, when, and for how long; and execute those seemingly endless mechanics demanded by legalities and economics. Mom asks overwhelmed, "Where am I now that I need me?"

These parents are doing their best to set up two homes, working out the division of responsibilities, time, and fun. But, like many people, their strong emotions about their personal relationship often pollute their jobs as parents, and they are unaware of how damaging this unconscious behavior is to their children and themselves. When the off-the-wall feelings get the best of this couple, the kids get in the middle and things seem to fall apart for a while.

Mom and Dad know they need help. Mom finds a class on divorce adjustment, Dad joins one on parenting. They each count on friends who have two-home arrangements for their children for advice and helpful readings.

Johnny and Suzie are living most of the time with Mom and spending long weekends and some evenings with Dad during the early months. Their reactions to the separation vary: Suzie has said nothing at all, but her asthma is still severe. Johnny's reaction has been open and angry. He is talking back to both parents, is cutting classes, and getting into fights.

The parents have lost touch with their children's needs, especially their needs for time with each parent and to be out of the middle of their parents' problems. When the parents settled down enough to bring in some important order to the house and a flexible routine, some of the tensions and fear let up immediately. Other difficulties took far longer to even out.

During the first part of this stage, the knottiest issues remain unsolved —property, monies, the children. Finally, as feelings cooled and the parents became more adept at applying the principles of a working relationship to their discussions, they developed their own negotiation style, settling all but two issues themselves. They used a mediator to come to agreement on these remaining questions and put together their own "Parenting Agreement" that contained all the necessary legal elements for joint physical custody. When necessary legalities were finished, everyone breathed a sigh of relief but also felt the sadness of the formal end of the marriage. When fears fade, the next stage begins. For this couple, two years elapsed from the beginning of Stage Four to the end of Stage Five. Other couples may take more time to get through these two periods of time, but few people make it in less time.

STAGE SIX   *Mom's House, Dad's House*

The Reshaping Process
Settles Down:

Two one-parent households
("I've survived! I'm coping.")

Life is calmer now and the sobering demands of the new life become clearer. Suzie and Johnny have settled into new neighborhoods and have become accustomed to their new life-style in two homes. They continue to meet and trade information with contemporaries in similar family situations. Mom has a full-time job and has obtained excellent after-school care for the children, easing her most pressing guilt feelings about being a working mother. Dad has long ago moved out of his bachelor pad into better quarters, and the children live with him on a regular basis. He is far more confident of his role and his parenting style. He and Mom are talking about the possibilities of the children living the majority of the time with him for a year or two.

During this stage parents cement a relationship where they respect one another's territory and parenting style and rarely find reasons to interfere. Old hot spots occasionally flare up between them, but these incidents are less frequent. The parents know now how to keep their children out of the middle and are well along on the job of separating being parents from being former lovers. They know now how to tell the difference between marriage and parenthood.

Somewhere in this stage, most people experience a series of "flashbacks" to the off-the-wall stage triggered by a change in circumstances, such as remarriage or a move away. But a solid working relationship can keep these replays short and manageable.

Dad has had an important love affair and Mom is going out more. Despite a few secret thoughts of getting back together, each knows that reconciliation would not work.

These parents are coping fairly well, but they have not yet found this life-style as satisfying as the promise of their original Dream. Mom asks, "Is this all there is?" Their tasks are to continue to solidify their new lifestyles and their working relationship and to develop a loyal circle of compatible friends. Until a strong support group can act as an "open" family (if not for parents at least for the children), parenting and re-evaluation tasks can increase, often becoming burdensome. Extra caring is important to the stability of all families—regardless of the parents' marital status.

STAGE SEVEN   *Mom's House, Dad's House*

From Coping to Creating:

Two one-parent households

Stage Seven is a creative breakthrough for many families. Now that they know how to separate their personal lives from their parenting functions and how to nourish their own new family integrity and solidarity, their new life-style is flourishing with a sense of continuity and security. The two families are not just coping, they are creating. The incompatibility that led Mom and Dad out of their marriage is clearly evident now in that their life-styles are different and their emotional expressions divergent.

A new man-woman relationship established during this stage can be born in freedom, not in the frantic need for another parent, an old view of family, or "getting back to normal."

Mom and Dad long ago stopped competing for the good-guy prize and no longer worry that one will turn the children against the other. Occasionally, they still disagree about the children, but that's par in any joint venture—especially when the partners were once lovers. They have learned tolerance, and everyone is the richer for it.

Suzie and Johnny are now Susan and John—growing up with two homes and both parents. Their parents' individual friendship and family circles have greatly expanded in recent years, even more so since their father's remarriage. Susan says, "I get love and advice from a lot of people." John says his rooting section, when he plays on the school basketball team, has doubled in three years. Next year they will live most of the school year at Dad's house, with long weekends twice a month and all summer with Mom.

Mom and Dad say the arrangement gives them both "adult time" as well as parenting time. Though partners in autonomous parenting, they may now feel that they have little in common save their joint history from the first three stages. They have rebuilt their trust and respect, but from a distance. A few couples become good friends in this stage; others remain working partners. Often there remains a private recognition of affection for each other, an acknowledgment of their shared past, but the emotion is carefully monitored lest it lead to misinterpretation.

These parents, just like those who are parenting solo, have formed a network of strong bonds with people in similar circumstances. These people also reached and found new ways of relating to their children and reorganizing their families and new ways which allow them to be responsive and responsible parents, as well as lead adult lives.

Stage Seven is worth the wait. Here there is a new form of parenthood and adulthood, a special blend of old and new which was forged by the need to survive, but sustained by a renewed faith in intimacy and family life. The new families and personal integrities are mature. The homes are stable.

Remarriage and a New Family History

Remarriage can take place at any of the last three of the seven stages. During Stages Five and Six, however, the adjustments to a subsequent marriage may be more difficult. Unfinished emotional business from the old marriage can overburden a new union's chances for success. People who remarry thinking it will heal hurts and solve problems may find that remarriage attempted too soon creates new difficulties instead. Remarriage doesn't automatically solve anything, and with four out of every ten remarriages ending again in divorce, the happy ending may not be that at all.

Remarriage is often interpreted as Stage One—a return to the one-home, one-authority version of the American Dream. But, Stage One cannot be re-created. Remarriage means Stages Five, Six, or Seven or later stages. The only true way back to Stage One, where the children have both natural parents under one roof, is to remarry the other biological parent!

When a parent remarries a new family history begins. If there was History 1 with the original marriage, then History 2 is the new single life. Remarriage means another family reorganization, History 3. For example, the new family may come together with four different ways of celebrating birthdays or other holidays, or cutting the pumpkin at Halloween. Each way competes for its place in the new family history and its precedence in family rituals. These blending experiences occupy the first year or two of the remarried family's history and, while the process is complex, millions of people have successfully navigated these waters to reach a satisfying new family life. Remarriage is a watershed, no doubt about it. And once the situation settles down, it can be a boon to the two-home arrangement as long as the new spouse is an additional parent and not a replacement parent.

The Crisis Periods for Parents and Children—Stages Four and Five

Stages Four and Five are the critical crisis periods. The body and psyche are under stress. This time has great potential for good or ill with and without a two-home arrangement. The crisis periods can last as little as six months or as long as two years or more when complications develop. These stages occur when life-changing decisions need to be made, but when judgment is often impaired and resistance to illness is down.

These two periods are so important that a series of future chapters details the symptoms, treatment, and homework for you. There will be guidelines on how to identify stress points, how to increase personal resources, how to clean out the painful wound the end of your marriage has caused, and how to help yourself heal and avoid making poor judgments.

You and the Other Parent

Building a new working relationship between you and the other parent is, as was shown before, a paradoxical process of separating your old role as a lover from your continuing role as a parent; marriage from parenthood. This is what I call the "retreat from intimacy" and the development of a new businesslike working relationship. In the chapters that follow you will see how this works and how you can put it into practice.

It helps to remember that you don't have to love your former mate to have a businesslike relationship any more than you have to love your mechanic to get your car fixed. Be patient with yourself during this disentanglement process. It takes time and is sometimes discouraging, but it is something that can be learned, and it yields to persistent effort. Give your past a chance to settle, your feelings a chance to cool, and your skills a chance to increase.

When the Other Parent Will Not Consider the Two-Home Arrangement

When the other parent is out of the picture, hostile or apathetic toward the idea of two homes, you have a series of steps to take and then a number of options to exercise. First, take some time to read a special section in Appendix I, Reinvolving the Drop-out Parent or Becoming Reinvolved, then return to this place in the book and continue reading each chapter as was suggested in Chapter 1. You will find in each chapter that the techniques and guidelines for parents usually work to end the hurt and guilt whether or not the other parent ever comes around to seeing a two-home view of things. Once you have satisfied yourself that you have digested the concepts as thoroughly as necessary, you have a series of options before you—either attempt to reinvolve the other parent (or convince him or her that you should be reinvolved yourself), or develop a two-home arrangement with a relative or friend—adding an Aunt Alice's House or Tom and Joan's House instead of a Mom's House or Dad's House.

Guidelines for Your Progress from One Home to Two Homes

1. Understand the seven stages and the way family histories can change.
2. Weed out any negative or unrealistic beliefs and find your own meaning of family, of home, of parenthood.
3. Respect the crisis periods of the transition, learn how you function during times of stress, and increase your personal resources.
4. Let the emotions of the end of your marriage run their course and evaluate your past.
5. Learn how to separate your role as a former mate from that of a parent.
6. Set up your own home (or reorganize it if necessary), establishing your new family rituals, customs, and rules.
7. Aim for a good "Parenting Agreement" and a privately negotiated settlement about the children.
8. Strengthen ties with supportive others—friends, family, associates, or if necessary, seek new ties.
9. Watch your language as you proceed along this road since it can describe your status, your self-esteem, and your accomplishments. As the next chapter shows, how you say things can determine how you feel about them.

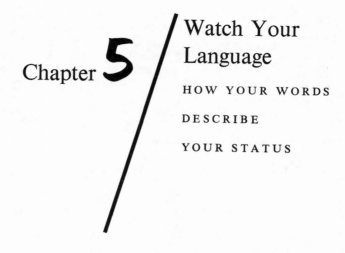

Chapter 5

Watch Your Language

HOW YOUR WORDS

DESCRIBE

YOUR STATUS

Here is a familiar scenario. Someone asks a divorced man whether he has a family. He is likely to say something like this:

"I used to have a family, but my marriage broke up three years ago. My wife has custody of the kids and they only come to see me on the weekend."

His former wife might describe her situation this way:

"I have three children but I am raising them alone. They visit their father on the weekend. Our marriage failed three years ago."

Now suppose we changed the parents' script:

Father: "I have a family with three children. They live with me on weekends and with their mother the rest of the time. Our marriage ended three years ago."

Mother: "I have a family with three children. They live with me during the week and with their father on weekends. They have two homes. Our marriage ended about three years ago."

Stinkweed Words, Rose Words

It is remarkable how much difference the substitution of a few words can make in the meaning of the statements. In the first case, father and mother are using what I call "stinkweed" words, words that are unpleasant, negative, or defensive. In the second, they are using "rose" words, words that connote satisfaction, confidence, and a sense of pride in parenthood.

In this case, the words that make a big difference are the positive

48

phrases "have a family" and "live with" instead of the apologetic "used to have a family," "custody of the kids," "raising them alone," "come to see me," and "visit." (Remember, outsiders visit; families live together.) Since the two-home approach is not yet well established, it is equally important to say that the children have two homes—Mom's house and Dad's house—rather than the one home of the old days. Finally, as a way to relieve any guilt or shame that might be lurking in one's insides, it's important to say that the marriage ended rather than that it failed or broke up.

Most parents sit up and listen attentively when those shabby old phrases are picked out of everyday speech and placed end to end. No matter how one looks at it, the language applied to divorced parents and their children usually puts them at odds, not at ease, with their society.

The broken-home label and the use of divorce as a scapegoat for society's basic problems don't just stop with everyday language. They are entrenched in much professional language and attitudes as well. For instance, pick up almost any professional journal on the family before 1975. The divorced family is referred to somewhere in its pages as a "broken home," rather than as a one-parent family, divorced family, or just a family. It takes little imagination to understand how parents or children must feel about coming from a "broken home"—not good. And other words will make them feel worse. "Fatherless home," "motherless home," "incomplete family," "failure of the marriage," "shattered family," "unfit parent," "awarded custody," and "visitation rights" are thinly veiled insults that undermine self-confidence and promote a sense of societal disapproval.

To family therapists, the phrase "broken home" once elicited associations such as lack of caring, not whole, inoperable, separated, and torn. My own pet peeve, though, is "reconstituted family" meant to describe the single parent who remarries. This phrase recalls instructions for fruit juice concentrate: Add one mate and get an instant family. Apparently, the family that existed before doesn't count as a real family.

Even the seemingly innocent phrases "single-parent family" and "one-parent family" can sound defensive. Why don't people simply acknowledge that such families are acceptable as families, period, and stop at that? Why not call a family a family instead of adding some kind of qualification by way of explanation about the parents' marital state? If the term "intact family" is reserved for the never-divorced, no wonder divorced men and women are sometimes uncertain of their claims to parenthood!

Many single people haven't realized how the day-in-day-out use of stinkweed words injures them and their children. Their sense of self, family, and parenthood is undermined. At their worst, stinkweed words can set the scene for all-out war between parents, with battles over property, children, and who was to blame. At their best, they connote second-class status worthy of pity or condescension. Of course, not all children accept the labels at face value. One bright child with divorced parents told me he did not come from a single-parent family, saying "My parents are single, but I'm not."

Here's a beginning exercise for parents. The very next time someone asks you, "Do you have a family?", regardless of whether you have legal custody or not, answer yes. Don't add, "I'm divorced" or "I'm a single parent." If you are a parent without legal custody, don't add "but my children don't live with me." Stake your rightful claim to family life and parenthood. This claim is yours and you deserve it. Try saying yes without excuses and explanations. Simply by changing certain everyday words, you can improve your sense of identity, strengthen your sense of family self-confidence, and acknowledge yourself as a person who is a parent and heads a family, whether you are single or remarried.

What the Children Hear

To a child, getting married and having a family means people get presents and have parties. Most words about love and family exalt oneness and sharing in a "real family" where a mother and a father live under one roof with their kids. The average child accepts this easily.

Getting divorced is the reverse of all this. People get sad, yell at each other, and do other scary things. There are no parties and definitely no presents. One of the parents goes to live somewhere else and nobody says they are going to be happy, not even after a while.

When parents divorce, the child knows the family doesn't look the same anymore. And it certainly doesn't feel good to a child to hear a teacher call his or her home broken, or hear the doctor calling the child a victim of divorce or parents stating that their marriage failed. What does all this mean to a child? With negative labels come negative conclusions. The home is broken. The parents are failures. The child is, at least partially, deserted.

Divorce as a Crime

Children are also confused by legalistic language and all the mystery surrounding courts and the judicial system. For most children, courts exist to decide who is the good guy and who is the bad guy—who's supposed to be punished for breaking the law. Somebody's to blame somewhere. When you are a child, it's easy to imagine that divorce is some sort of crime.

If a child were unlucky enough to overhear a lawyer talking to a parent before going to court, he would hear such tidbits as "the best defense is a good offense" (and any sports-minded kid knows what that means!), or that most dads "drop out" after a year, or that Mom has to "protect her best interests" so she can be prepared to "raise her family alone." How would you feel if you heard this as a child? Would you be afraid? Would you wonder whether you were loved or would be cared for? Would you feel helpless?

Divorce as a Contest

It isn't bad enough that Mom and Dad go to court like criminals. One day Mom returns from court and announces that the judge awarded custody of you to her but gave Dad visitation rights. It isn't particularly reassuring when Mom hastens to add: "What this means is that you will be living with me and visiting Dad on Saturdays." To many children, including teenagers, it can sound like a contest in which they were the first prize.

Children don't like to talk about these things. But occasionally their confusion erupts in statements like: "Daddy sold me to Mommy for two hundred dollars a month," or "Mom won the car, the house, and me."

Even parents who avoid court battles must still deal with words such as custody, visitation, awarded, child support, investigation, and unfit. These all sound as if they pertain to prisons, wardens, and probation instead of to families. These words confirm the conclusion that one parent has all the authority, responsibility, and rights, while the other parent must meekly obey all the rules of procedure in order to gain access to the institution.

Many professionals—counselors, psychologists, judges, and attorneys—are as deeply upset with the current adversary language of courts and institutions as any single or remarried parent. These people would be only too happy to replace the harmful and degrading words with terms that more accurately and humanely describe evolving life-styles.

The broken-home myth dies hard, however. Even though the legal language and professional literature are heavy with cold or negative labels, some single and remarried parents use words that perpetuate the suspicions that surround society's attitudes about the broken home. These parents, like some professionals, have not yet been convinced how crucially important it is to clean up the language we use to describe our new family system.

A New Vocabulary

All of us urgently need to develop a new vocabulary to describe family life after divorce. Although the beginning word list below is short, you may find it hard to master. If you can convert completely from stink-weed words to rose words in two or three months, you will have accomplished something very important for yourself and your children. If you start adding your own new words to enlarge this beginning vocabulary further, you will be one of our real pioneers.

Beginning Vocabulary

Instead of Saying:	Try Saying:
Visiting	Living with
I have children but they live with their mother/father	I have a family
The children's mother/father left us	I have a family
The children are seeing (or visiting) their dad/mom	The children are at Mom's house/Dad's house, at their other house with their other family
Motherless, fatherless, split home, broken home, incomplete home	The home, the family
The children have one home and their mother/father visits	The children have two homes
The marriage broke up, failed	The marriage ended
Wife, husband (ex-wife, ex-husband)	Children's mother, children's father
Custody and visitation agreement	Parenting Agreement
Remarriage, reconstituted family, blended family, combination family	Family (or second family, third family, etc.)

Instead of Asking Children:	Try Asking:
Where do you live? (questioner knows only that parents are separated)	Where do your mother and father live?
Where do you live? (questioner knows one of the parents)	Where is your other home? Where does your other family live?

We have talked about most of the words on the list. There are some others that need our attention. It is important to stop talking about your wife or your husband after divorce. Ex-wife and ex-husband don't do such a good job either. Saying former wife or former husband or first (or second) wife is somewhat better. But saying children's mother or children's father is best of all. The point is that words can help you separate your old role as a mate from your continuing one as a parent. Referring to your former intimate relationship with the words *husband* and *wife,* even with *ex* or *former* in front of them, reinforces your old life together and all those emotions connected with it. Saying children's mother or children's father will help you focus on the parent-parent relationship. Perhaps later, when your emotional divorce is complete, you can use terms like "my former wife" or "my first husband."

Old Habits

All habits take time to change. But when other people resist your changes by providing roadblocks of scorn or reproach, changing a habit can be more difficult.

The other day, I watched a little girl attempt to answer a playmate's mother's question. The mother asked, "Where do you live?" knowing full well that the child was presently living with her father during the summer. When the child replied that she lived right there in the same apartment complex and then with her mother in a neighboring city, the woman replied, "Oh, I know that, but what part of the city?" The child wasn't fooled. Her friend's mother knew she was living with her father now. Why did she ask her where she lived? Wasn't her father's home her home too? And, if the woman wanted to know about her other home, why didn't she just ask about it straight out? Couldn't she have asked, "Where is your other home?" or "Where is your mother's home?"

In other situations, resistance to a new set of words comes more painfully from children's friends or from a parent or grandparent. Teenagers might resist some of the two-home vocabulary because of peer pressure and acceptance of what is "in." There are no songs on the charts about two homes or cooperative parents. Church groups do not extol the virtues of parents who develop two homes.

Children of all ages might straddle the fence of words because they assume that one parent would be hurt or vengeful if the child referred to the other parent's house as home. Some parents or grandparents send out strong implicit messages that say: If you talk about the other parent at all, you must act as if that parent is unimportant. You must act as if your *real* home is with me and you love me best. Such hidden agendas thrive on stinkweed words. Some older children may think, "I'll do what they ask, but I don't believe it for a minute." However, it takes an especially strong child to make such a distinction. Most children find themselves in the mire of the loyalty struggle, the worst affliction for children of divorce. They want to look out for their parents' best interests and to please those they love. But one parent is saying that such love can be proved only if the children dump or demean the other parent, or if they lie about how they feel. Parents and grandparents who place children in such a double bind not only undermine the children's respect for them, but do their children a grave emotional and moral injustice.

Your own feelings may also stand in the way of the new vocabulary. It is perfectly natural for a parent who has the children most of the time to resent hearing that the children live at the other parent's house, when according to the old way of talking they only visit here. You can get a barometer reading on your own degree of anger if you try the following exercise. Ask yourself how you honestly feel if you say, "My children live with me during the weekend (or the week, whatever your circumstance), and the rest of the time they live with their other parent."

If the children live with you the majority of the time, do you feel comfortable or uncomfortable with such a statement? Does it make you feel less alone, less burdened, less as if you had all the weight of responsibility on your shoulders exclusively? Or do you resent changing your language habits because you do not want to share the term "live" with someone who doesn't share equally all the heartaches and the hard work of raising children? "They don't live with their father," said one angry mother, "they play with him. With me they work and face hard reality. I resent him being the hero while I'm the villain."

This mother's barometer reading on anger was high and for good reason. She was in a lopsided situation and the term "live with Mother" was one of her few rewards. But her anger cost her a good deal.

Advantages of a New Vocabulary

If your children live with you on weekends, do you feel more like a bona fide parent when you say: "My children live with me"? Or do you resist saying they live with you because you really don't feel like the traditional parent with daily authority over meals, clothing, and homework? "Just saying 'live with me this weekend' gave me a terrific boost of parent confidence," one father said. "I started thinking like a parent instead of a host with weekend guests."

This exercise doesn't just tap feelings of anger or of hope, but brings to light other emotions and attitudes that are worth your attention. Even if the rose words seem hard to say, say them and see what happens. Pay attention to what feelings and attitudes come up for you and your children. Write down the results, if you can.

In changing your vocabulary from stinkweed words to rose words, it's good to remember that old habits carry with them the old attitudes of society. I have found myself in social conversations where I use rose words only to be corrected by someone who insisted that I use the stinkweed words. "You mean they visit you in the summer, don't you?" When I assured the questioner that the children lived with me, they then jumped to their next conclusion, "What a pity you lost the court battle," or more indirectly, "Why aren't they living with you all the time, dear?"

Perhaps the most touchy situations are those with friends who react to your use of rose words with "Oh, you know what I mean" or, worse, accuse you of trying to make a bad situation look better with verbal whitewash. "You know full well that one weekend a month and two months in the summer doesn't make a home," said one father who objected to the use of rose words.

These are real times of test, for they reveal the biases and show the true colors of your friends and family. Sometimes you can answer "I know what you mean," or shrug. When you do, probably nothing has been gained and you might feel an unpleasant aftertaste. But you could answer with a polite but firm "That is the way you see it. But I see it another way."

We all need approval and acceptance, especially from those close to us. But going along with their stinkweed words is not, in the end, going to be to your own advantage. With some effort you can work out your own ways to educate yourself and your children. In so doing, you may find that the rose vocabulary genuinely interests others who find its positive approach refreshing and worthwhile.

Sometimes people don't take the rose words too seriously. "If it's as easy as that," they ask themselves, "how can it really work?" If you fall into this category, remember, using new words is a little like caring for your teeth. You have to brush and floss regularly before the results show in a good dental checkup. It's the same way with getting rid of stinkweed words. The changes are subtle but important. They take a while to show up.

Rose words can definitely be a boon for parents. They create an atmosphere in which parental cooperation can develop more readily. "When I said the children 'visited their father,'" one mother said, "it didn't occur to me to ask him to attend a parent-teacher conference at school. But when I started using 'lived with their father,' it dawned on me that maybe he did have a right and a responsibility in this area, too. Now I feel far freer to ask him to pitch in and share and he feels freer to say 'of course,' and to initiate responsibilities in other situations too, like the medical checkups and the children's summer camps."

The new language of two-home families can also be carried over into legal agreements and subsequent marriages, as I show in future chapters. But you need to use it every day until it permeates your thinking and becomes an unconscious habit.

Language plays a fundamental part in shaping our values and our priorities, in giving substance to our beliefs, and in defining boundaries. What we call ourselves and what we are called can shape what we become.

Words exist to serve, not to oppress. If a word or phrase describes the life you live, keep it. If it doesn't, toss it out and find a better one. It is our responsibility to ourselves, our children, and to all the others who will eventually join us, to use words that work for us, not against us.

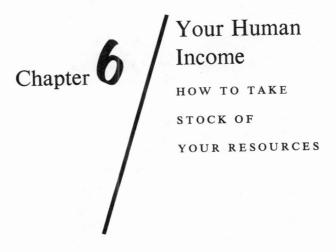

Chapter **6** / Your Human
Income

Getting a divorce means the release from one kind of a legal relationship and the beginning of a new one. This legal release does not promise future happiness or fulfillment. It only signals the official beginning of your family reorganization and the process of disentangling your role as a lover from your role as a parent.

During this period doubts and questions crowd a person's thoughts. What's going to happen to me? Will I make it? Will I botch it up? What can I count on? How will the children take it? As a thirty-eight-year-old man with a five-year-old daughter put it, "The question that haunted my life before I separated was, 'Would my life be any better than it was when I was married?' "

These reactions are valid and to be expected; look at the avalanche of changes that inevitably accompany separation and family reorganization.

Changes Brought About as a Marriage Ends

- Your way of life changes from being married to being single.
- Your intimate relationship changes from having a long-term committed relationship to being unattached.
- Your parental role changes from being one of a set of parents under one roof to being a single parent.
- Your identity and self-image change, now undefined by marriage.

57

There may also be changes in:

- Neighborhood—the one who leaves adjusts to a new area, while the one who stays adjusts to new circumstances in the same environment.
- Personal habits—eating, exercise, sleep, sex, and household habits: who takes out the trash, who does the wash; from sleeping together to sleeping alone.
- Occupation and income—usually less money to live on, or a need to change jobs, to train for new work, or to resume work.
- Social circles—friends may take sides or drop away in time. Few friendships remain exactly as they were when you were married.

Any one of these, by itself, is a big change. In ending a marriage, these changes come together or in rapid sequence, draining energy and building up pressure. It is very much like a form of culture shock, like being thrust into a foreign country. This is especially true for the parent who moves out of the original family home. The parent who remains still has the familiar surroundings and the responsibilities of the children's routine. "It has some of the feeling that all is going on as it was before," said one mother, "but one of the members is missing."

Still more layers of potential stress can come from society, from your friends or family, and from your own attitudes. Guilt, stigma, discrimination, the legal process, and the legacy of the broken home all take their toll. "No welcome wagon for us," said one young mother, "not at school, church, at work, or in court." Furthermore, the new single parents need to meet new people in the same boat, people who can provide them with examples for their own lives. While successful two-home parents exist, they don't wear signs that say, "Watch me." As one woman said quietly of her divorce after twenty years and three children, "The experience of ending a marriage is like childbirth; you have to undergo it to understand how intense it can be. I know now what they mean by killer stress."

Stress

Stress and Illness

When stress gets too high, the body's natural resistance to illness is weakened. If the pressures are not dissipated appropriately, health problems follow. Parents who work hard at the office and return home to another four to six hours of work and responsibility have no time to relax and recuperate. Not surprisingly, this unbalanced life often affects their health. Furthermore, when an unbalanced life is combined with highly stressful events such as death or divorce, people may be more susceptible than usual to heart disease, hypertension, strokes, cancer, and other life-taking illnesses. Stress is not a disease, but it can cripple nonetheless.

Stress and Decisions

For many people a high level of stress reduces their ability to make measured judgments. Yet many decisions demand attention, poor judgment or no, and the advice and suggestions of well-meaning others only seem to add to the problem. "My brother is going through a divorce," said one man, "and his judgment is awful. He distrusts everyone who tries to help him. How can he make life-long decisions this way?" When people most need their wits about them they are all too often at their wit's end.

Everyone has a limit, and even the most stable, easy-going personality can be immobilized by too much too soon. Regardless of age, income, or education, the ending of a marriage nearly always brings stress—lots of it. There is usually too little money, too little time, too little rest, too many decisions, and too much responsibility. Relationships can become strained, resistance to illness goes down, and judgment deteriorates.

Your Human Income: Resources for Coping with Stress

When stress wrings your heart and body, extracting your inner resources, how can you replenish your inner self and regain that important balance and perspective? Answer: Increase your human income—the way you are meeting your basic needs for support, survival, and human nourishment.

Here is a quick survey to give you a rough estimate of just how much survival and human income you think you have to meet the personal stress that comes with divorce. The questions focus on basic survival and human needs and how well you feel you are meeting these needs.

Before you take the survey, look at some sample situations and answers. For question 11—"Do you have an operating circle of acquaintances, friends, or neighbors who can help you out, and vice versa, when needed?"—one man, John, rated himself 2. He has about six bowling acquaintances. He hasn't thought about whether they would help him out when he needed it. He simply doesn't know. John can't think of other people he might call on. He thinks his bowling acquaintances would help out, but he's never wanted to put them to the test.

Jim, on the other hand, has a group of friends that he calls his divorce buddies—people he worked with who went through divorce about the same time he did. He knows he can count on these people (and vice versa) because they have come to his aid in the past. He gave himself an 8, adding that he could always add more friends to his circle.

Jane is naturally quiet and reserved. She does not make friends easily. She is new to the area and knows no one; her family lives thousands of miles away. She gave herself a 1, but when questioned said that she fully intended to get that score up to a 5 by the end of the month. She was already planning to get to know her neighbors well enough so that she could count on them in emergencies.

Your Survival and Human Income

Answer the following questions using a scale of 1 to 10. Rate the happiest, most satisfied yes you can give a high of 10. Rate the saddest, most dissatisfied or resigned no a low of 1. A rating of 5 can be your personal average.

- 10 = The best possible answer for you. The way you are meeting this need is ideal; it suits you perfectly.
- 5 = An average answer. This need is being met but there is ample room for improvement.
- 1 = Things couldn't be worse! Either you are not meeting this need at all, or you are as yet unable to meet this need in a way you feel is best for you.

How Do You Rate Your Survival Income?

( ) 1. Can you pay the rent, afford nourishing food, purchase adequate clothing?

( ) 2. Are you relatively safe in your home, your neighborhood, and at work?

( ) 3. Can you obtain and afford medical care when you or the children are ill?

( ) 4. Can you obtain and afford child care during the whole week?

( ) 5. Can you obtain and afford help at home?

How Do You Rate Your Human Income?

( ) 6. Can you take a day off for rest or recreation every week?

( ) 7. Can you see a movie twice a month or take a ride somewhere out of the area for a change of scenery?

( ) 8. Can you afford a sitter so that you can take two days off a month to be an adult without being responsible for your children (if they live with you most of the time)? Or can you afford to be with them forty-eight hours consecutively once a month (if they do not live with you full time)?

( ) 9. Is the children's other parent involved in parenting the children; and is this parent taking on reasonable responsibilities?

(   ) 10. Are you and the children's other parent on good working terms?

(   ) 11. Do you have an operating circle of acquaintances, friends, or neighbors who can help you out, and vice versa, when needed?

(   ) 12. Do you have a group of friends or relatives who can share some of your family life like birthdays and special occasions?

(   ) 13. Can you give and receive affection from this group?

(   ) 14. Does this group on occasion share with you some of the parenting of your children?

(   ) 15. Do you have at least one really close friend you can share just about anything with?

(   ) 16. Do you have at least one person you can really count on?

(   ) 17. Do you have a mate or lover with whom you can give and receive affection and/or sex?

Now, add up your scores. Scores above 90 show you feel you are operating with a reasonable income using your own standards. The higher you score the better, of course. However, scores below 90 suggest that you take some important steps to increase your survival and human income level so that you can decrease or dissipate your present stress level. The higher your income the easier stress may be to handle.

Survival and human needs* are common denominators to everyone, regardless of degree of sophistication, education, or financial income level. Sometimes the threat of losing security can be just as stressful as actually losing it. Just as the body needs food, the spirit needs security. The shipwreck victim can exist on a case of canned sardines, but he can go crazy watching the sharks circling the perimeter of his rubber raft.

The challenge is to minimize the stress by identifying first where it comes from; second, what basic needs are either not being met (or are threatened); and finally, to change the situation for the better.

How to Increase Your Human Income

Major changes happen at some time to everyone, married or single, and both experts and laymen see the management of stress through action and attitude as important. The following Ten Basic Rules bring together some of the guidelines found most helpful by parents and professionals in our workshops and classes.

* Survival needs: food, water, air, shelter, sleep
Human needs: love, friendship, belonging, security, self-respect, a sense of purpose or meaning. (Adapted from Maslow's hierarchy of needs.)

Ten Basic Rules

1. Don't Go Through This Period Alone

Support and acceptance by other people are absolutely essential during big changes. Support is perhaps the most important of all the ground rules. At least one other person must care enough about you to be supportive, to listen, to give you feedback, and to truly care. Two people are better than one, and a group is best of all, especially when your children are welcomed and accepted in the group too. Seek out your friends, but be careful here. Sometimes old friends take sides or have a vested interest in your not changing at all. It could be that for a time you will need to create new friendships better suited for this time of change. If you are isolated for the moment, call on your minister, a counselor, or a hot line. Despite the popular beliefs in rugged independence and making it alone, to go through a crisis completely by yourself is risky. Isolation can raise the already dangerous stress level, leading to later complications and delaying your progress. Sometimes membership in an organization can be a temporary substitute for close friends, but it is not an adequate replacement for a personal friendship. Remember, "Sorrow shared, half the sorrow; joy shared, double the joy."

2. Learn What's Going On

Use your head; ask questions; pay attention. It is important to know when you make any change what you are getting into. Also, finding out what's going on usually puts you in touch with new people—some of them in the same boat as you. When you ask questions or observe people in somewhat similar situations, you can pick and choose among what you see, thinking: "This is a little like my situation," or "That one has totally different problems." You gain a clearer perspective.

This sharing of a common condition need not take the form of baring your innermost soul. Just your physical presence at a meeting or lecture where you can learn what's going on is action enough until you are ready for deeper, more personal involvement. Given half a chance, other people will share their knowledge with you and your own investigations will give you extra clues. In the meantime, gather information, make observations, and ask questions. The more alternatives you can line up to choose from the better.

3. Look for What Works and What Doesn't

Give a plus to an action or attitude that promotes personal and family growth, a minus to those toxic signs that bring pain and dissent. There are many red lights during the first two years, and observing them in others (and asking your friends and other singles about them) can help you avoid defeatist attitudes and keep you from getting unnecessarily bogged down. One divorcing woman remarked during a workshop: "Nobody told me life was a series of situations to confront and review. I was taught to see situations as problems, as a sign that *I* hadn't done something right. Now I see that if I want to reshape my life, I have to forget about problems and failures and look at what works and what doesn't."

4. Care for Your Inner Self

Provide for your basic human needs, especially those which lead you to a strong sense of self. Since the complexities of what I call The Process bring many role changes, you will face yourself alone, no longer a married parent or a married person. Your own self-esteem and reshaped identity will respond to acceptance, respect, affection, and a sense of belonging and feedback from those you respect, but you need to give these to yourself as well. Make time for your inner self, for contemplation and for quiet periods alone when these many changes can have a chance to sink in gently. Respect this period of your life. Listen to yourself; your emotions are not tyrants, but are parts of your being that have a right to be heard and to be cared for.

5. Take Care of Your Body and Find Safe Ways to Blow off Steam

What's good for the psyche is also good for the body. Respect the need of both to take "time out" for rest and recreation. Big changes take enormous amounts of energy; if you don't rest, stress gets the upper hand. While stress can kill, it more often maims, especially when people don't take time to eat, exercise, and rest. A crisis period can lead to the overs— overdrinking, oversmoking, overeating—with no energy left for those activities and health schedules that will really help you to withstand stress and resist illness. Now is the time to check with your doctor, especially about the right amount of exercise for you.

Baby yourself with a good book, an afternoon with friends, a quiet walk. Find safe ways to blow off steam, ways to let some of the inner pressures escape. Some people jog, play tennis, take up bowling. Other people work out at the gym, play the piano, join baseball teams. Whatever is your way, you'll know it's working when your body feels better and your problems seem smaller.

6. Keep a Positive but Realistic Perspective

A positive but realistic frame of mind is an important key to making anything work. This does not mean blindness to problems, or a Pollyanna view of life. It does mean taking a long view of your experience every once in a while and making conscious efforts to shake off any negative, doomsday feelings. Your situation is similar to others', but it is also uniquely personal. *You are your own best judge of what is happening.* It's your life and you are ultimately responsible for how you see it and for what you do with it. Furthermore, the latest research strongly suggests that people who best withstand the stress of crises have supportive contacts with others and a determination to focus on the hopeful rather than the depressing sides of a difficult situation.

7. Increase Personal Skills

You might agree that you need more friends, knowledge, awareness, better perspective, and that you should care for your body and your inner self. But how do you do it? Know-how can be acquired. Reach out to other people; ask them what they do. Observe others thoughtfully. Take classes. Use the guides described in this book.

Reorganizing one's life usually requires a far more sophisticated set of specific life skills than were needed in marriage. Your relations *are* more complicated now and can all profit from a stronger grasp of personal skills.

8. Watch Your Language

The vocabulary you use to describe your circumstances is tremendously important to your children and your own sense of dignity and direction. It's your responsibility to make a vocabulary that accurately and humanely reflects your circumstances and life-style. If a word or phrase does not positively reflect your new status, get rid of it and make up your own rose term. Remember, we often become what we are called.

9. Use Your Sense of Humor

Even if you are in a crisis period now, try to lighten it up with the humor and laughter that can so mercifully release pent-up tensions and renew a sense of hope and perspective. As serious as a crisis might be, it can't always be taken seriously. Play with your children, relax with them, enjoy being together. The months and years will go by quickly enough. The times together will be the ones most likely to be remembered and cherished. These will be the times that will say "family."

10. Encourage Your Children to Explore These Rules for Themselves

These basic rules are not just for grownups; they can be encouraged in children as ways that they too can learn to weather crises. Your example during crisis periods is not only a good teacher for your children, but it can give your children a sense of confidence in your ability to cope with massive changes and in their ability to "take after my Mom" or "be like my Dad."

These basic rules cover a lot of ground, but an action in one part usually affects other parts as well. One action meets more than one need; one insight influences more than one attitude.

How Much Change and Stress (Can/Should) You Take?

The higher the stress, the greater your need to protect yourself and to be good to yourself. But changes don't happen overnight, and sometimes all the talk and action of reshaping lives is just too much, too soon. That's your clue to stop, take a rest before going on. During great change people are very much like sponges; they can absorb just so much at one time and no more. Later, after drying out a bit, more change can soak in.

1. Get some *real* rest by *not* thinking about your problems. Give yourself some breathing room. Cope with your situation at your own pace, in your own rhythm.

2. If at any time you question your resilience, your durability, talk to a friend or a counselor, or find a hot line. Use all the help you can get during those first couple of years. It is available, and you deserve to treat yourself to the best.

3. Respect this period of your life. It probably wasn't in your original blueprint for your life, but it's here now, so give it your most creative attention.

Chapter 7

The Emotions of Ending a Marriage

HOW THEY HELP

AND HINDER

THE WORKING

RELATIONSHIP

"I didn't know it would be so hard to get a divorce," said Lois, a twenty-nine-year-old mother of an infant son, separated for three months. "I thought Barry (the baby's father) would go along with my idea for two homes. People told me he'd be angry at me for wanting the divorce but I didn't believe them. Now Barry is hostile, resentful, and I'm so mad I don't care if he never sees our son again. I'm even tempted to tell my lawyer to go for sole custody!"

Lois's surprise and reflex reaction are familiar to parents after separation. The intense emotions of divorce erupt. Resentment, blame, and anger obscure and threaten original goals of cooperation. Barry's anger at his child's mother is as predictable as Lois's nearly automatic retaliatory response of threatening sole custody.

How Emotions Hinder a Working Relationship

If these two knew little about post-divorce emotions, they could easily fall back into the one-home, sole-custody quagmire. They might abandon the prospect of two houses and be trapped behind the all-or-nothing road-block discussed in Chapter 2. Thinking that they are obviously no longer the perfectly civilized couple, they can only be the battling "exes."

Unfortunately, most people are unaware of the dynamics of these emotions and how they can affect judgment. They plunge ahead, riding the crest of their intense feelings, making decisions on property, children, and support monies. They lose their tempers, their perspective, and their shirts.

66

They jeopardize a good working relationship, delay their emotional divorce, and painfully complicate their legal business.

This chapter will take a broad view of what the emotional process of major changes can look like. The common stages, symptoms, and treatments will be described so that you can make this period work for you instead of against you. The family life you save will be your own.

The Wounding and Healing Process of Divorce

The end of a marriage and the initial process of family reorganization are like a psychic wound, one that needs to be properly cleaned and cared for or complications may develop. The healing of this wound takes place in stages. First, letting go of the emotions and experiences of a past relationship is like cleansing a wound—it hurts to do, but it does need to be done. Certain later stages are critical for new growth, and a new blow can reopen the area and cause even further damage. The entire healing process can be fast or slow, relapses few or many. How long it takes depends on how well you take care of yourself. How well you take care of yourself depends on the kinds of information you have to work with.

You can make the most of the increased natural energy and marshaled courage of this crisis for your own and your children's benefit. Wisdom can grow during change. "After I finished those first two years of my divorce," said one father, "I felt I could handle anything. But before I understood about the stages of the process, I thought I was going off the deep end."

Getting a divorce is not something people plan to repeat. Consequently, sure that it will never happen again, they may not want to pay much attention to the process itself. Divorce may not occur again, but other life crises, such as the end of a serious love affair or the death of someone close, most certainly will. All such crises share common elements and call for similar personal skills; learning those skills for today's world is as important as learning business math.

Some of the material on the emotions of ending a marriage and reorganizing your family life has already been touched on in other chapters. Before going over the actual stages of this process to relate it to your own experience, take a look at the underlying purpose of the crisis period —the job of emotionally reordering your life.

The Symptoms

Survival and Emotional Reordering

The major tasks during the first two years are, first, to assure your physical survival and, next, to set your emotional self in order. Nature helps us survive by giving our body the extra energy of "flight or fight." The crisis puts our bodies into a kind of automatic red alert that increases our internal rpm. This special energy can be both healing and destructive. Higher rpm prepares us to meet drastic changes with more adrenaline, courage, and often more energy. But, unless we give ourselves adequate times to idle, to rest, or to proceed at a measured pace with a higher human income, the acceleration can also speed up the depletion of our bodily resources as well.

Review Work and Releasing Strong Feelings

Review work combines going back over your history, re-evaluating as you go, and then—most importantly—releasing the emotions still stored in your memory, muscles, and nerves.

Review work shows itself as a natural inclination to be preoccupied with the past (or with some present incident that seems to reflect the past) and to find yourself in the grip of strong feelings about these bygone events. Some say, "I keep having these conversations in my head and all these feelings come out." Long-forgotten episodes can come up for review, touching and releasing any stored emotional charge left over from the unresolved past. "After twenty years of marriage, I found myself recalling things sixteen or seventeen years old," said forty-five-year-old Dorothy. "I remembered the times he was angry at me when I was pregnant. I felt abandoned.

"Feelings welled up in me as if it were yesterday. I cried about them all over again. Then I got angry. I could see now that from those early slights, I had long ago begun to distrust his love for me. On one hand, my review work gave me a lot of insight into my marriage, but it confused and angered me as well. Why hadn't I ended the marriage then? Why had I gone on to have more children?"

Your preoccupation with the marriage, who was responsible for what and what this means to you now, is very natural and healthy review work. But it is *work,* like grief work after the death of a loved one. Similar in many ways, review work is also very different in that the other party is alive and a continual reminder of the old marriage, of the unanswered questions, of the still unsettled past. "We live in the same small town. I even see him on the street sometimes," said one woman. "I wonder, what is he saying about me to people? Is he blaming me for the breakup? I get upset just thinking about it." If marriage is the process of selection, then divorce can be seen as being "deselected." And the living reminder of this deselection is the children's other parent. The sense of failure and disappointment is sometimes crushing. It obscures the job of gradually separating your marriage from your parenthood.

Review work usually means having to deal with feelings of failure and of guilt. These feelings come together with thoughts of how, given another chance, you might have behaved differently. One mother doing review work said, "I feel so damned guilty now. I didn't try to have a relationship with him, I did take him for granted. I'll never be that way again."

Along with guilt and failure come feelings of being unloved, unwanted, or totally alone in the world. Some say painfully, "Who am I if I am not loved?" or "No one in the world finds me important anymore."

Usually review work permeates much of the first six months and then lessens, although occasional flashback periods bring up unexplored areas again over the years to come. The easiest (and most peaceful) response to review work has been described by a few people as simply coming to no definite conclusions. Not all questions have answers and not all whys are worth pursuing. Asking, "What's going on here?" is a more helpful question to ask than "Why?" Release and peace do not necessarily depend on taking a course of action on a position, but simply on acknowledging the experience.

Releasing Strong Feelings

Give the feelings that come up a safe outlet through physical exercise, sports, activities, absorbing hobbies, or meditation. Any activity that will allow you to release pent-up energy and give your mind and body a chance to heal is a good idea. But do it—regularly. Many people find that lots of physical work and activity—as much as their doctor will allow—is a wonderful way to release strong feelings safely as well as a chance to take up that sport they have admired or that fitness plan they've been promising to follow. As the body responds to self-care, self-esteem and self-confidence increase. The review work seems easier, more constructive.

Repeating Themes: Your Old Skeletons

When, as Dorothy reported, a memory and a feeling reappear repeatedly, you can be sure you have stumbled on an old skeleton from your personal closet, perhaps from your life before your marriage, perhaps during your marriage.

Pay special attention to these relics—they give especially important clues on how to accelerate and stabilize your growth in the future. Keep a notebook or a journal on these reruns—a simple sentence will do. (Some of Dorothy's reruns were: "Feel abandoned again." "Why didn't I end the marriage sooner?") Old skeletons are often overlooked, but their usefulness for your own personal stability and growth and for a sub-sequent marriage cannot be exaggerated.

Your Automatic Brakes: Denial and Numbness

Because too much change and stress can be dangerous, a peculiar but completely understandable phenomenon occurs. Numbness begins and the mind either ignores or denies certain facts. This denial and numbness are the psyche's way of resting, of making the present work for you. It is a natural way of letting change proceed at an acceptable pace. It is as if, like a swollen sponge, you have absorbed enough for now. Denial isn't necessarily a refusal to see reality, but a set of brakes unconsciously applied to the accumulation of too much change too fast. The transformation from being married to being a fully integrated single person and parent does not happen in a single day, but gradually over a period of months and years. Even the most adaptable person will find this a long journey. Denial is not intrinsically bad, and appears to some extent in almost everyone during the first two years. It will work for you by helping you to slow down, letting your sponge of change dry out a bit. It will work against you if you never go near the water again.

The Stages of Emotions

The emotions of ending a marriage seem to come in stages. Progress through these stages releases energies that can work for you or against you. The same neutral energy that gives some people the courage and motivation to make positive changes can in others create illness. Some people stop smoking, lose excessive weight, change careers. Others lighten their personal load of debilitating habits, attitudes, or beliefs. This is how these emotions can work for you. The energy is there and the right choices are usually within reach. But you need information in order to recognize and choose the right alternatives for you.

The emotions of divorce often divide themselves into two major time periods. For this reason, I've called the first period of time the "first wave." This usually lasts about two or three years. It begins before the separation when the relationship's future is in serious doubt. It often ends many months later, after the end of the marriage, when the new single identity, roles, and life-style are fully integrated and the largest share of the emotional divorce is nearly completed.

The second time period, the "second wave," is a series of brief re-lapses or flashbacks spontaneously triggered by certain events or devel-opments. This second wave comes after that first two- or three-year period.

Each time period is unique, bringing its own symptoms, danger signals, and effective series of treatments. This chapter will describe the stages within the first two or three years, what to look for, and what to do. A later chapter will do the same for the second-wave time period.

Before going into detail about the first-wave stages, take a brief look at the chart below that gives a bird's-eye view of the stages of emotions and re-evaluation process. Then, let's begin with Stage One—where your relationship first began to show signs of serious trouble.

The Stages of Emotions and Re-evaluation

THE FIRST TWO TO THREE YEARS   The First Wave

1. The period just before the actual separation: the beginning of a crisis period
2. The time of the separation: a crisis period
3. The eruption of strong emotions: a crisis period
4. The adult adolescence of testing new roles, new identity
5. The more mature identity and new life-style

AFTER TWO OR THREE YEARS   The Second Wave—Flashbacks or Relapses to First-Wave Feelings and Actions

6. A general, deeper re-evaluation and awareness of what the new life has brought about
7. When the other parent remarries, recouples, or again divorces
8. When you remarry, recouple, or again divorce
9. When the other parent has another child with another mate
10. When there is a change or threatened change in legal arrangements, such as custody or support
11. When one of you moves away from the area
12. When there is a big change in personal circumstances (increase or decrease in income, status, health)

Treatments for Healing the Wound

The best treatments for all stages are easy to remember. Follow the Ten Basic Rules given in the last chapter. Be especially conscientious during the first three stages, they are crisis periods. In Stage One, the stress level may rise to a peak just before the decision period and stay there. This high level may remain high through Stage Two and find a different or an even higher level in Stage Three.

First, do your review work. Preoccupation with the past will run its course eventually, but it does need to run its course.

Second:

1. *Take care of your body.* Baby yourself; pay attention to your diet, rest patterns, and exercise patterns.

2. *Have several friends (even if they need to be new ones) with whom you can share your feelings and companionship.* Or enlist a trained professional. You may not feel like company, but you should be able to have it if you need or want it.

3. *Identify several more friends you can use as sounding boards for decisions.* Your judgment may need perspective during this time.

4. *Note your old skeletons, those repeating themes that the review work returns to and that generate so much feeling.* Keep a brief journal.

5. *Find safe and healthy ways to release your bodily tension and your strong emotions physically.* Sports or exercise approved by your doctor can complement private emotional release, as can writing in your journal or pounding the pillow.

6. *Drive very carefully.* You may be accident prone.

Stage One: Preseparation

The Decision to Part

Most relationships, like human beings, go through an initial period of being under the weather. Many speak of this uneasy period in their marriage, saying, "something wasn't quite right," but feeling unable to put a finger on just what was wrong. Aware that a primary relationship is the backbone of emotional stability, people hesitate to admit a serious marital rift, even in the face of a deteriorating sex life, loss of communication, conflict of opinion, and even evidence of dishonesty. Most people deny the symptoms as long as they can.

"My initial reaction was to deny that my feelings had anything to do with the relationship between my husband and me," said one mother of three teenagers. "I assumed that the trouble was my imagination or my attitude, or the kids. We would avoid each other, then unexplainably become very close for a few days. It was awful, and crazy. We tried individual therapy, finally marriage counseling."

Eventually, even with such bold attempts at denial, one or both of the partners becomes aware of the marked erosion of mutual trust and respect. The future of the relationship is now in doubt. Usually during this time one or both spontaneously begin an assessment of the relationship—the review work—sometimes together, sometimes in counseling or therapy. In some cases, this strengthens the relationship; in other cases the review work strengthens the individuals for the separation to come. But we have all seen how the emotions that accompany the decision can work against a person. The strong feelings that many people experience add to their tension to an intolerable degree. Such crushing pressure is written on haggard faces and leads to bouts of anxiety, depression, hostility, and recurring illnesses. The decision period eventually begins. If a mutual decision to part is not reached, one partner becomes the potential leaver and the other the one who is left. The prospects of being left usually add more to the frustration, disappointment, and despair. The leaver may feel guilt and relief. Despite the feelings, plans for the reality of separate futures need to begin.

Stage Two: The Separation

The actual separation can be both a relief and a shock. The relief from tension and discord is accompanied by physical and emotional shock, an enveloping sense of loss. The old life has finally stopped.

The relief of finally acting on such a momentous decision helps some people, and they feel liberated, in touch with the possibilities of their new life. These are often people who covered a lot of emotional ground in the first stages and/or who initiated the separation. Others are less fortunate. They may feel relief from the hostilities and the indecision, but they are in shock and need time to recover. "Before the divorce, I knew everything about everything. Then when the marriage didn't turn out the way it was supposed to and the family life I loved was gone, there I was without a series of alternate game plans. I was paralyzed," said Gary, father of three.

Some who can accept intellectually the fact that the relationship has ended may strongly deny the depth of its emotional impact—even in the face of physical numbness, perhaps a tightness in their throats, a hollow sensation in their abdomen, a loss of appetite. Sandy described her separation experience this way. "He moved out, reluctantly. I was relieved, but numb. Looking back now, I can see where the separation shock began and then wore off, but then it was hard to define. I couldn't sleep, cried a lot, had a couple of minor car accidents."

Other people find that the shock of separation raises their stress level to the point where some physical weakness is triggered into an acute crisis requiring medical attention. Myra, describing her siege of illness after her separation, said, "Three weeks after we separated, I landed in the hospital for emergency surgery. Then, a week after that, I landed in the emergency ward again, this time for a transfusion. I regarded myself as a walking soap opera for a while."

This separation stage can bring with it three dangerous side effects:

· Poor judgment
· Accident and illness proneness, poor reflex actions
· Depression

While these tendencies come and go through this stage and the following stages, they can be at their peak in Stage Two. For this reason, it is advisable to try to get through this stage as quickly as possible. It can last for several hours, several days, or several months. If it lasts more than a few weeks, seek professional help.

The Wall Between Stages Three and Four

It is not uncommon to find people who continue to deny certain feelings and who, for a while anyway, hide behind a barrier of stubborn denial. Those who deny the separation—keeping it a secret from family and friends—may do this in an effort to insulate themselves and keep the way open for a reconciliation. However, pretending that he or she is on a business trip after the legal papers have been filed is not a good use of denial!

The other typical form of denial that forms a barrier to the next stage is the denial of strong feelings. Men most often deny their grief and sadness; women hide their anger and resentments. Usually this denial of strong feelings means a bout of depression. Denial acts like a big cement lid on a bubbling pot of very real and active stored feelings yet to be released through review work. Such conflict is a danger signal worth paying attention to. If you do your homework and if the depression still doesn't lift, consult a trained counselor.

This threshold between the shock and denial stage and the next stage of strong emotions can be difficult for some people to pass over. But the lowered income, changed or new employment, child care, new circumstances, and the absence of a regular sex life are all realities that increase stress and demand attention. Eventually, little blocks of the new reality will penetrate the numbness and strong emotions will escape, sometimes so strong that past restraints and traditional courtesies fly right out the window. For this reason, the next stage is characterized by out-of-control emotions.

Stage Three: Strong Emotions

Because this period is both natural and nasty, this stage has been nicknamed "off the wall." It may be a time when softspoken women want to scream obscenities and throw things at their estranged husbands; a time when tender, caring men often spy on their estranged wives, producing wild accusations of deception or whoring. Former partners may develop a deep distrust of each other which all too often spills over into the legal arena. People may act in ways they never have before and never will again. Behavior can be exaggerated and atypical. Barry, for example, had never acted so hostile during his marriage nor had Lois been so vindictive. The once-stored anger can be released and aimed toward the separated spouse. Such destructive feelings and behavior often combine with intense feelings of loss and longing to have things the way they were.

Max described this experience: "I was unbelievably angry with her. The separation was her idea, but the divorce was finally my doing. I suppose my manhood demanded that I do something, that I act. I couldn't conceive of so much pain. But at the same time, a part of me longed to have her back. I felt that if I gave her a long enough lead, eventually she would come back to me. A part of me loved her, still does. That part wants her to grow and be happy . . . and I wanted to ensure that my daughter would get good care."

If the parents haven't experienced a "bargaining" period before now, one of them may attempt reconciliation and promise, "I'll go to marriage counseling" or "I'll do whatever you want." When the bargaining fails, the emotions become even more intense.

These strange emotional roller coasters are common at this stage, causing many people to fear permanent emotional instability. Others mistake the symptoms as signs that they are being punished for their failure, or as proof that they still love their former mate. The degree of feeling frightens some people, and confuses most others. As one mother of six said, "It's as if all of me is in pieces, flying around in the air. But these pieces aren't landing, they just keep going. I'm scared." The off-the-wall emotions often collide with the hiring of an attorney by one or both former partners. The adversary system can act as a catalyst or a foil for these feelings, and the combination may be deadly. Even the most conciliatory and mediating of attorneys find it difficult to convince out-of-control clients that the legal process is not the appropriate arena for their intense feelings of fear, spite, or anger. Such clients would say: "Things got much worse when I hired an attorney." While anger and disappointment are projected (and sometimes worked out) through the legal process, this is a very risky way to go.

During this period, it's common to think that *you* are okay but *your ex* is out of control. Actually, you probably are *both* out of control. This is the worst possible time to make any permanent decisions—especially legal ones. Thinking and believing the worst about each other is one of the chief hazards of this stage, and such thoughts, exaggerated and extended, can lead to serious complications.

"Junkies"—A Serious Complication

The off-the-wall stage lends itself to a peculiar but understandable effect—people can get hooked on the strong emotions. For some people, these intense and very real sensations make them feel alive and powerful when they may otherwise feel empty, numb, and powerless. Since rebuilding a new life takes time, everyone has a period when the emptiness gnaws away at their insides and at their hearts; the powerful surge of feeling is often a familiar, if not welcome, ally.

The junkie can be hooked on anger, depression, grief, blame, guilt, hostility, or revenge—any feeling that can keep a person obsessed with the other parent in either past or present times. A junkie doesn't work out the feelings in safe or structured ways; he or she wants to keep the feeling.

How can you identify a junkie? By the amount of time in day-to-day living spent thinking about the other parent, the situation, or about who is to blame. While the off-the-wall stage produces a certain amount of such absorption, junkies wear their obsession like a badge of courage or of principle.

How Junkies Begin

Many people do and say things after separation that they "didn't have the guts" to when they were married. "She got her way when we were married, she's not going to get it now." "He bullied me when we were married, I won't let him bully me now. He can just talk to my lawyer instead." Here is a composite case history of how junkies can begin.

"I was afraid that my husband would stop child support, or stop seeing the children if he knew why I wanted a divorce," said Portia. "So I didn't talk to him at all. I told him he had to talk to my lawyer instead."

Greg, Portia's separated husband, sought in vain for the real reasons his wife wanted a divorce. He described her to his friends as unstable and uncaring, with deep emotional problems that kept erupting in demands that he leave the house. Sometimes he wanted to punish Portia for "kicking him out." Typically, he made statements like, "She thinks she knows everything; but she's not going to get her way." Then moments later, "I hate her lawyer." Greg is so angry when he says these things he is out in the hinterlands of communication. His feelings become so intense he sometimes crosses the border and becomes inarticulate.

Both Greg and Portia played a series of blame games that gave meaning to their addiction to strong feelings. Greg's complaints and accusations about Portia were part of the "see why I divorced" series. Portia's complaints were more covert. She kept repeating: "See what I had to put up with? He is totally unreasonable." Both are hooked on their strong feelings.

Ordinary self-help treatment rarely reverses this damaging set of circumstances. Junkies need professional help.

Danger Signals and What to Do About Them

Men and women quite frequently feel a surge of unreasonable and irrational feelings during the off-the-wall period. What will they do with the feeling? Some men talk openly about "slapping some sense into her" and women talk about "making him pay dearly for what he's done." If these are your statements, it's important that you discuss this with some trustworthy person, preferably a professional. If you have a friend who talks this way, be alert and strongly urge professional intervention.

There may be thoughts of suicide or even homicide when serious complications develop. These are danger signals and must not be overlooked. If you have such feelings, or if you have a friend who expresses such feelings to you, immediately contact a suicide prevention center, the nearest free clinic, hot line, neighborhood health center, or the emergency room of the nearest hospital, fire department, or police department. Tell them you are going through a divorce and are temporarily out of control. You need a trained ear to listen. You need advice. Sometimes one contact is enough. Sometimes you may need a series of sessions. *Do not ignore* the following danger signals.

- Poor judgment and accident proneness
- Extreme feelings of anger, depression, distrust, and revenge
- Unwillingness or inability to express these strong emotions safely
- The ever-present temptation to take all this frustration and strong emotion into the legal arena
- Illness or physical symptoms that increase under stress

You can help yourself by doing *all* of the following:

- Enlisting personal aid—a friend or professional. Do not go through this alone.
- Staying away from your estranged spouse
- Finding at least one safe way to release the pressure of your strong feelings
- Avoiding long-term legal decisions

Review your Ten Basic Rules again and look at how you can raise your human income.

Avoiding the Traps

How can you avoid getting hooked on the blame game/junkie syndrome? Here is a typical case history told in the words of Anne, drawn from the similar experiences of dozens of men and women who managed to avoid the traps.

"The first six months were a combination of many things: relief on rediscovering my own integrity, and a feeling of coming back to life; relief that I could hold a responsible job; relief to meet men interested in dating a mother of three. Though my children reacted intensely to the separation and divorce, we all got through the worst time together and began to stabilize our family life.

"But along with these good discoveries came a terrible anger and resentment, a longing to have been able to work things out in the marriage. I wallowed in self-pity at being overburdened with these children with so little time for myself, with no cash reserves, no family close by to help me. Then came self-hatred for my self-pity, anger at the past, ambivalence about my new life. I was depressed, and then outraged. I was out of control, full of denials and intense, conflicting feelings from almost continual review work. It was hard to separate my feelings as a former wife from my feelings as a parent."

The anger and hurt can last a long time. Anne, for example, didn't trust her estranged husband at all after he refused to see the children for three months. The children were hurt, angry, bewildered, acting out their fears at home and at school. To make matters worse, Anne found that few people expected the children's father to honor his parenting responsibilities. Anne reported, "The lawyer said, 'You can't make him be a father. If he doesn't want to, he doesn't have to.' People expected that he would 'not care' and I almost went along with it because I thought the worst of him then."

Anne's story of her treatment for this stage is typical of what worked for others. "With the help of friends, good information, some new perspectives, and some badly needed practice in communications and business relations, we avoided a legal battle, and I've been grateful ever since. But I did have to let those strong feelings out somehow. So I took up jogging, tennis, washed floors, wrote pages I never read again. Sometimes I took my anger out on the kids, sometimes on myself. Only once in a while did I lash out at their father. One close friend, in particular, continually reminded me that I was going through a process, one that I could really learn from and grow through. She was right."

There is no mystery to safe passage through this stage, but everyone needs to find their own way to clean out their wound so new growth can take place. What works for you may not work for your friends. Whether it's karate, cleaning house every day, or running in place to the morning TV, find what works for now and do it. It's important to check with your physician before you begin any new exercise or sporting program. In the words of one man, "People thought I was crazy, but I ran to the hills almost every day and yelled my guts out until I healed it through. But it worked."

Stage Four: Adult Adolescence (Living in the Present) and Stage Five: New Maturity

The first stages clean out the psychic wound and prepare one for the healing process to begin. The past needs to be put to rest to make room for the new identity. The adult adolescence period is set in the present.

You'll know you've reached this stage when you've become restless with the past and seek present challenges. If deep feelings still exist, the past will continue to fascinate you even if only temporarily. People often find, however, that living in the present makes it easier to ventilate their feelings from the past. The present, paradoxically, can be an excellent and rather safe stage for this expression.

"There I was, happily shopping for some cheese and wine for a tête-à-tête with a new woman friend," reported one man of thirty-four, "when I came across my former wife's favorite kind of wine. I immediately had this vivid memory of the two of us together and almost cried then and there. Then, it was over and, although I felt stunned, I was okay. The whole thing took no more than five minutes and it didn't spoil my evening. Five months earlier it would have."

A withdrawal from the past means living in the present and the present has several overriding realities:

· Being single and no longer legally attached to a mate
· Being a parent
· Being single *and* a parent without any definite expectations from society on how this is to be defined

The present can also bring with it feelings of euphoria, an exhilarating "I did the right thing!" One mother said, "I feel guilty because I'm so happy now." One father put it, "The worry, the loneliness I expected. I didn't expect to have such happiness emerge from the midst of it."

The Adult Adolescence

The term "adult adolescence" usually elicits broad smiles and knowing expressions from parents and professionals alike, as most people anticipate a discussion of the free-wheeling sexuality of the adolescent, only this time with the power and experience of an adult. This is a beguiling fantasy, only sometimes realized in real life. But the adult adolescent's reality is a combination of wisdom and naivete, experience and innocence. Of course, today's divorced adult has more freedom to experiment sexually with less censure than perhaps ever before, but concurrent adult responsibilities for a family don't vanish.

The symptoms in this stage, when the adult adolescent may behave like a gregarious, naive thirteen- or fourteen-year-old, are described by Marie. "I felt like a teenager again. I was excited about life. I felt attractive, flirtatious. I had coveted piano lessons and skiing when I was married and had never done either. I immediately signed up for both. I changed my clothes and hair style. I made many new friends and wanted to be out all the time. Sometimes I found out about being single the hard way. The first time I was asked to dinner, I expected dinner, not a heavy sexual pass. The unspoken singles' codes and rules took time to learn."

Singleness is a new skill, learned by careful observation, groping, testing, and listening in the company of other singles. People need to find out about themselves as social and sexual beings. Common questions are: "Will other people like the new me?" "What will new sex partners be like?" "Can I handle the changing values?" "What will my children think? My parents? My neighbors?"

A different personality, more reserved than Marie's, would meet the adult adolescent period differently. Another person might be slow to meet new people, saving social times for old friends, a group outing or sporting event, and keep new acquaintances to a minimum.

Adult adolescence is a matter of style and preference, each choice carrying peculiar pitfalls and advantages. In Marie's gregarious style lies a danger. Her fascination with her new life might lead her to neglect her children's basic needs. A more reserved style ("the hermitage," one father called it) brings the danger of isolation and a different type of parental neglect. No rules fit everyone.

The symptoms of the early adolescent period are:

1. Resurgence of your original teenage symptoms and mannerisms. Exuberance, shyness, etc. (Some old skeletons may emerge here as a result.)
2. Need for friends, a reference group, a social group to pal around with. It's another world, now.
3. Preoccupation with yourself, your interests, your emerging identity, your appearance, your attractiveness
4. Increased interest in sex and willingness at least to consider some experimentation and to test yourself out in this new world
5. A sense of excitement about your new life

The danger signals are usually the following:

1. Ignoring the basic needs of your children
2. Ignoring your own needs for a balanced life

3. You becoming the teenager in the family while the real teenagers or younger children become your parent
4. Getting in with the wrong crowd of singles and taking on a pace or a life-style that you are not ready or suited for
5. Getting engaged or remarried too soon

Treatments are:

The basic rules again, the importance of human contact, with groups and with friends, taking care of yourself, taking "alone time" to let things settle. A new identity rarely happens in a vacuum. While others do not shape your identity, they do give you a mirror to work with. The problems with parents and children will be explored in the upcoming chapter on setting up your home and meeting your children's basic needs. You can meet your children's needs and your own at the same time. It is possible to meet your needs for freedom and exploration while also assuring your children of their security and continuity with you as their parent. Finally, the "quick replacement danger" is minimized by your own awareness that a too-soon-permanent relationship will start out with two strikes against it.

The reaction of the former mate to the new identity of the "adolescent" varies from anger to astonishment. "She's a mother! She shouldn't be dating like a teenager," scolded one former husband. "He's lost thirty pounds, looks fit, tan, and handsome. I had no idea I was married to someone who had that man deep inside of him," said a former wife unhappily.

The adolescent period may go on for some time, but like a true adolescent period, the early stages of wide fluctuations of testing and retesting give way to greater stability. The time comes when even the accepting single world will shun a single who remains too long in the irresponsible adolescent stage of experimentation. Indulgence is not granted indefinitely. A thirteen-year-old's behavior differs from a nineteen-year-old's behavior, and the greenhorn single is expected to grow up and mature.

The Mature Identity and New Life-style

The key during the later adolescent period is to pay very close attention to what you do and most particularly to what you are feeling. A sense of comfort and ease with yourself often signals your deeper self. You can meet your needs for respect, affection, belonging, and self-actualization in less fragmented ways. In time, being a good parent to your infant emotions can enrich your life ten-fold.

Mellowing applies to people as well as to fine wines. The wise are not emotion*less,* but rather emotion*full* with passions that have matured in their subtle richness and body. The feeling side of human beings seems to be like anything else in nature; it needs a chance to be and to grow up, to age, to mature. Then like fine wine, feelings need air to let out the sharpness and to give excess acidity a chance to evaporate.

The psychic wound caused by the divorce has been cleansed in the first stages of the process, and the last stages progress to those of the healing and mending process. The divorced person develops new growth, with some residual scars and some tender spots. In theory, at least, the final healing brings the ability and the willingness to take the risk to love and care for another in an intimate relationship. In practice, most people take risks early in their separation to make new attachments, although, in the early months, these attachments are less intimacy than sex, less relationship than exploration.

The making of new friends or of new intimates is pivotal to the maturing identity and the evolving life-style. The reconstruction of your own personal community, your sense of family, and the gathering around you of people who support and nurture you are critical to you personally and to your children too. Such rebuilding is important to the natural conclusion of the healing of the psychic wound of divorce.

The Final Stages of Uncoupling

Anne described the final stages of her wounding and healing process. "Eventually, the children's father and I cooled down, finished our off-the-wall period, and began to act like parents instead of angry and revengeful lovers. He wanted to be a parent again. This time I could be respectful and courteous instead of suspicious. Over time, he developed a second home for his children (his way, not my way), and next year they'll be living with him most of the time while I set up the second home for them.

"We've both traveled a long way. It took three years for the marriage to end. Another six months getting through the initial shock and crisis period. And finally about another two years exploring myself as an unmarried person and as a partner in parenting. Now I have established a new life and a new self-image, and am now well finished with most of the flashbacks. Parts of me are so different from what they were five years ago that old friends are amazed. I still have occasional flashes of looking at the children and thinking, 'Why couldn't it have worked out?' But I feel that's normal. After all, I was married sixteen years, and we have three children together. We don't divorce memories, we just learn how to live with them."

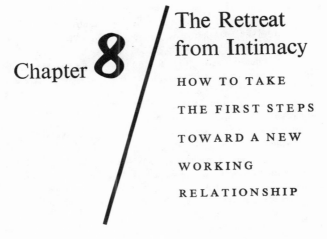

Chapter **8** / The Retreat
from Intimacy

HOW TO TAKE

THE FIRST STEPS

TOWARD A NEW

WORKING

RELATIONSHIP

"When I was married, I had a good idea of what was expected of me as a wife," said forty-year-old Peggy, separated after eighteen years of marriage. "But now that I'm separated, I don't know what is expected of me. Do I ask him for dinner when he comes for the children? Do I go along with his request to have the kids an extra night on the weekend? And what about sex?

"When I am angry with him, the answers are all no. But when I'm not angry, I don't know what to do. My confusion returns and nothing is solved."

Peggy has not yet separated her role as a parent from that of a wife. When she can make the two roles distinct and separate from one another she will probably say no to sex with her former husband, no to all but very special invitations for dinner with her and the children, but a good many yes's to the father's requests for extra overnights for the children at his home. Until Peggy can make this role distinction, however, she has only her anger to help her make decisions.

Negative Intimacy

Anger might allow people like Peggy to say no unequivocally for the first time in their lives. It might even be the primary emotion that propelled her out of her marriage, but it is not a wise basis for long-range

83

decisions. Furthermore, anger can tie former lovers together as securely as love, perpetuating an intimate continuing relationship.

The old saying, "Love and hate are very close together," was never more true than during the early days of ending a marriage.

After a heated battle anyone might say, "I can't stand this hostility. It hurts, it's destructive. How could he/she be this way after all we've meant to one another?" Yet, despite firm resolutions to stay calm the next time, another violent disruption appears. Why does this happen?

Living a long time with another person leads to a form of emotional investment and understanding we call intimacy. To oversimply, when feelings are loving, intimacy is positive. When feelings are neither positive nor negative, intimacy is neutral, nonexistent. When feelings are destructive, negative intimacy arises, a term coined to describe the attachment of antagonists. Most couples divorce because their history together has become too negative or neutral with not enough positive intimacy to act as a healthy balance.

Most parents grapple with their leftover negative intimacy during the first years of separation and divorce. They quarrel over custody, the children, money, blame one another, yell at the kids, and sometimes feel depressed, resentful, or revengeful. Such parents have not yet separated their parental roles from their former roles as lovers.

You can find practical ways to relate to each other without being permanently hobbled by blame games and negative intimacy. This chapter deals with simple skills, giving pointers for everyday behavior and know-how that most people have but don't yet know how to apply to a graceful retreat from a marriage. To begin with, take a look at how negative intimacy can fit into the larger family picture.

That Old Family Feeling

Each family develops its own private rituals, rules, and customs, its own unique blend of positive, neutral, and negative intimacy; a powerful blend I call the old family feeling. The family feeling is an emotional climate that says, "This is home," "This is what a family feels like," "This is how family members behave." In families, people learn what can bring a smile or a frown to another's face or how to hurt or soothe another, much of it subtly communicated in tone of voice, a look, or a gesture. Parents know how this works, even if it is an unconscious knowing, and so do the children.

After separation, the old family feeling is disrupted. The new family feeling has not yet emerged and people can feel lost. Until the new family climate is pulled together under the guidance of the parent, the old family feeling, and the parents' negative intimacy, no matter how boring, destructive, or sporadic, will continue to dominate and even escalate. This is especially true if the old family feeling is primarily a negative one, and family members don't know how a positive family climate works. The family needs to develop a new family feeling, one that will be as positive as possible and free from the parents' negative intimacy.

From Intimacy to a Working Relationship

People can move from intimacy to a working relationship. The how, when, and where of their meetings can change. So can the why and what of their communications. Before shifting gears, people need to understand the mechanisms of relationships, far more clearly than they did previously. Much is fuzzy about what you can or cannot do. "I know I'm attracted to playing all those blame games with my former wife," said one twenty-seven-year-old father of twin sons, "but what do I do instead? And how can I do it when I'm so damned mad at her, or feeling so hurt, that I can't even talk with her?"

If he didn't have children, the answer might be to leave town. But, tempting as it is, flight is rarely the best answer. The only way out is through. We have seen, in Chapter 7, how this applies to the wound of separation and divorce. You don't pretend the wound isn't there; you help it heal. The same is true of learning how to relate to the other parent. You don't pretend you don't have a former lover. You learn how to relate to the children's parent in a new way.

By looking at the way human relationships vary from acquaintanceship to intimacy, you can begin to see how to retrain yourself for your new role as a former lover and a present partner in parenting. Remember, it's not a sign of personal failure to feel confused about how to relate to the other parent now—the situation is confusing.

The Differences Between Relationships

Relationships usually develop according to their own unique sets of rules and expectations, marked by varying degrees of personal investment. Acquaintances don't become friends overnight. People first meet as acquaintances. If subsequent meetings prove the relationship worthwhile, friendship might begin. Over months and years, if all goes well with the friendship, the relationship might enter that of true intimacy. Most people understand this progression instinctively and are familiar with how it works in daily living. If it were to be plotted on a scale from low to high, it would look like this:

Emotional Investment and Intensity in Relationship

Acquaintanceship   **Friendship**   **Intimacy**

Lowest ─── Highest

You have more invested emotionally in someone you have known for fifteen years than you have in someone you met last month. The progression of relationship carries with it a gradual increase in an investment of self and of emotional intensity. In a good relationship trust, loyalty, and respect grow.

This difference in relationships is something we all know about. But a more sophisticated understanding of this difference can help you teach yourself how you can relate to the other parent in a new way, one that discourages negative intimacy and encourages a new working relationship.

The Three Basic Levels of Relationships

The Acquaintance and Business Relationship

An acquaintance is the druggist, the mailman, or the person you just met at a party. You both follow an implicit and explicit set of rules. When you talk with the druggist, you give him the prescription and he fills it. He makes out the bill, and you pay it. If the druggist asks how you are, you answer, "Just fine, thank you," even if you have had a miserable day. Business associates do business efficiently, courteously, while keeping a low emotional profile.

The more at stake in a business relationship, the more explicit you must become: You operate with written agreements and formal information. If a ten-cents purchase of chewing gum gets a cash register receipt, how much more important are explicit agreements or clear information that involve time, money, and perhaps the future.

On a personal level, despite the cordiality and familiarity that develop over the life of a business relationship, the axiom "Don't mix business with pleasure" usually holds true. Here is a shorthand way of looking at this type of interaction:

Acquaintance or Business Relationship

No assumptions
Formal courtesies, public meetings
Explicit agreements, contracts, structured meetings
Little confrontation, low risk, low emotional intensity
High personal privacy, low personal disclosure

Friendship—The Natural Next Step

"There are friends, good friends, and close friends," said a ten-year-old child. "I walk to school with friends, I play with good friends, but with my close friend I can do everything and she knows my secrets." This child already knows that friendship comes in many shapes and with many boundaries. She already knows that many are called but few are chosen for the highest place of honor.

If a relationship moves successfully through an initial testing ground, it changes into a beginning friendship where trust and respect are building. The relationship is both formal and informal. Sometimes you make explicit agreements, and sometimes it's acceptable to make assumptions. Your assumptions about one another grow with your friendship. You are occasionally private, no longer totally public; you disclose personal information to each other and your feelings of closeness grow.

Friendship

Increase in assumptions and expectations
Growing trust, loyalty, respect, understanding
Increased emotional exchange and personal disclosure
Increase in private meetings, shared feelings

As the serious friendship grows closer to intimacy, you peel off more and more protective layers, possibly revealing insecurities and faults. You can be deeply moved or hurt. When tender spots are revealed and then accepted, the friendship can deepen and another step toward intimacy is taken. When these same spots are ignored or found wanting, hurt and anger arise over a friend's insensitivity and lack of caring. When your deepest fears and faults are revealed, will you stay friends? Will respect and trust remain?

On such touchy issues many relationships falter. Unable or unwilling to go those additional steps that will mean intimacy, people fall back either to a less demanding form of friendship or all the way back to acquaintanceship or less. "I was so disappointed in him," said one woman of her previous lover, "I didn't want to know him at all."

But when the next steps taken are successful, intimacy becomes another option to add to your repertoire. You can be partners, friends, and now also intimates.

Intimacy

Intimacy has been described as an intense exchange of caring and sharing; a "safe place" where you share honesty, understanding, vulnerabilities, dreams, aspirations, and joys and, often, common values and goals. Intimacy requires a deep emotional investment and intensity; it is extremely personal and private. Couples who have the capacity for intimacy do not spend all their time this way. They also spend time structuring daily tasks as working partners; they spend companionable time as friends as well. Many people can burn out their relationship with continual demands for intimacy. In positive intimacy, though, respect, trust, loyalty, confrontation, feedback, and support flourish. Paradoxically, risk decreases with independence and increases with dependency. Once the bottleneck of tentative intimacy has been passed, risks diminish, for the established trust and respect encourage a continual honesty and personal ways to settle minor disagreements.

Many couples find themselves tangled in the web of negative intimacy after years of delight and satisfaction. They are restless and act disrespectful and annoyed with one another. Fear of losing such a treasured relationship can undermine love further with overdependency that requires continual reassurances and tests of love. Dissatisfactions creep in, and perhaps one person will begin to test the other's involvement. Such scenes will eventually endanger the future of the relationship. It may be more and more difficult to rebuild positive intimacy. What can they do now? Must they just erase the good with the bad, the compatibility and sharing with the incompatibility and withdrawal? Must shared history simply be ignored, or can they find some way to show respect for their once valid emotional investment? The answer is a move away from intimacy back to acquaintanceship.

Intimacy

Positive Acceptance	Negative Rejection
Positive assumptions, expectations	Negative assumptions, expectations
Trust, respect, loyalty	Distrust, disrespect, disloyalty
Privacy, informality, and confidences are protected	Privacy, informality, and confidences are not respected
Implicit agreements and assumptions are positive	Implicit agreements and assumptions are negative
Supportiveness	Competitiveness
Disclosure	Disclosure in order to hurt the other
Security, comfort	Insecurity, discomfort
Maximum intensity of emotions and feelings	Maximum intensity of emotions and feelings

Building a New Working Relationship: The First Steps

Successfully ending a marriage means a move away from intimacy. Your marital life may have been sweet, bland, or sour, but it was probably intimate, and divorce means a definite—even if slow—ending of that intimacy.

Two principles guide this new working relationship:

1. *Think of the working relationship as something brand new, something to be built from the ground up.* You don't return to the way you two related before you married.
2. *Think of the relationship as one in which you transact business.*

For example, try thinking of your parenting relationship in this way. You and the children's other parent are just starting to do business together. Each of you must earn a good name for yourself. People do business together only as long as their transactions are mutually beneficial. That's just good business sense. Principles of good business can be a great aid to parents in establishing sound communication and negotiation skills so that they can come to reasonable agreements about their children's welfare. The business relationship between divorced parents usually works. It is not only the most effective, but also the kindest and most rational road to emotional and economic recovery for both parents and children.

Doing Business When You'd Rather Do Battle

Often, after I introduce the concept of the business relationship to a group of parents, one will groan aloud and say something like, "I hate (or distrust, or resent) my ex so much there is no way I could ever do business with him [or her]." If you react like this, think of your situation in another way. Pretend you are a diabetic on a frontier outpost. The only source of insulin, by a twist of fate, is controlled by someone you distrust. If you don't find a way to do business with this supplier, you are courting death. The supplier, moreover, deals only in insulin and needs your patronage to survive. You may look for ways to get out of such a miserable situation, but you nevertheless have to have *some* business transactions with this person until you get yourself in a better situation and can deal from a greater position of power. In short you must do business with the supplier, like it or not.

While such feelings as deep distrust or sadness are normal parts of the separation process, you can't afford to let them endanger your life or your future. The daily tension between you and the supplier will go on. If you don't pay your bill on time or if you get an inferior batch of insulin, complications multiply. What happens today will affect tomorrow. In your best interests, and that of your children, learn how to develop this working relationship now. As strange as it sounds, the supplier needs the buyer just as much as the buyer needs the supplier.

If all this seems unfair, it probably is. Divorce is one of the most unfair processes people experience. But seeking justice and emotional satisfaction from a former partner instead of negotiating a business arrangement is not going to make the result fairer. Real justice depends on a lot of honest hard thinking and work, not on your or the other parent's lofty sense of fairness.

"I'm Reasonable But He/She Is Impossible."

"This relationship is hopeless, he's totally illogical." "I'm willing to be reasonable, but I know she's sick emotionally." "We have so many bad feelings between us that we just have to talk through our lawyers." If these statements could be yours, remember that such comments usually reflect a natural tendency when emotions are out of control to see the other parent as the troublemaker, yourself the innocent bystander. Even if you are correct, the attitude alone will surely prolong the emotional divorce, keeping you attached by such emotions and beliefs to the children's other parent. As one mother said, "I have to decide: Do I want to be right? Or do I want to be free? I decided I wanted to be free." If you make this choice, then you are on the path to building a working relationship.

Who Should Begin?

The retreat from intimacy can be initiated by both of you or just one of you. Usually one begins alone while the other balks or invites or baits a return to the old ways. Even though it would be ideal for both of you to back off at the same time, such timing is uncommon.

When only one of you begins to take on the behavior of an acquaintance and then that of a business partner, the other parent may protest loudly and convincingly. "It feels awful not to have you tell me what is happening in your private life like you used to," the reluctant new single may say to the one retreating. "After all those years together to treat me so coldly is deeply cutting. Didn't we mean anything to one another?" The wail is genuine, the question penetrating.

If you are the one retreating and your separated former spouse touches you in your heart of hearts, pleading for you to stay in a close relationship, say gently: "I feel many of these same things. But we are just prolonging the inevitable. Let's try to honor what we had by respecting one another in this new way. We have decided to live our separate lives from now on and this is part of what we have to do."

Sometimes a retreat is not so poignant and the bait is hostility, accusations, and threats. Negative intimacy is hard to shake when each of you knows how to hit the other's vulnerable spots. But remember it takes two to battle and the hostile ex-partner will be shadow-boxing if you keep on doing your homework well.

Developing a working relationship as parents is the most former lovers should ask of themselves. Friendship is unnecessary. For some parents, however, two or three years of a successful working relationship bring the additional dimension of a renewed friendship. When this happens, the parents often consider themselves part of one another's open or extended family. However, even then this friendship doesn't take precedence over a solid businesslike working relationship.

When to Begin

Developing a working relationship is serious business. Hasty decisions or misplaced parental demands can do a great deal of harm. Some parents learn about the retreat to a working relationship and think, "I can do that easily. All I have to do is be businesslike." Similar to teenagers with no driving experience or training, they jump into the driver's seat of this new idea, step on the gas, and back right into a tree. So before you make any important moves, take the following self-survey and see what you come up with.

	Seldom	Occasionally	Often	Usually
1. Do you ever find yourself calling the other parent "my wife" or "my husband" in conversation or in your thoughts?	4	3	2	1
2. How frequently do you mention the other parent in conversation with others?	4	3	2	1
3. How often do secret "if-only's" and "the only thing wrong is because of the other parent" type of thinking crop up?	4	3	2	1
4. How much do you depend on the other parent to support your needs in your single life?	4	3	2	1
5. How often do you find yourself thinking about the other parent during a typical week?	4	3	2	1
6. How much of your internal thinking about yourself revolves around a re-evaluation of your past relationship with the other parent?	4	3	2	1
7. Are there unsettled issues between you and the other parent that are major problems?		YES		NO
8. Are there unsettled and *unspoken* issues between you and the other parent that are major problems?		YES		NO
9. Are you and the other parent involved in *any* legal action against one another at the present time?		YES		NO
10. Do you have a key to the other parent's home? Does he or she have a key to yours?		YES		NO
11. Do you keep or store possessions in one another's homes—furniture, art, appliances, jewelry?		YES		NO
12. Do you keep memorabilia and love souvenirs from the former mate in a prominent place in your home or office?		YES		NO

Move away from Intimacy: A Self-Survey

Answer questions 1 to 6 with seldom, occasionally, often, or usually, and 7 to 12 with yes or no. Then, ask a good friend of yours to answer these questions about you. Sometimes we don't realize how we appear to others or don't realize what we do or say. It's worthwhile to get another opinion.

How to Score This Self-Survey

THE FIRST SIX QUESTIONS   Four or more answers of "seldom" or "occasionally" usually means that you have either completed or are well on your way to a successful emotional separation from the past. A score of 18 is excellent. One "often" answer is not indicative of an emotional tie, but two "often" answers and even one "usually" should draw your attention.

THE SECOND SIX QUESTIONS   More than two "yes" answers to these questions falls into the same category as a "usually" does in the first six questions.

Most people have one or two unsettled issues or habits between them. Some of these are kept around almost as pets. But negative or emotional involvement that goes much beyond this limit is a sign that deeper issues need attention before the retreat from intimacy can be complete.

Checklist for Your Move away from Intimacy

The Way Out

1. *Watch your language.* As I explained in Chapter 5, the first step is internal and can be repeated many times a day until it becomes automatic. This very important aspect is the one most frequently overlooked. Think of your relationship with the other parent in new words, using new words. Do not think or refer to your "husband" or "wife" or even "ex-spouse" or "former spouse." If you refer to the children's other parent as your "wife" or "husband" you are still thinking married, not single; still thinking intimacy, not business relationship. Your feelings may not deny it, but your words should not encourage it. Refer to your children's other parent as "the children's father" or "the children's mother." This language can help you and the children to place your new focus where it belongs—on the parenting. The right words can help your "cooling down" process, help your retreat from intimacy, and reassure and re-educate your children and yourself.

2. *Begin to think now in terms of "acquaintance" or "business relationship."* Remember the characteristics of an acquaintance or business relationship: courteous, relatively formal, low-keyed, public. You keep your personal life to yourself, you expect your meetings to be structured, and you expect explicit agreements, whether verbal or written. The next chapter will go over this in detail.

3. *Help yourself to privacy. Give the other parent privacy.* If you find yourself asking friends or the children questions about your former mate's new life, try to stop it. If such information is offered by others, politely change the subject. As for details about your own new life, keep them private.

Often people are curious about the other parent's private life, especially in regard to sex. A father may be infuriated by the thought, "Is she sleeping with somebody now, in my house?" "Is he having a good time partying," a mother wonders, "while I work two jobs to keep body and soul together and a roof over my children's heads?" Keep your normal curiosity within bounds. If you want to share the details of your private life, keep them for your close friends. Don't ask for trouble by waving the red flag of sex before the other parent.

When curiosity about the other parent's sex life grows excessive, negative intimacy erupts in distorted fantasies about the other's behavior, often promoting inquiries to friends or the children about the other parent's whereabouts and actions. If this happens, try to remember that you *are* getting a divorce and that knowledge about the other parent's private life is your way of holding on to your former intimacy. As much as you may want to know what is happening in that other bed, you—and your children —are bound to get hurt if your curiosity persists. When it comes to sex, rumors are rampant and truth is scarce. Not only is the other parent's private life no longer your business, but the version you get will surely be distorted.

4. *Your time with the children is you and your children's together.* One of the ugliest blows children suffer comes when one or both parents sees their time with the children as "baby-sitting" or "dead-time," instead of valuing it as their own private time with the children.

Some fathers refuse to see their children because they are angry at the mothers, wanting them to be overburdened without a break from parenting and without a chance to make or pursue new love relationships. Blinded by jealousy and revenge, such parents call themselves "baby-sitters." They forget that they have their own distinct parent-child relationship quite separate from the other parent. They are obsessed with being a former mate instead of a parent.

Mothers likewise can dole out times that fathers can be with the children like lollipops—Dad gets to be with the kids if Dad does what Momma says, and at Momma's convenience. "He has a girlfriend now. His be-

havior is a bad influence on the children when they see the two together."
Mom's hooked too, and, like Dad, is putting the kids in the middle.

These maneuvers all imply competition, revenge, and jealousy, and
drag out the anguish and bitterness of divorce. Manipulation breeds "negative intimacy." Such behavior does not characterize an acquaintance/busi-
ness relationship. Also, it can be very damaging to children.

5. *Show common courtesy and respect even when you don't feel he or
she deserves it or needs it.* Common sense says, be courteous to new acquaintances, withhold rash judgment. But common sense is often missing
when it comes to divorce. Bring yours back and use it. It is hard to be
courteous and formal when inside you have feelings such as, "I distrust
you," or "You are cruel and heartless," or even, "I still love you, I don't
want to let you go." Although you may be right in thinking that a good
blow-up will temporarily clear the air, more often it's like scratching poison
ivy. You may feel better for the moment, but the task of stopping the
itching and bringing your poor skin back to health still lies ahead of you!

6. *Act like a guest in the other parent's home.* "How do I act in the
other parent's territory?" Easy. Like the guest you now are. Wait to be
invited in, ask for permission to use the phone, the bathroom, etc. Even if
the answer is, "Of course, you don't have to ask . . .", ask anyway . . .
every time. A parent who wouldn't dare barge past the secretary into an
inner business office might not show the same courtesy to the new partner
in parenting; he or she might step in uninvited and even "share" the food
in the refrigerator. The principles are the same, even though the circumstances are not. Respecting one another's territory and privacy is very
important, especially during the first two years. Yes, it can be hard and often
sad to back off and be impersonal, but nowhere near as hard as it could be
if you don't respect the new regime. If you are not invited in, painful as it
might be, don't pout or have a tantrum. Either wait on the doorstep or in
the car. This waiting can be very painful for both parents, inside and outside
the house. Though time soothes, there is no easy way during the first year.

Children will want to invite their parents into the house, saying "It's my
house too, and you can come in." Despite the truth to the statement, you
will be wise to instruct them to get permission from the other parent, again,
every time. It's a wise formality. It builds respect with the other parent and
shows your children that you have that respect for their other parent.

7. *Don't expect appreciation or praise from the other parent.* Approval
and appreciation for a job well done may be found in the business world,
but it is hard to come by in the early stages of a working relationship between parents.

Parenting alone for the first time can be lonely. You may long for the
support or approval of the other parent. Perhaps you need advice on a
problem or appreciation for your tactics or decisions. When Olga, for
example, asked her son's father, "What do you think about my decision

to punish our son by denying him TV for a week?", she was hurt when he answered, "I think it's a stupid thing to do. You never could control him."

If you are going to fish for support, remember that you may get a kick in the pants instead of a pat on the back. You are not yet entitled to expect any kind of support in your new relationship, and while the move away from intimacy goes on, the strain of the separation throws tact out the window. What you do in your home is your business. It is also your problem.

During those first months when tensions are high, better look to friends and close family for support and appreciation, even in child-rearing decisions. If you can tactfully lend your approval and support to the other parent, do so. If you can't, try to withhold expressing your *disapproval* until you know how to do it without rocking the boat too much.

8. *Intimacy is implicit and impressionistic, while a business relationship is explicit and detailed.* A mother might say, "I don't need to be explicit for the children's father, he knows what I mean when I say I'll pick them up on Monday. Or at least he should, we were married eleven years!" This woman is still drawing on her old "intimacy account" with her former husband. It's time she closed that account and started saying explicitly what she plans to do and where. For example, "I'll pick them up on Monday at my brother's house after the children have had breakfast—between nine-thirty and ten o'clock."

9. *Expect to feel strange about the new relationship at first.* Remember that many people feel strange about beginning a new relationship with an old lover. "I feel like a hypocrite," said a mother of two. "I want to tell him off and here I am being courteous and businesslike." Control of your behavior at this stage earns a plus, and if you feel the mismatch between your feelings and your actions, join the crowd. This facade of a neutral civility may be very thin sometimes. But as the months pass this will change. Emotions will have cooled, the retreat from intimacy will be well on its way, and the working relationship will have developed its first solid beginnings.

10. *Look at the retreat from intimacy as a path, not a tunnel.* You may feel you don't need to follow these guidelines very often. If you are newly separated you may even find that the guidelines don't always bring you the relief you hope for. But, as one father put it, "It isn't that the business approach is the only way you interact, but it *is* what you put into practice as soon as you start getting emotional or tense. It's not all you do, but it is what you get back to."

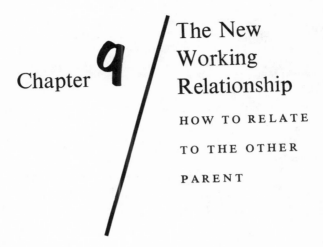

Chapter **9**

The New Working Relationship

HOW TO RELATE

TO THE OTHER

PARENT

"The greatest disappointment of the first months of divorce," said one woman, "was my realization that—like it or not—I had to relate to the children's father. I had wanted him out of my life completely. I never wanted to see him or hear his voice again. But, when you have children together, that is not the way it works."

The last chapter put forth guidelines for your move away from your former intimacy. This chapter will look at how to approach your new working relationship. There are ground rules for autonomy, for respect of one another's territory and authority, for communications between you, and for negotiations within your new working partnership. Appendix I elaborates on the more complicated problems of eventually developing a working relationship with the dropout parent who wants to become reinvolved, or reinvolving a parent who is a parent in name only.

Again, here is a reminder that any actual changes you are considering in your present relationship should be set aside until you read the rest of this book. Don't be in too big a hurry to make changes. Let the information and ideas soak in before you make any big changes or draft a legal agreement. Some parents, in a hurry to reach a final arrangement, assume that all they need is a good legal agreement. They feel that the law will not only set the stage for a parenting relationship, but will guarantee it. But, consider this: When parents learn how to communicate and establish ground rules after divorce, their legal agreement will probably be an excellent one, and a good working relationship can result. But if they haven't mastered some basic skills, the best legal agreement in the world will not succeed in practice. Chapter 12 has more on this.

Ground Rules for a Working Relationship

Your Territory, Independence, and Autonomy

The most important ground rule for your new working relationship is also crucial for your move away from your marriage and your shared intimacy. This important rule is that you each delineate and maintain your separate territories. Put simply, Mom's house is her bailiwick and Dad's house is his. *What you do in your own home, and how you parent the children there, is your business. What the other parent does, likewise, is her or his business. When the children are living with you, you have authority and responsibility.* To preserve autonomy, you must maintain your own territory courteously and firmly—and you must keep your nose out of the other parent's territory as well.

How Independence and Autonomy Can Work

Each parent has the same rights and prerogatives. No fair making plans on the other parent's time! And, don't let the children talk you into changing times with the other parent "just this once." Exchanging times requires both parents' consent.

Dad is living in the original family home with three children, ages five, seven, and twelve. Mom is taking them to her new place this weekend, Friday after school. When the twelve-year-old says he wants to go to a baseball game on Saturday with his pals, Dad tells him to call his mother for permission. The weekend is Mom's time to make decisions and take responsibilities. If Mom says no, Dad should not make use of this opportunity to malign "mean old Mom."

Or suppose Dad has been given four tickets to a children's theater on Mom's Sunday. Before he whets the children's appetite for the theater, he tells Mom about the tickets. It's dirty pool to put a load of guilt on Mom's back because she wants to have the children during her time instead of giving up the afternoon to Dad. If Mom is unwilling to change plans, Dad should step back. If he really wants to smooth the waters and build everyone's sense of trust, he can give the tickets to Mom!

The noninterference principle can strengthen the parent-child relationship and enhance the emotional climate of family life. It lessens nasty side effects like competition, nosiness, and manipulation. Noninterference gives the children a sense of security and continuity. Children know what to expect and eventually see how two homes with no fighting works.

When parents adhere to the noninterference principle, parental co-operation is strengthened, and the children see a new, different, but still united front from their parents. Noninterference is the workable way to respect your partner in parenting and to share authority and responsibility. Children need not play one parent against the other to feel power. Child power through manipulation is a frightening substitute for parental strength and responsibility.

Your Own Style of Parenting

One outcome of autonomy is that each parent is free to develop a personal style of parenting. You no longer have the right to judge the other parent's adequacy as a parent or to insist on certain behaviors that meet your own standards. And you are free to insist on this same autonomy for yourself. Here is the type of thing that can happen when parents overstep their boundaries.

Eloise, a mother of daughters aged five and six, thinks that their father, Vince, is inept and unfit as a dad, even though she knows that he loves his daughters. Eloise insists that Vince present for approval a detailed schedule of projected activities for each of his weekends with the girls. This is a surefire way to insure trouble from the girls *and* from Vince. He may eventually seek custody himself to escape from Eloise's iron control and from the humiliation of parenting on her terms. Or Vince may just give up and fade away.

Maybe Eloise is right when she claims that Vince knows very little about child psychology. All parents can use improvement. But while her relationship with Vince remains strained, she cannot appoint herself instructor for his parent education. A friend might encourage Vince to upgrade his parenting skills, but any intervention by Eloise will probably only arouse resistance as long as Vince is resentful of her.

Every parent, married or single, makes mistakes. It's unreasonable to expect perfection of any parent, especially those now trying to relate to children alone for the first time. If Vince were able to communicate with Eloise, he might say something like this: "You weren't born knowing everything about being a mother! You made some mistakes in feeding the girls and training them. I have a right to make a few mistakes and to learn on my own, too."

Protecting Your Child

Because of your emotional involvement, you may be unable to distinguish the parent who is merely inexperienced from the one who is dangerously incompetent or abusive. A parent who raises welts or breaks bones is far more dangerous than one who swats a child's bottom when exasperated. Child abuse can and does happen during times of emotional turmoil. It is every parent's responsibility to exert self-discipline at these times and to protect the child if the other parent is obviously abusive.

If your child is in any physical danger during this period, *seek help immediately.* Do not attempt to act without outside help when you know that a real risk exists. If you are uncertain how to proceed, call a hot line, the emergency room at your local hospital, your family doctor, or a therapist for advice. You may need a professional counselor to help you decide whether the child is really in danger or whether your fears have been magnified during the emotional upheaval of divorce. If you find that your child is not in real danger, let the other parent alone. Cool it and pay more attention to your own relationship with your kids.

The New Working Relationship: Basic Principles of Communication

Very often it isn't what is said, but the way it was said that causes the trouble between parents. When you are just a few steps on the path away from intimacy even the most innocent gesture can press on a bruise from the past, triggering a full-blown angry reaction. No matter how firm Jim may be in his resolve to treat Jane as a business associate, he reacts to a certain rasp in her voice as he would to boiling oil down his back. His wrath rises, and instead of remaining coolly detached, he suddenly reacts with furious intimacy. Both are temporarily "off the wall."

Fortunately, fundamental methods of communication can be learned. With a little effort and practice, many people can control exaggerated responses and diminish their vulnerability. Taking the following surveys, whether in a single sitting or one by one, will show you how to rate your own current status. The process will also give you some tips on how to increase your own communications skills.

Checking Your Communication Style

The style of communication between intimates or former intimates operates according to a complex dynamic. But your answers on the following questions can give you some important information about your style, and some instant feedbacks on what you might do to strengthen or improve it. The Notes suggest further reading.

In order to answer the following questions, think back only to the last four or five times you had reason to have some communication with the other parent. Ask yourself *how* you made this contact. Ignore for the moment why you did it, what the message was about, or how you felt about it all—just concentrate on *how* you got the message to him or her.

Did you talk to him or her yourself—by phone, in person? Did you write a letter, send a note? Did you pass along a message through someone else like a friend, a spouse, or a child?

Communications: Self-Surveys

I. YOUR MESSAGES: DIRECT OR INDIRECT   As you think back over the last four or five times you have had a message to give to the other parent, how did you pass that message along—directly or indirectly?

_____ Direct: You talked directly to the other parent yourself,
No. of Times   face-to-face, by phone, or wrote a letter/note in
                       a sealed envelope.

_____ Indirect: You asked someone else—a friend, child, rela-
No. of Times   tive, co-worker—to get information for you or
                       to give a message to the other parent. Nothing
                       was written down. This was word of mouth only.

After you have scored yourself you might think about the other parent's communication style with you. Is it direct or indirect?

Donna sends messages frequently to the children's father, but never in person. Over the past two weeks she has sent messages to him twice through a third party (his brother) and twice through one of the children. None of these messages has been written; all have been word-of-mouth. She has a score of 4 indirect messages.

Dennis has a different communication style. He has talked directly to his child's mother twice over the past two weeks, once on the phone and once in person. He has all direct scores.

Jay lives 900 miles from his children during the school year, and they live with him during the summers and holidays. He talked to his children every week directly but realized he had talked to their mother directly only once during that time. He had asked the children to tell their mother information for him three times. He wanted to avoid talking to her on one occasion. The other two times it seemed the natural thing just to ask one of the kids to tell Mom for him. He had 1 direct and 3 indirect.

2. YOUR SOURCES: DIRECT OR INDIRECT   Where do you get your information? Think back over the past. Try to remember where your information has come from about your children and your former mate the last four or five times. For example, Donna gets her information about the children's father from his brother, sometimes from the children. The brother also gives Donna information about how the children behaved the weekend they were with their dad. Donna gets her information indirectly, and over the past two weeks, she has gotten such information four different times. Dennis, on the other hand, usually gets his informa-

tion directly. He asks his former mate questions himself, often in phone conversations or a note. For example, he asked the children's mother, "Do you want me to send extra jeans along with the kids this coming weekend?" Another parent might be indirect in the same situation and ask the children, "Did your dad say he wanted me to send extra jeans along with you next weekend?"

Remember as much as you can about where/how you got your information and record below your source of information.

Direct: "I find out from . . ."

From my former mate _____times
From my children   _____times

Indirect: "I find out from . . ."

From relatives   _____times
From friends   _____times
From children (about
the other parent)   _____times

How to Score

Now look at your scores in 1 and 2. If you have higher direct scores than indirect scores, you're on the right track. The higher the direct score, the more you are tending to your own business yourself rather than involving other people in your responsibilities. The higher the indirect score, however, the greater the chances are that you are ducking your own responsibilities or passing them to others. The children, when asked to carry a message by word of mouth, are the worst mode of communication. Notes passed back and forth with the children as messengers can work out all right as long as the notes are in a sealed envelope. Otherwise, you are putting your children in the middle. "Tell your mother that I'm going to be late next week," Father might say, as he drops the kids at the front door of Mom's house. Or, "Tell your father I'm waiting for the support check and he should send it with you when you come home." Regardless of how legitimate the message, using the children as messengers is strictly a no-no. Never send bad reports by the children. Do your own work, Mom or Dad, and leave the kids out of it. Your best bet is to develop your mode of direct communication. Second-best is indirect and written. The worst is indirect and verbal.

Indirect communication usually signals some kind of game playing. Sometimes the style is artful, based on the implicit knowing that characterizes old intimacies. At other times, it is clearly manipulative or a flat-out power play. If a person won't be direct, you can't get a straight answer. You may have to wait around, possibly losing your temper or your advantage while you do.

3. RESPONSES FROM THE OTHER PARENT: HARD OR EASY   Answer the first four questions by circling a 1 for a definite no and a 5 for a definite yes. A 1 is the most dissatisfied, difficult, and hard no you can give, 5 is the most satisfied, reliable and easy yes.

	No				Yes
1. Is it fairly easy to contact the other parent—that is, if you had to get in touch with him or her for an emergency, could you do it readily?	1	2	3	4	5
2. When you have a request or a question for the other parent, do you feel you will be given a fair hearing?	1	2	3	4	5
3. When you ask a question or look for a response from the other parent do you get a response within a reasonable amount of time?	1	2	3	4	5
4. Generally speaking, how would you rate your communications with the other parent? Give yourself a 5 for a pattern of excellent communications, a 1 for the poorest or if you have no contact at all.	1	2	3	4	5
5. When the other parent at first wants to avoid an issue, or avoid talking to you, can the two of you eventually work this situation through?	1	2	3	4	5
6. When *you* want to avoid an issue or to avoid talking with the other parent, can the two of you eventually work this situation through as well?	1	2	3	4	5

How to Score

Add up your answers for these questions. A score over 18 is a positive sign, an indication that you can get in touch with one another when you need to and that you have brought about a degree of mutual respect.

If you score under 18, your sense of respect or of trust may be strained. If you review your communication style carefully in the next set of questions, you may find some helpful clues to easing the situation.

4. REVIEW YOUR COMMUNICATIONS, PAST AND PRESENT   *Think back on your marriage. At what time of day did you have your most positive exchanges?* When did you seem to have the most difficult ones? "The worst time to talk to Harry was just before lunch," said Laura, "and there didn't seem to be any really good time." Can you give yourself some idea of the best and worst times to start a conversation with the other parent?

Then ask yourself which mode of communication seems to work best, which the worst? Some people think they have their worst arguments face to face, others on the telephone. Some people hate getting letters and are calmed by a phone call; others find that meetings clear the air.

There are no clear-cut answers. You have to decide which mode works best for you. Write them down on paper—after you have the answers to these questions, ask yourself these questions:

What is the most irritating and maddening thing that he or she does, the mannerism, tone of voice, or topic that really sets you off? "He's evasive—he never gives me a straight answer," say some people. "She's a liar; she says she put the check in the mail and it arrives a week later with a postmark of two days before." "She whines." "He wants to talk about the separation all the time." Whatever list of irritants you make, spend some time thinking about how that parent can make you angry or upset. Then ask yourself what you do that sets him or her off.

Finally, ask yourself how you avoid talking about something with the other parent. Do you change the subject, refuse to answer the phone or letters, say you will get around to it (and then never get around to it)? Do you say, "I don't want to talk about it"? Do you get angry or feel like giving the silent treatment, perhaps forget it altogether? Whatever you do when you want to avoid an issue or answering the other parent's questions, it's useful for *you* to know what you *do* do. Once you have identified some of your own responses, ask yourself, "What does the other parent do when he or she wants to avoid talking to me, or answering questions?"

Give Yourself a Break

When you have answered the questions on each of these self-surveys, you have gathered important information on how you can communicate more effectively with the other parent. Try to remember the fundamental rules. *Be as direct as possible, get your information as often as possible from the other parent directly, and know what he or she does that pushes your anger buttons.*

As mundane as it sounds, just knowing what is happening is half the task. At first you may not be able to change what you do or say, nor how you say it. But you will know what you are doing rather than remaining oblivious of your own actions. Change takes time for everyone. Give yourself the benefit of the doubt and try out this new way of communication for a month. See if it will help you and your situation.

Basic Business Principles for Parents

It isn't always easy for two people to do business together. If you have worked for more than a few years, chances are you have worked for a difficult employer, or supervised some hard-to-manage employees, or dealt with the demands of unreasonable customers. In business we often take pride in our ability to operate successfully under difficult circumstances. And when your own happiness and that of your children are at stake, learning the skills of doing business with someone you don't like and don't even trust is vital to your future.

Here are some of the basic business principles parents can use:

1. Effective businesspeople keep their feelings in check. They don't mix business with pleasure . . . or with displeasure.
2. Effective businesspeople conduct business through an orderly give and take in which both adhere to a common set of courtesies and expectations.
3. Effective businesspeople expect proof of sale or agreement.
4. In business, effective people give the other person the benefit of the doubt when it comes to motives but nevertheless expect delivery of promised goods and services.

When the participants are honorable, transactions are finished quickly, a sense of accomplishment results, and both parties feel they have made a good deal. They hope their next encounter will be equally satisfactory. Each successful transaction helps to cement the foundation on which mutual trust is built. Even under the best of circumstances it takes time to build a good reputation.

1. *Keep your feelings in check.* In business relationships, one's feelings are not to be confused with the job to be done or the goal to be reached. People say, "Don't mix business with pleasure." In part, that means, "Keep your private life and private feelings to yourself." In order to succeed with cooperative parenting, you simply expand the rule: Don't mix business with *dis*pleasure either.

The impersonal business relationship seems incongruous between people who have shared bed and board and are the co-parents of children. Yet there is a bitter-sweet dignity to this posture, which allows you to close the book gently but firmly on your past lives together.

Men, trained in the subtleties of business, often understand the concept of controlled emotions well. Once they are introduced to the concept of a working or business relationship with their former wives, they feel more comfortable. Women sometimes seem to have been socialized to negotiate with feelings instead of with words and formal processes. However, these women catch on quickly once they understand the rules of the transaction. For both men and women, the fly in the ointment is the ever-present danger that the feelings simmering below the controlled surface will erupt in that businesslike discussion and bring it to a most unbusinesslike end.

2. *Be orderly.* Good business, like communications, requires regular schedules, protocols, business hours, expectations, and much recordkeeping and memo writing. As cooperating parents, you prepare for each

business transaction with thought, study, and self-control as if you were preparing to talk to an associate about a situation in the office. You would not want to remind the associate of past misunderstandings. You must be willing to put the past behind you in a realistic manner and promote a meeting of minds. You make appointments to see your associate instead of just popping in. You write a memo at the end of your discussions. You don't leave the meeting expecting that you or your associate will remember every detail accurately. These principles work for parents as well.

3. *Make no assumptions. Have everything explicit.* Avoiding assumptions means checking your understandings with the other parent. Have everything explicit and put it in writing. With agreements, get a confirmation or a corrected version from the other parent. For example, a father might assume that he is going to continue bringing the boys to Little League games just like he did when they were living together, and since he has been living with the boys every other weekend, he will continue to take charge of their Little League activities.

It's Dad's job to put these assumptions about Little League in a note and send it off to Mom asking for her confirmation or her version. When feelings run deep and strong, it's hard to remember objective details. Memos after separation are a must, and more details on them are given later in the chapter. Remember, you wouldn't purchase a new carpet without all the details in writing. Don't enter into a long parenting period with a vague "We'll take care of it when it comes up" statement. Check out your assumptions, write them down, and then get verification.

Dad's note or letter to Mom could go something like this: "I've made the assumption that during the Little League season I'll be responsible for seeing that the boys get to the games and practices and back home, and the costs that come along with all that. I've also made the assumption that the every-other-weekend schedule that we've had is to continue indefinitely, or until we come up with other arrangements. If these don't check out with you, I would like to know by the end of this week so that we can come to some other arrangement."

4. *Give the other parent the benefit of the doubt.* This is a close cousin to the make-no-assumptions rule. When one parent is late picking up or bringing the children, think first of a flat tire, or heavy traffic. Don't immediately see the delay as a deliberate attempt to ruin your plans.

Suppose you hear from a neighbor that the other parent is going out of town the weekend that he or she is to be with the children. You wonder, "Is this parent going to cancel the weekend with the children at the last minute?" Furious, you are ready to pick up the phone and make some accusations. Take a deep breath and back off. Do your best *not* to assume that second-hand information about the other parent is accurate. Better instead to say nothing or to call after you have calmed down.

The bad feelings that accompany separation and divorce can bring about rudeness, emotional outbursts, broken promises, outright dishonesty, and invasion of privacy. In business, difficult situations are managed whenever the stakes are high enough. If you adopt business and communications principles, you can go a long way toward moving away from negative intimacy while also building a new working relationship with the other parent.

5. *Use businesslike communications and recordkeeping.* Good business communications principles apply to parents developing a working relationship. Business is conducted in many ways: in person, by mail, by phone, and sometimes, when the going gets sticky, through attorneys. Rarely does a business transaction take place with an unauthorized third party (friends, relatives, or children) carrying information; apply the same principles to parenting. Communicating is your job. Try to make plans yourself, by mail, by phone, or in person. If in-person communication becomes too uncomfortable, retreat to the phone or the mail. This is quite acceptable. Just write that you're trying to keep your feelings out of these important discussions, but you hope to resume personal contact later. Give a generalized explanation—not the details.

6. *Don't take the other parent for granted.* As simple as this guideline may seem, it may also be the most important. Building trust with the other parent does not mean you can take him or her for granted. After divorce, this becomes a dangerous form of disrespect and can rapidly lead to trouble.

An Example of a Good Working Relationship

Brian and Pat, who have children ages nine and eleven, have been separated for about six months. The children live with Pat about two-thirds of each month. Twice a month they live with Brian over extended weekends, from Thursday night through Monday morning. This division of parenting is a tentative arrangement. They've agreed to try for two months and then appraise the result. They are both still in the off-the-wall stage of emotions.

Usually Pat and Brian communicate by phone and use the mails to verify their arrangements. They need to write memos and keep records because Pat has a reputation (with Brian) for being forgetful. And Pat claims Brian often changes plans at the last minute. Writing memos is a time-consuming bore, but it prevents accusations and excuses. The parent who slips up cannot shift the blame. Each agreement is confirmed by the memo on the desk or on the kitchen bulletin board.

Brian has a free afternoon coming up next week and wants to spend it with his daughter Tricia. He calls Pat at work and asks, "Is this a good time to talk to you, or should I call you later?" Pat replies that she's free to talk now. Secretly she just wants to get the talk over with.

"I have a free afternoon next Thursday," Brian says, "and I'd like to spend it with Tricia. I'll pick her up after school and have dinner with her, then bring her home around eight o'clock. How does that sound to you?" As he talks, Brian hopes he doesn't have to convince Pat.

Pat agrees; Brian is relieved and he mails Pat a note that outlines their agreement and contacts Tricia to see how she feels about Thursday. Tricia is delighted and father and daughter make their private plans. Brian's note reads:

"Here is my understanding of today's phone conversation. On Thursday, January 12, I will pick Tricia up after school and take her to dinner. I'll bring her home at 8:00 P.M. I'll call the sitter on Thursday morning to explain that Tricia won't come home after school. If I have any of these details mixed up, please call me. Otherwise, I'll assume this is your understanding as well. Take care of yourself, Brian."

Brian marks his calender and makes a copy of the note before mailing it to Pat. There is no need for future phone calls between the parents and far less possibility of misunderstanding. Brian now has a direct line with Tricia about Thursday and each parent has a memo to remind them of their agreement. If Brian wants to change plans, he will have to repeat the entire procedure. Pat and Brian followed these guidelines:

Checklist for a Business Discussion

Style of communication: Direct. Neither children nor friends transfer or mediate information. All information comes directly from one to the other.

Expectations: A business occasion only. No expectations for emotional support or approval or taking the other person for granted.

Preparation for discussion or transactions: Set up appointment, ask for most convenient time.

Content of discussion: One or two items, about children only. No personal disclosure, keep a low profile.

Style of conversation/discussion: Informal, but on the subject; courteous; caring without being personally drawn in; specific, rather than vague; questioning, rather than judgmental reacting.

Time of phone calls: During normal working or business hours.

Recordkeeping: Notes or memos made after each conversation to record details of agreements.

Verification of agreement: Note sent by one or both parties itemizing the contents of the agreement reached. The other party corrects any misconceptions.

* * *

Pat and Brian could have sabotaged their exchange in many ways. Brian might have called Pat late at night, and either parent might have been discourteous on the phone. Brian might have failed to send the memo. Pat might have forgotten to post it as a reminder for Tricia.

Let's imagine how such behavior might affect an ordinary business relationship. Suppose a person calls you at home, after you have gone to bed, to complain about the details of a contract you are negotiating. When you tell him you will discuss it on Monday during business hours, he becomes discourteous. He finally agrees to a Monday-morning appointment —but he doesn't show up at your office. When you finally get together, he snarls at you and makes snide remarks about your personal behavior. Would you buy a used car from this man?

Think of the many ways people in business can be irritating. They don't return telephone calls, are late for appointments, misrepresent their services, and don't keep agreements. They bring in the personal aspects, stray from the subject at hand, challenge your competence or integrity, and downgrade the competition. Former mates are especially adept at sabotaging their own transactions by using such provoking, unbusinesslike behavior.

How Memos Help

Most parents find "those damned memos" irritating but very useful. "The memos shaped me up," one mother said. "I couldn't blame the children's father for my own negligence." During periods of emotional upheaval, people are forgetful. They remember feelings and snatches of conversation but forget details that have not been recorded.

Some people try to communicate only in vague speech and nonverbal signals, as if they are afraid to commit themselves to any specific details. When Brian agreed to bring Tricia home at eight o'clock, he made a commitment not to keep her out beyond her bedtime. Keeping such promises is essential to building trust in the cooperative parenting relationship. He showed his willingness to abide by the agreement when he put it in writing. When Pat received the memo, she accepted it as a routine business procedure—not a sign of scorn or distrust. (Some people misunderstand this feedback process when it occurs in private communications.)

Writing memos eliminates some of the verbal cues that cause tension in an oral communication. "I knew he was going to give me a hard time," one mother said, after a telephone call from the children's father. "His tone of voice was icy and disdainful." Familiar voice tones, gestures, and postures tell us what might be happening inside our former mates. But as accurate as we might be about his or her thoughts and motives, mind reading and second-guessing do not belong in business. Focus on words, not feelings.

The Working Relationship and Your Children's Respect

The businesslike relationship will be a boon to your children as they watch a minor miracle occur. Their parents—two people they love deeply—are learning how to work together, despite feelings of anger and disappointment. This new ordering of priorities is a model of civilized behavior. You can teach them by your example how to devise an effective working relationship without sacrificing personal integrity.

Mom's House, Dad's House

Chapter **10**

HOW TO MAKE

THEM HOMES

Put yourself in your child's place. Your parents have announced that they are separating. What would they have to say or do that would (1) help you feel things would work out all right, and (2) show that you would now have two homes instead of one?

Parents in workshops frequently respond by saying: "I'd want to feel that my parents knew what the heck they were doing." "I'd want my own things, my own place in my second as well as in my first home." "I'd want my friends, my school, my pet." "I'd want to stake out my own territory in each place." By the time the list is half-way finished, one person in the group will say, surprised, "This second home sounds like a real home." Right. The second home *is* a real home. And instead of competing with the other home, it can help stabilize life after divorce in both places.

Building security and continuity into two homes does not have to remain a mystery. Nor need the parents feel that they will make the effort only for the sake of their children. The two-home plan can become the mainstay of the parents' own stability as well as the basis of family solidarity. The reorganization offers work for head and heart. The head has to organize the essentials of life, the heart has to give it meaning and warmth.

The first set of guidelines in this chapter will be valuable for any parent, with or without custody, with shared custody, with or without the beginnings of a new working relationship. These guidelines can help you organize your home and redesign your independent relationship as a parent without consulting the other parent. Your place is your territory, your responsibility, your independent domain. You can make it a real home for you and your children. Even fathers with limited visitation rights who followed this first set of guidelines have reported over and over, "I feel like a real father again."

The second half of the chapter will look at those decisions that need to be made between you and the other parent—which one of you will live where? How important is it to keep the original family home? If you keep it, who will live there? How will the time be divided between Mom's house and Dad's house? What about the other adults in the children's lives—teachers, coaches, doctors, and dentists? These considerations will probably be part of your first negotiations with the other parent.

Setting Up Your Own Home

A Sense of Belonging: My Own Things

The common grumble of parents when children return from being with their other parent is that shoes, a favorite toy, or a jacket have been left behind. The first knee-jerk reaction comes: The other parent or the child has been inconsiderate, thoughtless, or deliberately provoking. Actually, as we have seen, this forgetfulness probably stems from the child's need to stake a claim to some territory, a sense of belonging in his or her newer home.

Children will know they belong in two homes when they no longer need a suitcase to go from one home to another. This holds true even if they spend as little as three days in one home. The time spent doesn't matter, the sense of belonging does.

Children need their own space, even a drawer they share at the bottom of their parent's dresser. They need their own nontransferable toilet articles and two or three changes of clothes. They need their own place for toys and personal effects and a place to sleep. In short, at least some personal things belong in their second home and stay there. Sleeping bags rolled up in a closet can be good beds if these are their own sleeping bags. A house, a yard, and an extra bedroom are just trimmings. The sense of "my own things, here" matters.

Many second-home parents simply take their offspring shopping for new clothing, sleeping bags, and toilet articles. These purchases offer a way to participate in the organization of their second home. If money is a problem, perhaps parents can agree on which of the child's articles of clothing and personal belongings can be transferred permanently from one home to the other. Whenever possible, honor the children's preferences. If they want to carry their favorite pajamas back and forth, let them. They may change their minds after a week or two and make a switch. This maneuver usually tests out Mom's and Dad's reactions, a trial-and-error way to learn what will feel best but also what the parents will accept. Allow reasonable time to try out different schemes; observe what is easy and comfortable for the children and then agree on rules. "Usually one or two things transfer," said one parent. "Our eldest wears the same hats back and forth. Our youngest carries his blanket and teddy bear."

Remember when your children have their clothes and things in two homes you also get rid of the "suitcase conversation" with the other parent.

Ground Work

Ground work designates the time parent and child take walking together around the new home(s), exploring, familiarizing themselves with landmarks, meeting neighbors and potential playmates, discovering busy streets and—most importantly—determining boundaries for roaming without an adult. Ground work is the most basic settling-in work parent and child must do in a new neighborhood, but it may be the most ignored task of parenting. It takes no more than an hour to do and should be done by each parent at each home. Benefits are widespread and long-lasting.

Lecturing the child as you march over the ground won't do the job. Nor is this an activity to be delegated to baby-sitters. Parent and child do it together. Like other shared activities, ground work gives a sense of security, while showing the neighbors that you are a caring parent. One parent admitted her shame at living in the same place for four years and never walking the neighborhood with her daughters. "I realized I had been a four-wheel parent; if I didn't see it from the car coming into our driveway or going out of it, it didn't exist. I didn't know the names of my neighbors two houses down!" When the parent walks these routes with the children, he or she can exchange phone numbers with parents of potential playmates and friendly local merchants. When Dad sends Eric to the store or neighborhood market for bread and Eric has not returned after a reasonable time, Dad—because he took a minute to get the market's number and to introduce Eric to the manager—can phone and ask if Eric has been there.

Such ground work establishes an automatic neighborhood watch for your children. Children gain a sense of security and of belonging; their parents gain peace of mind and real information about the neighborhood. Ground work takes only a few hours, but it pays off again and again in security and continuity for you and your children.

Order in the House

Parents feeling sad, remorseful, or angry can let daily routines and household organization go downhill rapidly during their own times of crisis. A little occupational therapy is in order. Pick yourself up and recover a bare minimum working order in your house. Set up a rough schedule that makes time for buying groceries and gas, for making and eating meals, for getting kids to school or to Little League, for rest and play and going to bed.

Paying attention to household management may sound like a dull remedy for the aches and pains of separation or depression, but both common sense and research support this approach as fundamental to calming fears and to the development of a new stability. A sensible routine, with regular meals and regular times for shared recreation, translates into home, into being cared about. "Knowing my kids needed that routine forced me to be orderly for at least part of my week. Even when I didn't think I could make dinner or read that bedtime story, I did it. It actually did make things easier not only for them, but for me, too."

This family and others who ordered their lives early on—despite their difficulties—seem to have an easier time of readjusting overall. Structure feels safe.

House Rules and Your Parenting Style

One wonderful benefit of your new experience appears as you renegotiate your relationship with your children. More than one parent, often the father, has reported that for the first time in his parenting life he is enjoying his children and feeling a rapport and depth of feeling for them that had escaped him earlier.

You may have compromised your parenting style when married; you need not compromise it any longer. You can set new house rules that reflect your needs as well as those of the children. If you want to take the phone off the hook during dinner, you may. If you want to have a quiet period for reading or headphone-stereo listening after 9:00 P.M., write it into the blueprint. If your natural inclination is to be a relaxed and permissive parent, consider tightening up during your first year, to help all of you settle into your new life. During the first year many children interpret limits as a reflection of their parents' personal stability and as a caring for family well-being. A set of house rules reached in a family pow-wow that promotes safety, health, and privacy for everyone can be periodically revised as new circumstances arise.

Safety Rules

Each home, regardless of how the children's time is divided, has basic needs. You need a clearly legible list of emergency numbers: the doctors', friends', and neighbors' numbers where the parent can be reached. Parents should familiarize children with fire escapes, routes in case of earthquakes or fire, meeting places for the family if separated. These essential routines take time. There's no need to alarm very young children with details of such information, but they should memorize their own addresses and last names, phone numbers, or the names of friends to call.

Chores

No home can function without somebody doing the chores. Besides being necessary, chores can help build security and solidity for the new family feeling, especially when parent and children work at the chores together. When the parent scrubs the sink, the eight-year-old daughter puts away the dishes, and the ten-year-old vacuums, the burden of housework is lightened by teamwork and the growth of a new family feeling. Participation builds solidarity, as all athletes who play team sports know well. Children of any age need the satisfaction of doing a job in cooperation with Mom or Dad. Chores are not a form of cheap labor for unpleasant tasks, but a preparation for an independent life as an adult. Completed tasks remind children that they belong; that they are functioning family members, trusted, appreciated, and most of all, needed to keep the household running. "I feel guilty having the children do work at my house," said a second-home parent. His misplaced guilt will not make them feel at home, but simple tasks and the resumption of a more normal parenting pattern will.

Children in divorced families often grow more realistic about the relation between caring and sharing, about how things get done in the grownup world. When children help cook meals, do the laundry, clean the house, shop, and eat the casserole they helped prepare, they know what their work accomplished. A sense of mastery and increased self-confidence can grow. Children such as these seem to be more independent at an earlier age than are children from families that have never faced any threat of division. They learn to get themselves around by bus or bike, to cook a whole meal, to stay alone or reach sensible decisions in a pinch when no adult is around to help. With less time and fewer adults to make decisions or carry out family chores, the children shoulder responsibilities at an earlier age.

Decision-making for chores and family rules is different in each family. Some parents prefer to make all the decisions, others allow their children to decide. A good midpoint leaves certain areas open to discussion, but the parent reserves the right for the final decisions, while the other areas are openly discussed by all with each child's preference given as much priority as possible.

Child Care

"If the freeway traffic is heavy and I arrive late to pick up my son after work, the sitter threatens me, saying that if I'm late again, I'll have to find another place for Bobby," sighed a tired father. "Then when my son announces that tomorrow he's to be at school at ten instead of the usual eight thirty, I'm faced with the problem of what to do for his safety between the time I'm due to be at work, nine, and the time he will be allowed at school. Doesn't anyone care about us and our needs?" This dad is finding out what working moms have known for a long time. The world of work and the world of caring for children are not compatible, and no one knows this better than the harassed working parent.

Aside from the problems of employment and income, child care is the number one concern of single parents. Most single parents whose children live with them most of the time are working outside the home. This usually means finding child care when money is at an all-time low. What to do? The choices are many: a neighbor with children the same age; a neighbor who runs a family day-care center in her home; an after-school day-care center in the child's school or at a local community center; a private sitter, shared with other single parents and rotating the after-school meeting place from one house to another.

Choosing Child Care

The quality of the care is most important for the children's development and for the parent's peace of mind.

If you are new at this child care search, or are looking for a way to evaluate your present situation, there is a detailed guide in Appendix VI, titled "A Guide to Choosing Child Care: A Checklist for Parents." Don't delegate this job of choosing who will care for your child. Visit the day-care center, the home of the day-care family, or the home of the sitter who may be coming to your house, and ask yourself the questions set forth in the guide.

Breathing Room for the Parent

Parents need time off to be adults. Taking time for yourself seems obvious, but is one of the most overlooked aspects of parenting, especially for singles.

In a world where so little is consistent, permanent, or secure, the continual presence of Mom or Dad seems essential for the security of a child. But think again—adults also need other adults for balance and perspective just as children need one another. The parent who never takes a break is courting trouble.

Unfortunately, most child care arrangements don't allow parents any breathing room. You rush to get ready in the morning, to get the children off to school or to the sitter's, to pick them up at night, to return home for dinner, homework, and finally, not until late at night, do you have some quiet adult time.

Even with a two-home situation, a tired parent can ask, "Is this all there is?" "I can hardly wait for the weekend sometimes," confided another mother of two, "when the kids will be with their father. At least he won't call me up, tell me the kids are sick so I have to drop whatever I'm doing and come pick them up." Parents need time to be adults, not just someone's mother or father.

Single parents, desperately needing balance and respite from constant responsibilities, need to examine their feelings and priorities. Granted you may have little time and energy left over for your adult personal life when you are running your home single-handed. But you need balance in your life, and your children need the renewal you get—and pass along—from the adult times you can carve out of every week.

A hovering parent can hamstring the child's development into the independent, self-sufficient individual he or she needs to be to survive in the tough grown-up world. Further, isolated adults can come to expect from their children the intimacy and understanding only realistically available from fellow adults.

Parents have been known to take time for themselves at the expense of their children's safety by leaving young children alone. Young children are not safe without a sitter, and the fact that they know it only adds to the dangers. No matter how conscientiously you may have taught and warned your children about what they should do in emergencies, they should not be left alone or asked to care for younger siblings when your usual arrangements have failed you. You alone are responsible for making certain that your children are under the care of a reliable adult at all times.

Even single parents on slim budgets can find time for themselves. Here are some successful ways other parents have worked out.

Free Nights

Three single parents agreed to bring their children together overnight once a week, either during school or on the weekends. This meant that each week two parents had one night completely free while the remaining parent had the three children. The children loved the expanded family feeling, and since each was an only child, all enjoyed observing different parent-child relationships, "staying over" at each other's homes.

This works best with three families, but two can also manage. Sometimes children can be picked up from school or child care by the parent whose turn it is, leaving the other two free. The trading can work on weekends, too.

Sometimes the second-home parent objects to such overnight arrangements, saying, "If the children can stay with another family, they can stay more often with me, too." But overnight arrangements with friends achieve more than simply free time for the resident parent. To see them as tricks to keep the child away from the second-home parent is to miss the importance of exposing the child to varying family styles and of supporting the child's natural desire to solidify friendships with his peers.

One mother whose former mate complained about their daughter's overnight visits with friends simply agreed with him. Now, the ten-year-old daughter has two nights a week away from Mom—one with friends and one with Dad.

What Are Your Priorities?

Since free time to be an adult is so important to effective child rearing as well as being a basic right for adults, one wonders why parents take out loans for a new car, clothes, or furniture, but not for child care? The time to have plenty of good child care, household help, and freedom to reshape your adult life is now—not later when the children are grown. Many parents find this concept perplexing, but those who forego other material possessions to gain the security and freedom of a housekeeper or a consistent sitting arrangement know the value of the support they buy. They aren't always coming home from work to face five or six hours more of housework. And when they open up the options to reshape their intimate adult lives, they can take more time to enjoy and relax with their children.

Keep in Touch with Your Children

Regardless of your children's ages, when you are away from home, even if you have a sitter or they are in day care, let them know where you are and when they can expect you back. If you are delayed, call and give them another approximate time to expect you. This simple information goes a long way toward calming children who have already seen one parent go out of their primary home. They need to be reassured (regardless of statements like "I don't care") where you are and that you are really coming back. "I started telling my teenagers that they could expect me home from work by five-thirty," said one single father, "or know the reason why. They were blasé about it, but if I came home at five forty-five and hadn't called, they let me know about it with: 'Where have you been?' or 'You didn't call!'

"It *was* important to them. At first I thought it was only because they didn't want me to be anywhere but home and at work, but that wasn't the whole story. They needed simple reassurance. They even tolerated my dating when they knew when to expect me home and what I expected from them during my absence."

Contact With Your Children: A Self-Survey

Communications with Your Children

When your child is living with you and you are working, do you:

1. Leave notes at home for your child (if the child is old enough to read)?
2. Phone your child from work once a day?
3. Get phone calls from your child to your work once a day?

During this last week, did you do any of those things listed above? If yes, about how many times? _____

When your child is not living with you, do you:

1. Call on the phone to the other home?
2. Send notes or letters if you are gone for more than a week?
3. Send tapes if you are separated for more than three weeks?
4. Have other ways of communicating?

During these last two weeks, did you do any of those things listed above? If yes, about how many times? _____

What Your Answers Mean

As before, there is no *right* or *wrong* answer. You decide if the answers you give satisfy you and reflect the way you contact your children when they are not with you. Children are concrete. They do best when they have tangible evidence of their parents' presence in their lives. Contact when you are separated is one way to provide that.

"Aw Mom, I'm too Old for a Sitter . . ."

Early teenagers often object vigorously to supervision, yet they need it as much as the younger ones. "My children are over thirteen," say some parents. "They don't need supervision when I'm at work or out in the evening. They would resent it and be difficult about it." Perhaps they would be resentful and difficult, but they may need an adult as much as the younger ones do. Older children, left alone after school and for long stretches of time during the weekends, often whine and crab over helping with housework or doing anything else. Such children need more, not less, adult caring and supervision.

"You should hear the way my teenage kids talk to me," a parent might say to me at a workshop coffee break. Sometimes a good friend will add, "They are snippy, condescending, and no help at all to her around the house. She works full time trying to keep a roof over their heads. They are totally unappreciative." When such parents come as private clients, the parent (usually a mother) often describes her life in this way. She wasn't often home in the evenings and was preoccupied with housework and errands on the weekends. There were few or no house rules, no regular communications, no working order. She had rarely done ground work with her children. No one seemed satisfied.

This mother can often regain control of her household and her life at home by beginning over from scratch. Instead of assigning chores to be done in her absence, she can make it a point to start being home two nights a week and to work along with her children. At least part of each weekend can be saved for family time. She can review her safety and house rules alone, then again with the children. Together they can discuss electricity, gas, and the locks, and agreed on house rules, such as quiet time—neither TV nor phone calls—after ten o'clock at night. A parent can call home every day after school to check in, and if the children would not be there, they can make arrangements to call at work. A final step is to find a neighbor who is willing to be a mainstay anchor, providing a place for the children to check in two or three times a week to leave messages on their activities and to care for them in illness. As parents take more control over the daily framework for the household order and safety, everyone's attitude usually begins to change. Tensions ease, there are more spontaneous fun times, and everyone feels more like a family again.

ANCHORS FOR TEENAGERS   An anchor comes in many shapes: a mainstay adult close by who knows what to do and whom to call in an emergency; a series of check-in phone calls between parent and child through the week; a routine that both can count on; and a good set of house and safety rules. The parent who takes the time to develop these anchors is improving living conditions for everyone.

An independent relationship between parent and child can be a joy in all families. When this bond is maintained or grows after divorce, children adjust more readily and parents set up new homes more easily. Things settle down and parents and children feel more "at home" in the new circumstance. In the words of one father, "I knew I had finally put my home together when I started reading to my daughters after dinner just the way I had when I was married."

Decisions with the Other Parent

In this chapter, decisions about setting up your home have so far applied only to your time with the children, your house, your territory. You must also consider the other parent in your children's lives. Who moves? How do you divide the children's time? What do you tell the schools, the doctors, the Little League coach? Who moves out of the family home?

The Family Home

Many parents start out convinced that the original family home and the familiar neighborhood provide an important sense of continuity for children during the first year of separation. My experience supports this view. On the other hand, this staying put may eventually put a psychological burden on the parent who remains. He or she may need freedom from neighbor's questions, comments, and opinions about the divorce, and from double-edged words about being the new single on the block. Houses can hang on to all the memories of the past. Each corner, each piece of furniture or china, can haunt the most dauntlessly practical parent trying to disentangle the new life from the symbols of the past.

How important, many parents ask, is it for children to keep the original family home as one of their two homes? For how long? There are no easy answers, only a few general guidelines:

1. Try to keep one of your homes your old address the first year.
2. If you must move during the first year, try very hard to keep the children in the same school unless they are already unhappy there.
3. If, after the first year or so, you must move, plan to do so at the end of a school year to minimize the disruption for the child and the difficulty for yourself.

Children moved from their schools, neighborhoods, and friends during the initial months of their parents' divorce have to make two enormous adjustments at once. Parents and children find life easier with only one major change at a time. Continuity of everyday patterns like going back and forth to school, playing with the kids on the block, and walking the dog helps steady everybody. If there must be a move away from the original home during that first year, make every effort to keep your children in the same school until the end of some definite school period, preferably the academic year.

Two-Home Geography: Who Is Where?

Another critical question for parents is where the two homes will be located. Are the two homes within walking or biking distance or do the children need transportation to go from one home to the other?

The easiest situation for the children is for you and the other parent to live close enough so the kids can travel between their two homes independently. If they can walk, ride their bikes, or take easy public transportation from one home to the other, they will feel far more secure than if they have to depend on others to make the arrangements and do the driving.

Generally, children do better when they can stay close to the original family pattern and setting, to old friends, to familiar faces and places. Adults, on the other hand, may be needing to expand, to reach out, to take new jobs. Women may be returning to school to retain far more interesting, important, or remunerative work, and such plans may entail geographic shifts (see Chapter 15). There are no automatic solutions, and even parents who initially moved away may move back.

How Long at Mom's House, How Long at Dad's House

Because each set of families must settle into its own unique pattern, there is no hard and fast rule for the division of the children's time between their two homes. Parents have, however, found two basic rules of thumb from which to begin:

1. Children and parents need a block of unbroken time together. This means time spent overnight, not just a few hours during a day.
2. Both parents need to take care that each becomes and remains a real parent rather than one a disciplinarian and the other only a recreation director.

In other words, both homes need to be fully functioning homes, not one home where children work and another where they play.

The importance of unbroken times with each parent can be understood when you look at the way children actually behave in each home. When a child gets used to sleeping somewhere regularly, he feels at home. When a child can find the bathroom, pull out a familiar toy, settle down for a bedtime story, read by Mom or Dad, both parent and child feel the return of family security and great joy in waking up in the morning to find each other there. Don't you remember being tucked in by your parents? The bond of continuity from such ordinary acts brings a precious togetherness that stays with your children all their lives.

Back to Normal

The faster you get back to the semblance of a "normal" routine with bedtimes, chores, house rules, and safety rules, the better chance everyone has of a quick and happy adaptation to this new life.

Of course, normal routines can also include doing something out of the ordinary, some special treat. Parents may feel at first that they must counterbalance the pain of separation and their fear of losing their children by promises of extra treats. And you might feel that these treats make the children look forward to seeing you, but if so, you are underrating your children's genuine affection for you as their parent. You also run the risk of degrading the precious parent-child relationship to that of entertainer and guest, with possibilities of recurrent disappointment.

Many parents have complained that the Sunday night ending to a weekend together is unbearably painful. In the words of one father, "The wrench of bringing the kids home on Sunday night is just more than I can take. Is there a way to get around this awful separation experience?" Yes, there is a way to get around it within a normal routine. Instead of bringing the children to their other home on Sunday night, take them straight to school on Monday morning.

One father says, "It's natural for a parent to bring children to school. I say good-bye to them more easily in the course of the routine. I go on to work and they go on to classes. There's no time to feel lonely." Other parents who have tried this plan say, "There's a natural rhythm to it," and, "I don't have to face their other parent. On Sunday, I can stick to the old 'school nights' pattern just like I always did and I feel more like a real parent this way."

Dividing Time During the School Year

Just how parents divide time with the children is very much up to the parents themselves. Sharing can range from a strict schedule of equal time at each home to a broader view of sharing as participation in child-rearing based on quality rather than quantity of time. The needs of your child should dictate your decisions. Pick and choose ideas from the following arrangements and create your own plan, one that suits your family best.

OPEN TIME BETWEEN HOMES   "Open time" means a freedom of movement between the two homes as arranged by the children. This works best when the children are in their teens and the parents are willing to make independent plans. The children make their plans with the parent they want to live with (for a week, a month, or a year) and then make plans with the other parent regarding their times together. The advantages of this are that the children make the arrangements and the parents may have little need to interact on anything but the annual major decisions regarding finances and education. Before this plan can work, however, both parents must believe strongly in the value of the independent parent-child relationship.

EQUAL TIMES AT BOTH HOMES   This equal time can be divided almost any way: three or four days with one parent, three or four days with the other, or two weeks and two weeks. This split-time or split-custody arrangement seems to work over long periods of time when the two homes are close together, the children are in their preteens or older, and when parents are especially careful to maintain regular schedules.

This split-time arrangement is highly controversial for infants and preschool children, although I know of one couple who arranged an alternating schedule with two months in one home and two months in the other. Their finances allowed for one housekeeper (who moved along with the children) and bedrooms for the children in each of the homes. This lasted about six months, until the parents decided to shift to a primary/secondary home arrangement.

ONE-THIRD IN ONE HOME, TWO-THIRDS IN THE OTHER   If thought out carefully, this arrangement can work well regardless of the children's ages. For about eight to ten days and nights a month, perhaps encompassing two long weekends (Thursday evenings until the beginning of school the next Monday), the children live with the second-home parent. This brings the structure and satisfaction of being together for four school nights. The children have a place and time to do homework and to share school life. The regular routine of Monday morning drop-off at school helps alleviate the sense of separation at good-bye times during the first two years.

When the eight to ten days a month are taken only on Saturdays or Sundays, parents report mixed reactions. The second-home parent lives with the children every weekend, but the first-home parent has no time to relax with the children when free from the work week. Both parents may end up feeling that the children interfere with adult social life.

ONE-QUARTER RESIDENCE IN ONE HOME, THREE-QUARTERS IN THE OTHER HOME   This is often a variation on the last arrangement—about four to six days and nights during a month's period. Usually the period begins on a Friday evening and ends on Sunday afternoon, without the advantage of the Monday-morning school ritual, but allowing some unbroken time for both parent and child to resume a more normal relationship and some of the weekend with each parent.

ONE DAY A WEEKEND   This arrangement allows the second-home parent a brief weekly contact with the child, but almost always encourages a guest-host relationship. Re-establishing regular parenting is difficult under this arrangement, unless the time includes an overnight stay.

Dividing Time During the Summer

Summertime for the two-home child can mean any number of experiences. It can mean a total two-and-a-half-month immersion in one parent's world, a split time between homes, summer camp away from both parents' peering gazes, or a continuation of what had been happening during the school year. Some fortunate children travel with one parent to different parts of the world, others settle into summer jobs or summer school or just hanging-out with the gang. The littlest ones keep going to day care or to the sitters, not yet old enough to participate in the summertime world. For some children the same divisions of time that held for the school year continue during the summer.

Often summer means that the second-home parent will have that two- or three-month-long continuous stretch of time with the children while the other parent has them on weekends. If the parents are separated by many miles, the summer home parent will have what one father described as "plain old parenting without a break."

There are infinite variations and each family designs its own arrangements for each summer. Some parents plan vacations with children, others without. Some children get one trip, others get two different vacations. Other parents plan their time off without the children. Still other parents work out divisions of summertime for the children to spend afternoons with Mom and eat supper and spend nights with Dad.

Summer camps come into the picture for many schoolage children, as do trips to other relatives or friends. The same principles apply, however. Whatever you agree on regarding times with each parent, remember that what one parent does on his or her time is not subject to the other parent's approval. Sometimes a parent will be upset because he or she assumed that the month the child spent during the summer with the other parent would be spent entirely with that parent. Instead, the other parent decided to send the child to camp for a week and to his grandparents for another. If this is the parent's time, this is also that parent's prerogative. This is his or her time to plan as he or she chooses.

HOLIDAYS   These times have a special meaning for many families and often require thoughtful preplanning. Appendix II outlines practical planning suggestions.

Post a Schedule

Post a schedule of (1) when the children will be at Mom's house and at Dad's house, (2) which parent will supervise which activity, and (3) what the parents will expect of the children. Make it simple, clear, easy to read, and then post it on the family bulletin board for everyone to consult. Chapter 12 has an example of one of these family schedules.

The Other Adults in Your Children's Lives

Have you met your child's teachers? Talked with his doctor? Compared notes with her coach? If not, do it now. Your child's professional guides don't see many parents—especially not many fathers. Since mothers have traditionally handled all their children's health, education, and extracurricular activities, the teacher may naturally assume that after divorce the mother will continue in the same role. "I'm sorry to say," said one junior high principal, "that I don't see much of fathers here—married or divorced. And when one does come in to ask about his child or want to see some official records, unless I have had some previous contact with him, I'm suspicious of his motives."

Each parent—especially each second-home parent—will have to initiate and maintain his or her own independent communication with the school and with other agencies or persons who supervise the child's activities. Investing a few hours a year in a phone call or written questions will reap enormous benefits for you, your child, the doctor, dentist, teacher, or coach.

If you have no written legal agreement and are in the process of negotiating one, now is the time to stipulate that all school and health records and information be made open to each parent on an equal basis (see Chapter 12).

If you do have a written agreement that denies access to records to the other parent, stop now and consider the great advantages of opening these records to the other parent. Customarily, the schools will allow the parent with sole custody to deny the other parent access to information about a child's educational progress, even though the denial of access to report cards and other formal records does not in most states fall under the custodial parent's legal authority. But because of the ambiguities, schools and other institutions such as churches, clubs, and medical treatment centers, fearing legal entanglements, are likely to refuse access.

Most institutions in your family's world have not yet caught up with your reality. Most schools, doctors, and clubs do not gather complete information about your child—only who will pay the bill or be the responsible one. Don't expect them to ask you questions—you will have to provide them with specific facts about who will have dealings with them and who will have responsibility. If you don't, no matter how good your working relationship with the other parent, your child will lose some benefits of your hard work in his or her contacts with community organizations.

How the Child Benefits

Here are some of the situations families and school personnel face and what can happen.

When thirteen-year-old Jennie was accused of theft at school, the principal's first thought was to involve both parents. But once he saw Jennie's registration card, he realized he did not have enough information to contact both parents. Jennie's registration card showed she lived with her divorced mother. There was no requirement, and therefore no place on the registration form, for information about the second-home parent, Jennie's father. Nor was there a place for parents to state their desires about the noncustodial parent's involvement in school matters. The principal didn't know how to reach the father—or even if he had the right to do so. Jennie's mother was not in her office, and the police were going to be at the school within the hour. Luckily, just when the principal was about to call a neighbor listed on the emergency card, Jennie's mother was reached and she was able to get to the school in time to be with Jennie.

The absence of information and some simple procedural guidelines had taken the principal's time and energy away from Jennie's needs and directed it to the unknown politics of the divorced parents' relationship. He wondered: Are the parents on friendly terms? Will the mother be upset if the father is called without her permission? Will the father be upset if he is not notified? Are stepparents involved? What about Jennie? Doesn't she have a right to her father's support and to the support of other significant adults in her family circle?

In contrast, when ten-year-old John broke his leg in a nasty fall from the monkey bars in the schoolyard, everyone at school knew exactly whom to call and for what, even though his parents were divorced. There was no need for a teacher to guess or tiptoe past parental discord. John lived most of the time with his mother, but his father and stepfather, also now divorced from his mother, were both authorized to make important decisions, to be present in classrooms, and to have access to all official records. In case of emergency any or all of the parents or stepparents were to be called. Given this clear-cut message, the school found it easy to cooperate.

HOW TO COMMUNICATE WITH ORGANIZATIONS   Each parent—separately—needs to have an independent communication with school and health professionals, to keep copies of children's health records, and to have open access to the children's records and activities. If your school district or individual school declines to give you this information or access, write a formal letter of complaint to them and get some action.

With the school, for example, parents can tell the school what they want instead of waiting to be asked. Parents with custody can write letters to the school specifying their preferences about the involvement of the other parent; if they choose, they can also formally or legally authorize the other parent to have access to privileged information and to assume authority when necessary.* These parents can also use the school emergency card to list the important people in their child's life by stating first the natural and stepparents as authorized people to call, followed by neighbors or friends. Parents without custody can show their continued interest in their child's school life with requests for a school calendar and duplicate report cards.

Parents say that phone calls and letters work very well. Say something simple like: "I am Johnny and Jane's parent and I want to introduce myself and encourage you to call me if I can be of any assistance. When the child is living with me, I may have occasion to call you, and this letter (or phone call) is a way of letting you know where I can be reached. Please call me if you have any questions." You can even give the school a number of self-addressed envelopes that the teacher can use to send you announcements of school activities and copies of your children's report cards. You can ask for a separate conference, and many teachers, encouraged by your interest, will be happy to oblige.

When you seek this information, it may be wise to drop a note or call the other parent to assure him or her that these actions are for information purposes and as a way to be prepared for times when the children, living with you, become ill. Stress that the main reason is your interest in the children and that this is a way of showing them that you are still involved in their lives.

This information is not to perpetuate disagreements with your former spouse; it's for you to become a better, more informed parent, and for your children to be assured of your involvement and knowledge.

Direct Contact

After you have made these independent contacts with the professionals you are free from the other parent. You don't have to contact him or her about some school function or a report card or for the doctor's phone number when your child is ill. Furthermore, you don't have to depend on your child's memory.

Be careful not to assume that your children can tell you their health history when with the other parent. A five-year-old running a fever of 101 degrees shouldn't be expected to recite to you the name of his ailment, medication, dosage, or suggested treatment. Not only may the information be dangerously incorrect, but the child may be unnecessarily frightened by

* Appendix IV has a special form parents can use with their child's school, itemizing parental preferences.

your sloppy parenting. It's a parent's responsibility to get this information directly from the other parent or from the child's doctor. This applies even when your child is a teenager.

The contacts and information point up other aspects of day-in day-out parenting and the ways of children. Parents find that children forget, lose, and otherwise mangle papers, report cards, belongings, prescriptions, and instructions, and that their absence or destruction is not a devious ploy by the other parent. Instead, it is nothing more than childhood at its forgetful, unconscious, or even mischievous self.

"We Both Care"

The strongest statement parents can make is to present themselves jointly to the school, the doctor, or the YMCA—either in writing or in person. In effect, they are saying, "Each of us is still concerned and involved with our children." It bears repeating: Any information about what you want must come from you. Don't wait to be asked.

Two-Home Rewards

Parents who set up two homes for their children often make comments like, "It made me feel I was a real parent again" or "I knew what I was doing and the children could feel it." When necessary steps are taken to reclaim certain responsibilities for our children, normal parenting is resumed. We break through some of these sex-typed barriers that have said that men cannot be nurturing and responsive, or that mothers in second homes have "given up their children" and have something intrinsically wrong with them. Giving your children two homes is different, but it can be highly successful.

For a brief review of the advantages of two homes:

· *Your relationship with your children is direct;* you need not go through the other parent. It aids you in establishing your own new identity by keeping your former role as spouse and married parent separate from your new life.
· *Your relationship with the other adults in your children's lives (teachers, doctors, dentists, neighbors, etc.) is direct.* You need not go through the other parent to exercise responsibility and caring.
· *You can retreat more gracefully from your former intimate married relationship because contact with the other parent is lessened and is limited to discussions about children.*
· *Your children are kept out of the middle.*
· *Your progress through the emotional divorce is eased by re-establishing your separate parental role.*

- *Your credibility as a parent increases in the eyes of your children and friends.*
- *Your children have two homes, two neighborhoods, two families, plus the security and continuity of their relationship with both parents.*

When children know that their parents have enough commitment to and interest in their welfare to set up two homes, they can feel that Mom and Dad are on top of this life crisis and that things are going to be okay. And then even perhaps, "Oh, oh, I guess that also means they are each going to get my report card!"

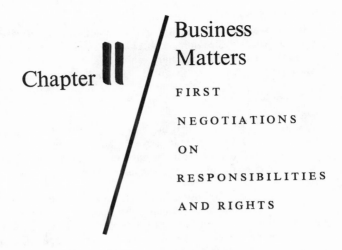

Chapter **11**

Business Matters

"A year ago I knew the two-home thing would never work for us. I couldn't even ask Sally for the time of day let alone arrange the time to sit down and make decisions. Things have cooled down since then and we've learned how to talk a little. There's a better chance now to get together on things about the kids. So now what? I've lost enough time as it is. I want to get started."

This man in his twenties echoed the eagerness of many parents, put off by bad feelings for months or years, to begin to reform their present situation. They had come to understand the need to build their own home and their own independent relationship with their children, to move away from their former negative intimacy, and to use direct communications. They were consciously trying to change their negative attitudes. But at the same time they were impatient to dig into the real issues of money, custody, responsibilities, and parental rights.

When such parents have not yet made their house a home for their children nor taken actions to change damaging behavior, I advise them to do so before proceeding with further discussions. But when they have taken these steps, they are certainly ready to prepare for their discussions with the other parent and to aim for some short-term trial agreements.

Are You Ready to Do Business?

The first steps should be taken very carefully.

Timing in these matters is important. You may be *willing* to do business with the other parent, but you *may not be ready* to make decisions with him or her. Your hesitation is natural—be patient with yourself. Any type of business relationship and negotiations has to take timing into account; you may be willing to begin discussions but you are not yet ready to complete them. This gradual unfolding is built into the process, thus the repeated suggestion that you read and then review the chapters in this book before making any moves.

Even when you are ready and willing to settle, your partner may not be. Common complaints heard are, "He keeps losing the papers for our meetings" or "She forgets to call me back." Such things keep happening when one parent is not yet ready to move to the next stage of the reorganization process, or when a power imbalance exists between the partners. In the latter situation, the only way to gain (or keep) a position of power is to stand pat or stall.

People trained in business know this matter of timing well. Their past experience has prepared them for the shifts in negotiations, the willingness to discuss, and the reluctance to settle quickly. They can draw on that experience now. Others with different past experiences may be prepared or motivated for this reorganization with a store of experience in human relations, tenacity or patience developed outside the business framework.

For example, some parents are unconsciously motivated by memories of their own parents' divorce. "My parents had a terrible divorce. I won't put my own children through what I had to suffer." "My father deserted us and I grew up without one. I won't let that happen to my own son." Look through your own past for any experience or belief that can motivate you to wait through the willing period to the settling period. While you are waiting for things to develop, remind yourself that, as frustrating as this period of time may be, it is also part of the pulling apart and reorganization process and, as such, just part of the price of divorce.

Getting Ready to Negotiate

First, take a look at the costs of raising children today and the many effects these rising costs exert on other parts of your life. Then, give yourself a break-down of what the real costs of living are today. Even if you do not develop a two-home situation, you still need this information. And your attorney will ask you for specific figures anyway.

Second, take a long and careful look at the "Master List of Parenting Responsibilities and Rights." It's a sobering list but well worth your attention, focusing on the points of your business discussions with the other parent. Know your feelings, desires, and position on such things as education, medical attention, and religion. Even if your desires or opinions change next month, you should know where you are now. Again, your attorney, if you choose to retain one, will ask for this information.

Third, when you have done all this homework, and it usually is a lot, reward yourself with some time off. Even if you have been reading this book off and on for the past few days or weeks, it's still a good idea to take a little break now and then. Let ideas soak in a bit before going on. When you think it's time, come back and pick up at the next step.

Fourth, read over, but do not actually put into action, the last section in this chapter, "Guidelines for Negotiations with the Other Parent." Unless you had a very comfortable "working score" in Chapter 3, have established direct communications with the other parent, and feel comfortable attempting these discussions immediately, it's far wiser to read the rest of the book and then spend time putting some of the noninterference and communications principles, and other guidelines, into practice.

Fifth, go back to Chapter 3 and retake that self-survey. If you now have a working score, you'll probably feel ready to begin your discussions for a short-term agreement. *Now use the Guidelines for Negotiations with the Other Parent for your own discussions.*

If you do not have a working score (or if the idea of discussions together leaves you feeling wobbly or very uneasy), find a mediator—Chapter 12 will tell you how—and use him or her from the beginning. (Or agree in advance to use a mediator if your discussions should get out of hand or if you cannot agree.)

Money: The Cost of Raising Children

The spectre of a bleak financial future often haunts the end of a marriage. At first few people can maintain their former married standard of living after separation. There are now two households instead of one, with the same amount of money to support them, and, from a practical point of view, many more unbudgeted expenditures, ranging from pick-up lunches and suppers out to consolation shopping binges or drinking sprees. The emotions of divorce seem to be at their zenith when the lowered standard of living combines with the need to talk about economics. An unequal standard of living and of economic opportunity between the two parents can encourage resentments and grievances. Financial issues, even more than others, can become the pot the emotions of divorce get cooked in.

Fantasies About Money and the Other Parent

When parents are caught in that unreasonable off-the-wall period and at the same time are feeling the financial pinch, some of them develop fantasies about how well the other parent is getting along. I have listened to some fathers say that the child's mother and the child can live comfortably on $300 a month "because she knows how to do this," or that money sent for the children is being used for new furniture. I have listened to mothers sure that the father has spirited away cash in secret accounts, angry that he has a new suit of clothes.

The truth is often overlooked in such tales. Parents are often deep in debt. Some work half-time attempting to change careers or to be trained, for the first time, for a job in the world. It's easier for people to keep their fantasies that everything is just peachy at the other house than to face the guilt that might surface when confronting the hardships that divorce has brought.

The fantasies serve one purpose—they avoid reality. They allow the parents to side-step their responsibilities to be specific about who contributes what for the children and their needs.

In reality, probably neither parent will be in the chips and, even if one has some money stashed away, it is unlikely the secret cache is the grand windfall the other imagines. Distrust or not, both parents will usually have to· rebuild their economic lives with reduced resources. Because of our history and our still inequitable levels of pay for some work rendered, this economic rebuilding is far more difficult for a woman than for a man. In spite of some changes, women still earn little more than half the wages men earn for the same jobs. Their eight hours of labor purchases about one-half the food that can be bought by a male doing the same work. This inequity takes its toll if the mother is the primary parent.

The parent with the lion's share of the child-raising responsibilities also has the lion's share of the costs. Without a solid two-home arrangement, this parent has less private time, fewer avenues to rebuild another intimate life, and less time and freedom to prepare for and build a remunerative career base than the parent living alone.

No matter how it works, divorce is an economic risk, and the decisions made about money are often intertwined with the questions of how responsibilities, time, and authority with the children are shared and protected. The old way was an all-or-nothing way: "You pay your support or you won't see the kids," versus "You let me be with the kids or you won't get your support check." The new way should be built on different leverage.

A Realistic Financial Picture: A Good Start

A realistic financial picture is one way parents can help themselves through the maze of competition and fears about money. A startling number of divorcing parents are unaware of how much money they spend on clothing, food, and other necessary expenses, and what proportion

EXPENSES

	PARENT ALONE	PARENT PLUS CHILDREN		
		Child 1	Child 2	Child 3
Housing (including insurance, taxes)				
Food, household supplies				
Clothing				
Child care				
Medical, dental (include insurance, drugs, eyeglasses, transportation)				
Education, basic (include tuition, costs)				
Education, college				
Utilities				
Transportation (include insurance payments, taxes, upkeep, fuel)				
Insurance				
Recreation and entertainment (include outings, vacations, sports, summer camps, toys, equipment)				
Cultural (include music lessons, classes)				
Allowances, personal				
Miscellaneous, incidentals				
Religion (include classes, events, donations, aid, special clothing)				
Miscellaneous, children (allowances, special events: birthdays, holidays, etc.)				
Taxes (personal, state, federal)				
Present spousal support				
Present child support				

actually goes for the children. This lack of knowledge seems to cause half the problems and misunderstandings between parents.

The list becomes important not just for an initial picture of what it takes to live with and without children, but for a good "guesstimate" of the more hidden costs of child rearing in both the primary and secondary residence. This same list can be a good help in determining the hot spots that might flare up around the triple issues of money, time, and energy. Finally, the list can be used as a personal check-up on your own financial condition.

It has been helpful for some parents to fill in this form from two perspectives: first, their present situation, and then what it would be like to be in the other parent's shoes.

If you have the secondary residence, check into the cost of housing with children, scan the ads, make a few calls, see what it feels like to hear the answer "no children, no pets." Take a look at the area—would you really want to live there with your children? Make inquiries about the availability and costs of really good child care and baby-sitters. Take the time to visit one of these places and look around.

The double assessment is time-consuming, but worth its weight in gold. Then evaluate your priorities. Where do you rank your children and their need to be with each parent? How high on the list is the two-home system? What about funds for adequate communications? for being together? child care? These items should be at the top, counted along with the survival needs of food, shelter, and clothing.

Financial Contribution (Child Support)

Once you have itemized your financial situation, determining your financial contribution to the children becomes far easier. The following is a traditional way of measuring support.

A *direct financial contribution* is the explicit sum you and the other parent agree on as a fair share for children's expenses. It is ordinarily a certain amount of money per child per month. When this amount becomes part of your legal settlement, it has traditionally been called "child support." It's money paid to a parent.

Indirect financial contributions are the paid costs of health insurance, partial or full payment of medical, dental, and drug costs, and provisions for college or school tuition. It's money paid for a bill.

Accounting for Contributions: Where Is This Money Going?

The contributing parent usually pays the other parent by check, and as one angry father said, "That money is going into the family pot!" True enough, there are no tracers on the dollars spent on the children's clothes and food, and a contributing parent can have good reason to be wrathful.

A parent could ask for an accounting of direct contributions to the children. The financial formality can help both parents avoid the suspicions that monies meant for the children are being misused. No parent has the right to a complete financial accounting of the other's income, but when it comes to money spent on the children, a simple statement may ease the strain between suspicious couples. There is a solution to this problem. Design your legal Parenting Agreement to include:

1. A simple accounting given to the contributing parent by the other parent that describes how, in theory at least, that contribution check is used. This can be done in one sheet and given to the other parent once every three to four months.
2. The contributing parent pays for costs directly. Instead of giving the other parent a certain flat amount that goes for bills, that parent pays the bills directly.

When Dad's contribution goes directly to the after-school day-care school instead of to Mom, he gets the satisfaction of the direct transaction and the sense of authority and importance that comes with it. Dad can also suffer with the vicissitudes of the rising costs of the child care, the increase at the end of the month. When no other money changes hands between the parents and direct costs are paid by the second-home parent, the distrust and uneasiness about money are often reduced.

The accounting is done simply. One mother took $150 she received from her child's father and gave him a simple one-page statement that read like this:

Per Month:
$125   After-school day care with Mary Milani, at 476 Holiday Road —basic rate, no overtime included
$ 25   Partial payment of housing per month

$150   Total

The father's response was one of embarrassment. Somehow he had not heard her when she had verbally told him the amount of the child care costs. The formal accounting sent to him in acknowledgment of his contribution made a difference in his attitude and in his later willingness to assume increased child care costs.

In many cases, the parent contributing monies to the child's other home is still stuck with the feeling that his or her money is being used by the other parent for their own personal benefit. The joint consumption by parent and child of food and shelter is part of living together. A brief accounting helps many parents to see where their contribution theoretically is used.

Master List of Parenting Responsibilities and Rights

When one parent saw this Master List with its responsibilities and rights listed one after the other, he said, "I've got to think about this to get a divorce? I can see why people stay married." When parents are married, their responsibilities and rights are undifferentiated and blended together. When parents divorce, this bundle of parental duties and prerogatives needs to be sorted out, one by one.

Parents who remain married are rarely forced to analyze their responsibilities and their children's futures the same way divorcing parents are. Never-divorced parents don't have to think about their child's college education when the child is five. But divorcing parents may need to make decisions about their children for a decade or more ahead. It's frustrating and debilitating to have to think in years when you are accustomed to thinking in weeks. "How do I know where I'll be in five months?" storm some parents. "I can't tie myself down to this kind of scheduling."

Start with Stort-Term Decisions

It is quite natural for parents to look at the Master List and blanch, saying, "I can't think of all these things now," or, "It makes me tired just to look at it."

The unevenness of the crisis months lends itself to a healthy fear of making long-term permanent decisions. The best alternative is to start with short-term temporary decisions. Come to agreements you can live with (or are willing to try) for two or three months at a time. When the two or three months are up, revise your agreement and make a second plan for another two or three months. Two or three such short-term agreement periods can give each of you a chance to weather the ups and downs of the crisis stages, give you experience in making and living with your mutual arrangements. Once you have both passed the crisis periods and have a good idea of what you want, you can negotiate a long-term agreement for one, two, or more years at a time. When that time comes you will have already acquired first-hand knowledge of how to negotiate with the other parent for what you want and what you think you can live with.

As you can see, the Master List contains more items than you need for a simple two-month agreement. But many items on the list may well arise in the next few years. So take a fast look at them all and put a few that are going to come up later on your back burner.

Some Ways to Use the Master List

This Master List can be used in a variety of ways: as an overview of parenting; as a way to order your thinking; as a way of preparing for discussions or negotiations with the other parent, your attorney, your counselor, or your mediator; and as a guideline for writing your own agreement. When you choose to use the Master List for purposes of mediation or negotiation, the following steps can be quite useful for all concerned.

1. Give yourself time to go over the list thoughtfully.

2. Do this first review without the other parent. This is your time alone.

3. When you are ready to get down to specifics, go through the list and *ask yourself the following about each item:*

 · Do I want to share this with the other parent? If yes, to what degree?
 · Do I want to divide this? If so, in what proportion?
 · Do I want to let this issue go by, leave it to chance?
 · Do I want this to hold for two months, six months, one or two years?

4. Then make two lists for yourself. Head two sheets of paper with:
THINGS I'M READY TO TALK ABOUT
THINGS I'M NOT READY TO TALK ABOUT

The Ready list includes those decisions and situations where you are clear about what you want, what you would compromise on, what is the least you could accept, and what would be the ideal arrangement. The Not Ready list is everything else—whatever is explosive, ambiguous, lacking in information. This list is for those items for which you need to put in more time, information, or thought.

5. Go through the Ready list a second time after you have completed it. Put a check mark next to those areas you think you and the other parent already agree upon. Try to find things for this list; this will be your business agenda for the next few months. The Ready and Not Ready lists will be of great help to your discussions.

6. Finally, put the lists aside for a few days and let your first attempt at this settle into your thinking. Then, review your two lists and make any changes that you think are important.

These six steps are often time consuming, but worth your effort and thoughtful attention. A word of caution: As you consider your desires and your hopes for your children and yourself, a number of feelings can surface, some pleasant, some unpleasant. As one man put it, "Just thinking about arrangements for summer camp reminded me of our troubles that summer we separated. It depressed me." It may be difficult to think because so many feelings crowd in. If this is the case, just take a few items at a time, limiting your thinking period to as little as fifteen to thirty minutes. Then go on to some other project and come back perhaps in a day or so to the next set of items. You may want to review Chapter 7 on feelings as well. Keep a record of each of your lists, dated and placed in your filing system. Your future discussions will generate new versions of the Ready and Not Ready lists, copies of which should also go in your records.

If you are attempting your first short-term agreement, do consider that the first agreement is not the time to settle anything "once and for all." For example, a mother and father may have had a long-term argument on the cost of the child's private school. Dad wants to pull his son out and use the money somewhere else. Mom wants to keep him in and have Dad pay the bill. If you have been disputing an issue, the first two months will most probably not settle it. If a settlement and compromise happen spontaneously, consider it a windfall.

Master List of Parenting Responsibilities and Rights

Religion

Affiliation
Training
Costs

Times
Transportation
Decisions

Education

Choice of school, teacher
Costs/supplies
Homework
Decisions: scholastic
Access to information/records

Teacher conferences
Report cards
Extracurricular activities
Emergency and registration card
information

Education, College

Costs/tuition/books
Living costs

Transportation

Medical and Dental

Insurance
Decisions on treatment
Appointments
Costs

Choice of doctor/dentist/therapist
Access to information
Transportation
Drugs, eyeglasses

Lessons and Cultural Enrichment

Outings, concerts, events
Decisions on enrichment
Transportation
Time

Lessons, training
Cost
Conferences

Life Skills*

Parental examples
Experiences
Time
Decisions

Training
Costs
Discussions

---

* Life skills can mean learning how to balance a checkbook, working in Dad's shoe store as a clerk, or taking on an apprenticeship.

Recreation

Teams
Outings
Time
Decisions

Camps
Transportation
Costs

Life Insurance

Mother
Child

Father

Wills

Mother: trustee or guardian
Father: trustee or guardian

Holidays (see Appendix II, Holidays)

Christmas
Easter
Easter vacation
Other religious or national holidays
Transportation costs

Thanksgiving
Decisions on time
Passover
High holy days
Other holidays (4th of July, Labor day)

Child Care

Choice of sitters
Transportation

Day-care/after-school care
Costs

Communications with Child by the Other Parent

Letters
Phone calls

Private phone
Other

Time Spent with Each Parent

School year:

Scheduled time with Mother
Unscheduled time with Mother
Scheduled time with Father
Unscheduled time with Father

Vacation/summertime:

Scheuled time with Mother
Unscheduled time with Mother
Scheduled time with Father
Unscheduled time with Father

Time Spent with Grandparents or Other Relatives and Friends

Transportation
Scheduled/unscheduled

Transportation for Times Between Homes

Provided by Dad
Provided by Mom

Other adults
Costs

Geography

Homes within _____ miles of one another
Agreement regarding future moves

Custody

Joint legal custory
Joint physical custody
Sole custody/visitation

Self-designed parenting agreement
(see next chapter)

Contributions
For children:

  Direct
  Indirect

For parent:

  Direct
  Indirect

Agreement Process

Ourselves
Mediator (in whole or part)
Counselor (in whole or part)
Attorney (in whole or part)

First Short-Term Agreement

For how many weeks or months?
Reviewed when?

Provisions for Catastrophic Events

Death of both parents
Protracted illness
Income changes

Other

A Sample Couple

Tony and Georgia have two teenage daughters, Sally and Cynthia, in private school. They have been separated for three months after twenty years of marriage. Tony's lists looked like this:

Things I'm Ready to Talk About

Education
Teacher conferences, homework, access to information/records, who checks up on Sally's grades. I want this to be either mine or shared with Georgia.

Medical and Dental
Insurance—I'll keep paying it; access to information and doctors—I want full access; share decisions on major health problems.

Lessons
Sally's lesson—continue as is, I'll pay the bill. Cynthia's disco—sore point; I'll continue but only for two months.

Recreation
Cynthia's softball team—I want to keep doing what I'm doing here and I'll take all the expenses.

Communications with Children
No restraints regarding phone calls or seeing girls after school.

Time Spent with Each Parent
School week and every other weekend at her house, every other weekend at my house beginning Thursday nights ending with my taking them to school Mon. A.M.; I don't know about the exact times.

Transportation
I'll pick them up at the house and bring them back.

Geography
I'm moving two miles away. It's even biking distance to school if I get hung up some Friday A.M.

Contributions
Direct contribution somewhere around $400. Indirect—the medical insurance, Sally and Cynthia's lessons, and the softball thing.

First Short-Term Agreement
Willing to do these things for two months only.

*Things I'm Not Ready to Talk About, or Compromise About,
or Think About*

Lessons	I think the disco thing is frivolous and I don't want it continued past two months. I won't compromise on this.
Religion	I want them confirmed in my faith.
Education	The cost of that *damned* private school. I want them in public school.
Education/College	I'll pay for tuition and living expenses only if the girls go to state-supported schools.
Life Skills	The girls are too sheltered by their mother.
Holidays	Not important now.
Custody	Definitely want joint custody, perhaps even split time.
Contribution to Finances	More than $400 a month is too much for me to keep up too long; I won't compromise on this. Georgia should go out and work.*

Tony has "Lessons" and "Contribution" listed on both his Ready and Not Ready lists. This gives a good indication of his probable trouble spots. He is ambivalent about money and how it is spent on the children. He is worried that Georgia will push hard to continue the lessons past two months and won't be satisfied with a contribution of $400. He uses his comments on the Not Ready list as a way of clarifying for himself what his limits for compromise will be.

Guidelines for Negotiations with the Other Parent

If you have strong scores on the communications self-surveys and are comfortable with your scores on the self-survey in Chapter 3, you may feel ready to begin your discussions and negotiations with the other parent on short-term decisions about your children.

The first rule is to be very clear about which things you think will be easy and which things will be tough. This rule can be called "easiest first, hardest last."

Look at your own ready list and put a big check mark next to the easiest decisions. In Tony's Ready list he had all the items checked except the disco lessons and money items. He had some more thinking to do. Did he

---

* Some attorneys feel that once Tony pays a high support amount (even temporarily) he may have to continue it in the future.

really mean $400, or would he go along for two months at $450 or even $500 just to keep some semblance of peace? He didn't reach an answer, but he was better for having thought about the quandary. (When Georgia has done the same kind of serious thinking, they can begin conversations. If she has not, then Tony must lead the discussions, saying he is willing to talk about the things they usually agree on.)

The second rule is to remember the principles of a business relationship (a review of the last two chapters before your first talks would be helpful).

The third rule is to digest the following step-by-step guidelines for your discussions:

Guidelines for Your Business Discussions

- Remember to choose a meeting time that is best for your partner and yourself. Don't make it the end of a long hard day or when you are hungry.
- Limit your discussion time to thirty minutes. *Stop* at the end of that time. Emotions often get out of hand after twenty-five or thirty minutes, especially if you are working without a mediator.
- Only cover a few items in one session.
- Start with the easiest decisions where you are most hopeful of agreement.
- Save the difficult decisions for the last meetings.
- When you discuss a subject, be specific about what you mean and how it would work in practice. Give each other real-life examples. Don't stop at generalities.
- When you disagree, look for the ways each of you could give in a little. A "Take it or leave it" attitude is not negotiation—reasonable compromise is.
- When you come to an agreement, write it down. A simple sentence will do, but it *must be detailed.* One of you act as secretary (you can flip a coin).
- When you come to a decision, put it away like a building block. Don't rummage around with the decision. Let it be.
- Think about how you will include your children in either your discussions or your decisions. Chapter 13 goes into the wisdom of, at the least, asking children what they think would work in arrangements that involve them.
- If you don't come to an easy agreement, don't belabor the point too long. The timing for its resolution may simply not be right for today.
- Do not insist that the other parent carry out an activity that you and you alone want for your child. (Georgia shouldn't be expected to transport

Cynthia to the softball game if Tony wants this to be his activity with her.)
· Expect some false starts and some setbacks. No one is perfect. After each meeting, make a copy of your agreement, keep one for yourself, and send one to the other parent for confirmation. Put your agreements in a file you keep for your working relationship. (This file should also hold your memos.)
· Make a simplified (and *edited*) copy of your agreement for the kids to read and use.

Tony and Georgia held their first meeting via telephone. Both had Ready and Not Ready lists, and Georgia's Ready list was fairly similar to Tony's.

First they established their ground rules of noninterference and respect for one another's territory, privacy, and parenting. This eased their tensions and served as a working basis of respect. Then they decided to talk about the three things they knew they agreed upon: medical/dental, time spent with each parent, and transportation back and forth from Mom's house and Dad's house. They flipped a coin and Tony got to write down and copy the results of the conversation. It was an easy first meeting. The first hurdle was over.

The second meeting was also by phone. Cultural items, including lessons, and then recreation were added to the list, and so was the question of money. A surprise to both parents was that the discussion went far more easily than they expected. A first good meeting can often pave the way for a good second one. The issue of money was difficult, but it was eased by the anticipation of a review in two months.

Objectives of Negotiations

· Using the guidelines suggested, both parents negotiate a trial period of one or two months and establish a regular but flexible schedule when the children will be at Dad's house and at Mom's house.
· Both parents agree on basic ground rules of autonomy, noninterference, and territory. They agree that when the children are with one parent then that parent is to take full responsibility for their care and welfare. The children are to clear plans with each parent during his/her time. Statements of noninterference by each parent are usually restated to reaffirm their respect of the other's parent-child relationship and of each other's territory.
· The agreement is written out and copies are made and signed by both parents. Each parent keeps two copies. One for the "Working Relationship" file, one to spare. Each parent independently (or in family con-

ference) describes the arrangement with the children, including the dates, times, and details regarding clothing, meals, and needed monies. The parents ask for feedback from the children. If there are serious reservations, the parents may want to confer again and make adjustments. Teenagers may be invited to participate in the agreement process. Younger children should have a chance to be heard—even if they don't vote.

· A simplified (and edited) version of the time schedule between the two homes and important aspects relating directly to the children's time with each parent should be written up and posted on the family bulletin board or refrigerator door. *This is most important.* It gives everyone a framework in black and white.

· When the trial period ends, adjustments are made in the schedule and another trial period is determined. (Often the original arrangement is extended with few changes.) Again, the agreement is confirmed by both parents, and written dates and times are posted for the whole family to refer to.

The pattern of the initial discussion is continued through the development of the subsequent Parenting Agreements, including the more permanent one that might be included in the legal court order described in the next chapter.

Your Own Discussion and Negotiation Style

These five Objectives of Negotiations, changed by whatever variations you and the other parent choose, can provide the initial structure for your business discussions. Your own style for these meetings will unfold as you continue to arrange your layers of agreements and disagreements.

Parents often develop informal agreements through discussions over a period of two to six months before they officially file for a legal end to their marriage. If they have established a workable style for negotiation, the legal process can be far smoother.

Times at Mom's House and Dad's House—February and March

Time at Dad's House and Mom's House:

Just like before. Every other Thursday through Monday morning will be with Dad, the rest of the time with Mom. Dad will pick you up after school on Thursdays at 4:30 P.M. and bring you to school Monday A.M.

Times at Dad's House: Feb. 14, 15, 16, 17, 28, 29
Mar. 1, 2, 13, 14, 15, 16, 27, 28, 29, 30.

Softball:

Just like before. Dad will take care of the league activities and will see to practice, transportation, games, and costs.

Ballet:

Just like before. Sally will make the arrangements with Mom for transportation and costs. When the lessons are during the time at Dad's house, Dad will provide the transportation.

Extra Times:

There may be times when one of us wants to spend extra time together. Let's talk about this when it comes up. If the time is at Dad's house, please remember to talk with him first, and if it is during Mom's time, please talk to her first.

Who Decides What:

When you are living with Mom, she will make the decisions. When you are living with Dad, he will make the decisions. If you want to change the schedule sometime, remember you will have to ask both of us about it.

Your Clothes, Belongings, Other Stuff:

You will have your own things and your own places at each home. If there are extra things you would like to bring to Dad's house, he can swing by Mom's house after he picks you up at school on Thursdays. Since you'll have your things in both places, there won't be much need to cart around stuff.

Dad's Work Number: 453-2578, Ext. 253   Mrs. Johnson's number 453-8556
Home Number: 453-8938
Mom's Work Number: 582-8927
Home Number: 453-9001

Chapter **12** / The Legal Business

"I had a great motivation to reach my own private agreement on custody directly with the children's father," said one mother. "I figured if I didn't make these decisions with him someone else would do it for me. And that someone else just can't know me or my situation as well as I do. The attorney can hassle the property agreement, but I want to control my private life myself."

This mother was reflecting on a fact inherent in our legal system today. When people cannot come to their own decisions, outsiders, less knowledgeable about their strengths and needs, will have to make the decisions for them.

This chapter identifies many of the things you need to know if you choose to negotiate either part or all of your own parenting agreement. There are guidelines for the minimum legal advice you must obtain on custody, the use of third parties as mediators, the actual process of negotiating the agreement with the other parent, and a detailed example of an actual Parenting Agreement complete with two-home terms you can use to design your own agreement.

The Ambiguities of the Law

While parents need to know what their rights are under the law—an important base of knowledge for private negotiations—what these rights mean in practice and how they would apply in specific situations often remain unclear. Parents ask lawyers questions such as, "What amount of

149

child support is my right?", "Could I have a chance to get sole custody?" "Joint custody?" The bottom line is: "If I took my case to court, what chance would I have that the judge would see it my way?" The answers to such questions may not be as specific as a parent would like. While there may be a range of acceptable child and spouse support payscales (when income level is X, expected child support per child is Y), the answers on other related issues all too frequently are: "It depends on the circumstances—the case you build, the judge, the county, the state . . .."; and even more: "I don't know—it could go either way." One byword for what parents can expect once they give up their own private negotiations and turn to attorneys and the courts is *uncertainty*. The only sure thing they can count on is that court appearances are costly. An agreement they can forge by themselves will save dollars and pain.

The Best Agreement Is the Parents' Agreement

Even though there are exceptions—where one of the parents is terrifically naive in business and the other one extraordinarily clever—it still holds that by and large the best and the most acceptable agreement on matters concerning the children and their welfare is the one reached by the parents themselves.

The law and its workings are a mystery to many, and attorneys have often told me how bewildered and confused their divorce clients seem. Often this is their first contact with the law or with an attorney. Some may expect that the attorney will know all the answers, take over all the unpleasantness of relating to the other parent, and somehow provide comfort for all the emotional issues surrounding the separation as well. The mere act of walking into an attorney's office is seen as either a declaration of independence, of defensiveness, of war, or as calling for a rescue squad.

Sometimes parents are taken aback when their lawyer tells them that, first, they not only need to present to him or her as complete a financial picture as possible (with past records, tax returns, and other formal documents), but that they have to figure out their own present and future financial situation. Second, they are asked to think about what they want regarding their children, and third, that unless the client wants to pay the hourly fee for being hand-guided through this process, the client has to do most of the work alone. Finally, when this information has been brought together, the attorney often suggests that the parents talk alone with one another, outside the attorney's office, about their custody and visitation arrangements. "I didn't need to pay seventy-five dollars an hour to do it myself," said one angry woman who had expected different treatment.

But attorneys frequently employ such tactics as part of a successful effort to get the parents to settle out of court. "The most successful family law practitioner," said one family lawyer, "is the one who knows how to promote a good agreement out of court, not the one who is constantly in litigation." Attorneys know that when an out-of-court settlement is not reached and the dispute must come before the bench, the best-prepared brief in the world will still be subject to the risk of unexpected events and the personal beliefs of the presiding judge.

When parents are thinking of handing over their decision-making to attorneys or, in the case of an unsettled dispute, to a judge, they could well ask themselves what the values and standards of these practitioners may be. How may the judge feel about fathers as nurturers? What about the sharing of parental authority, the two-home approach, the concept of joint custody? When laws are vague and outcomes uncertain, a parent's values can easily take a back seat to the values of those persons placed in a position of power.

People need attorneys. They need their expert advice on their rights under the law, an expert review of their decisions to date. People sometimes need attorneys to do the actual negotiations for them when their own efforts fall short. But people also need to be advised that the best settlement—after legal consultation—will probably be the one they themselves had worked out alone. It not only will be the most satisfying and reflect their own situations, standards, and values, but it will avoid the problems associated with the adversarial system.

The adversary process forces people to choose sides. The idea—however disguised—is to compete and win. In family law, the use of mediation and arbitration in the negotiation process can always fall prey to these adversarial principles, particularly when feelings run high as they do during divorce.

The problem is that the emotional off-the-wall stage, with its anger and accusations, has a need to blame someone or something. This natural but nasty time often coincides with the need to file the first legal papers. The combination can be lethal. The pain and bewilderment can transfer easily to the legal arena where the expectations of an attorney as white knight or hired gun can gum up the works. The law provides perfect ammunition to parental blame games, allowing the parents justification and ammunition for outrageous behavior. One judge described the disastrous results as "an officially required sadistic trip, often contributing to and even magnifying the problems already burdening the family, leaving them in an even greater state of conflict and hostility."

Guidelines for Parents

The way to counteract the quicksand of off-the-wall feelings, your own expectations of the law, and the nature of the system itself is to:

First: Recognize that emotional issues resulting from the divorce can complicate your legal business. At the time when you should be the most rational, you may have the least resources to do so. Keep your cool.

Second: Be aware of your rights and the law. Consult an attorney. But while you may want to retain your attorney as a consultant in your negotiations, do consider, at least initially, negotiating alone or with a mediator.

Third: If you are negotiating alone with the other parent and your discussions bog down, *think first of using a third party who will not take sides.*

Fourth: Separate your discussions and decisions about your children from those about your property and other financial matters. You may want to retain an attorney to settle property and other financial questions, but try to keep the decisions about the children for yourselves.

Your Rights and the Law—Obtain Answers to the Following Questions

1. Given your income and circumstances, what is the usual amount of child support per month awarded to a sole custodial parent?

2. Given your income and circumstances, what is the usual spousal support awarded per month?

3. Is there a joint custody law in your state? In which way and under what conditions will the courts now award "joint legal" or "joint physical" custody?

4. How could a paragraph be worded to prevent or discourage one parent's moving the child out of state and changing the original court order of shared parenting to one of sole custody?

5. Is there an attorney, mediator, conciliation court, or counselor who would champion your own private final agreement by supporting its incorporation into your court order? Would an attorney need to reword your own language into acceptable legal terminology?

6. What are the tax consequences of the different arrangements and how can you minimize adverse taxation?

The answers to the first two questions will help you understand your local legal guidelines. You need not follow these standards, of course, but you do need to have some idea of what might happen if your negotiations broke down and you had to take the more traditional route of engaging attorneys for the settlement.

Parents may choose to have their attorneys negotiate their child and spousal support arrangements for them, or they may choose to negotiate this between themselves. In either case, knowledge of local standards is important.

Answers about your state custody laws, how they are interpreted and implemented, are essential to your decisions about custody per se. You also need to know how you can safeguard for your future the mutually acceptable two-home arrangement of today. No matter how superfluous this information may now seem to your own situation, it should be gathered along with other relevant facts.

Since custody laws are not uniform across states, and parents cannot be confident that one state will uphold the findings of the original court, there is a danger that a disgruntled parent may seek to put aside a joint physical custody agreement filed in one state or avoid the consequences by taking the child to another state. There the parent may set up housekeeping and file for sole custody. While this is an extreme reaction, such off-the-wall behavior is child snatching, and even the fear of it can put an enormous strain on a relationship. Far better to plug the loopholes and equalize the situation in the beginning. A well-written legal paragraph in your original agreement can discourage a unilateral out-of-state move with a child.

The answers to the fifth question regarding the route your own private agreement could take once you have it in final form will help you decide whom to ask for advice when you need it.

Finally, the answers to the last question may save both parents money in reduced taxes.

Keep Emotional Control

The legal process married you. It also can divorce you, but it will not mend your heart or soothe your feelings. The expectation that the legal business will somehow make a person feel better is not likely to be met. Past chapters have given you some guidelines to consider and ways to soothe your feelings. The biggest rule of all, however, is: Don't let your out-of-control feelings cloud your legal status or your decisions. You can lose a great deal by that loss of emotional control and you may undertake actions that will prove disastrous to you, your children, and your legal case. For instance, if you threaten your partner with harm, you may lose your access to your children, gain an arrest record, and pile up more legal fees. If your feelings are leading you to a legal, physical, or emotional fight —run, do not walk, to a therapist or counselor who will help you find a way to work it out outside of the legal arena. If that counselor can work with your attorney, so much the better.

The Legal Issues

When it comes to legal issues, parents have four major areas to settle:
- *The dissolution:* the end of their marriage
- *Their property division:* the end of their common holdings as a married couple

- *The division of child-rearing rights and responsibilities and legal custody:* the end of their common parenting as a married couple
- *Their level of financial support:* the amount of contribution toward the care of the children (child support) and the other parent (spousal support)

Even though it has long been recommended that these areas be handled separately, tradition has it that a property and custody agreement are combined in one document and, for the vast majority of cases, presented as a stipulation at the time of the court appearance. The "backdrop of uncertainty," so well described by law Professor S. T. Mnookin, will continue to force parents and their attorneys into overlapping bargaining positions. Each needs a lever, and despite their desire to develop a trusting and effective working relationship, this leverage ends up being the money and the kids. Moreover, once the legal business is over, enforcement of the court order presents new difficulties. There is no way Dad can stop Mom from undermining his influence with the children or make sure she is home when he brings the children back at a designated time. Furthermore, in most states there is no way Mom can trace Dad to get overdue child support if Dad knows how to slip by the few safeguards the government provides.

Financial issues of support for the children and the spouse are never clear-cut. Child support usually requires careful discussion with an attorney because it interrelates with spousal support and property division. Some parents use their attorneys to reach decisions, others do it alone. However, the decisions about education, religion, time with each parent, and the degree and division of authority and responsibility (as listed in the last chapter) can be decided by the parents themselves, either alone or with a mediator. With some effort, parents and attorneys can usually remove the children from negotiations over property issues.

Custody, No Custody, Joint Custody

In Chapter 11, the Master List of Parenting Responsibilities and Rights identified the major decisions parents need to consider when they set about ending their shared living arrangement. Of all the questions to be answered on that list, however, the matter of custody taps most deeply into a mother or father's deepest fears and hopes for the future as a parent.

There is a significant legal distinction between the authority and responsibility designated to sole custody parent and those involved in joint custody. Psychologically and practically, however, the difference between the two terms is not just significant, it is enormous, and it often sets the tone for the parents' relationship.

The time you take to research your state laws on custody, and the pros and cons of different arrangements as offered by friends and professionals will be a top asset for your two-home plans. You may be in a position where you will have to educate your attorney (and the other parent) on the feasibility of two homes and the way the legal requirement for a definition of custody can be met. The Notes will suggest several books and articles that can give you a head start here, and the following brief review of the joint custody versus sole custody discussion will begin to show how your own Parenting Agreement can sidestep this issue and offer a viable, acceptable plan instead.

Legally, the term *joint custody* has long been clouded with ambiguity of practice and a most confusing inconsistency of terms and laws across states.* Furthermore, the word *joint* conjures up an expectation for strict and equal division of time and authority with necessary frequent discussions between parents. Often joint custody has come to mean half time at Mom's house and half time at Dad's. But neither frequent discussion nor an equal division of time need be true in your case unless you wish it to be. You can even share time and authority thirty-seventy or twenty-eighty if you like and still have "joint custody."

Sole custody on the other hand is legally far clearer. It's part and parcel of the one-home, one-authority tradition and has long historical and legal precedents to define its application in practice. One parent holds all the authority and most of the responsibility. Again, this strict definition need not be true if and when you design your own agreement.

Your parenting agreement, regardless of the new two-home terms or old legal custody terms you choose to use, should state your preference and then define *exactly* how you see this working in sum and substance. (How you can do this is described in just a few pages.)

Many parents who seek a two-home arrangement hope for as equal a legal status as possible. A good Parenting Agreement can provide this equality. Even if you do not have any desire to share equally the children's time or the costs and decisions that come with raising them, by using joint physical custody and then showing clearly how you two do want to share or divide your parenting, you forge your two-home intent in the strongest possible way.

If your state has provisions for joint custody, by all means investigate the necessary requirements and seriously consider obtaining this status. Look for joint *physical* custody, not joint *legal* custody. Joint physical custody means that authority can be shared between the parents equally. Joint legal custody means one parent has access to health and school records and a few other options, while the parent with *physical* custody has virtually all the authority that a sole custodial parent has.

* Terms such as "split custody," "divided custody," and "joint custody" could have different meanings in different locales.

The general term *joint custody* evokes genuine relief and respect from teachers, doctors, and coaches and others who are concerned with parental politics. Even joint legal custody, a far weaker form of custody than joint physical custody, promotes a sense of partnership, of equal access, and of parental interest. The statement heard occasionally that "joint custody doesn't mean anything" is simply not true. It might be a weak legal term when it is ambiguously or inconsistently defined or if joint legal custody is given to one parent and physical custody to the other. But even then it means something more than the sole custody/visitation arrangement.

You can avoid the old problems of joint custody (and the restrictions of sole custody) by giving these terms your own specific definition—what it means to you and how it will work. You give a term its substance. You define it, you clarify its meaning, you specify the times, dates, particulars (with the help of the Master List from Chapter 11.) You don't leave room for other interpretations. You write out how it will function in practice.

By shaping your own explicit version of what custody means to you, you give yourself and your children a most important cornerstone for your new life.

If you are just now beginning the legal process, you can start with joint physical custody and a Parenting Agreement. If you are long done with the court system, you can negotiate an agreement with the other parent and keep it as a private contract or instruct an attorney to use the new agreement to seek court approval to modify the original court order. The latter should be a simple procedure, neither complicated nor expensive.

Many parents who had an original sole custody to one parent and visitation to the other type of agreement never do bother to make the new privately negotiated Parenting Agreement strictly legal. They take a legal risk, but they feel it is worth taking a chance. The important thing, some have told me, is that "we finally got together and put being at odds behind us."

The Temporary Custody Decision That Is Not Temporary

"The attorney told me it was only a "temporary" custody order of sole custody—but I was stuck with it permanently." Countless times I have heard fathers who sought a permanent order of joint physical custody report that their desires were undermined by a temporary order that traditionally designated the mother as sole custodian. If you have a temporary order that gives one parent sole custody, beware. You would be wise to check into this pitfall. Often what now stands on the books will continue to stand, regardless of what was verbally promised out of court or explained in conversation.

The Objective Third Party

Counselors, Mediators, and Arbitrators

A third party can play an important role in your discussions and in your negotiations. You should, therefore, make certain what his or her approach is to divorce, to custody, and to reaching settlements before you agree to engage the services of any third party.

Counseling, mediation, and arbitration differ from one another in crucial ways. Counseling offers advice, alternatives, and, perhaps, some therapeutic intervention. Mediation differs from arbitration in that the mediator does not take sides and aids the parties in reaching their own agreement. But arbitration means that both sides present their case to a person who is hired and empowered to judge the case and make a decision. Arbitration hearings work like courts.

Counselors and mediators may be in private practice, members of the staff of a local family-service agency, or attached to local conciliation courts. Some of these counseling and mediation services are available only to those who are already in hot water—ready to take their disputes into the courtroom. But other professionals work as mediators or as family counselors with parents who are seeking an orderly and structured way to come to their private agreements away from the courtroom.

The use of a skilled third party can often be very helpful in the agreement process. A skilled mediator does not take sides, yet he or she can suggest alternatives for both. Today many professionals are sympathetic to the idea of removing domestic issues from the combat zone to a neutral ground. They may or may not be specially trained. The American Arbitration Association's Family Dispute Service offers counseling, mediation, and arbitration sources, as do some local agencies and conciliation courts. You will have to check with your local court to find out what services are available there.

Attorneys are usually in private practice and rarely are formally connected to the courts. Their services are available as litigants, consultants, counselors, advisors, and, less frequently, as mediators and arbitrators. Attorneys often decline the middle position of mediator because of the conflict-of-interest ethic and the fear of a malpractice suit later. Some attorneys join forces with other professionals, combining advisement with some counseling or legal work. An attorney–counselor team can be very helpful to divorcing couples.

Choose your third party with great care, knowing that the closer his or her philosophy is to yours, the happier you will be with the results.

How to Find a Good Attorney or Family Counselor

First: Ask as many friends as you can who they would recommend as an attorney (or as a family counselor) for a family matter. If you like, be specific and explain that it is for a divorce or working out a divorce. When a name is suggested, go further by asking the following questions:

"Have you used this person yourself?" "How did you hear about this person?" "What did you or your friend like most and least about this professional?" "Could you give me another name in case this person's caseload is full?"

Second: If you like the answers you received, you can make phone contact and, after introducing yourself, ask some pertinent questions. But don't be surprised or be put off if the secretary tells you to make an appointment so you can pose your questions in person. A counselor/therapist may be willing to answer your questions over the phone, but a successful attorney will rarely spend time on the telephone if he or she can help it. Think of how much free advice you can afford to give out during working hours in your own specialty, and remember that you are looking for a good attorney, not necessarily a cheap one.

When you do get to talk to an attorney or a counselor, take some time in advance to review the questions below and to prepare some basic information for the first meeting, in person or by phone.

QUESTIONS TO ASK THE COUNSELOR OR THERAPIST

1. How do you work in divorce matters? (As a therapist, mediator, counselor, arbitrator, or some combination?)
2. Would you act as a mediator or as a counselor for a couple who are attempting to negotiate their custody/visitation matters between themselves?
3. What experience have you had in working with couples who attempt to work out their own agreements and a working relationship? What percentage of your practice is devoted to this type of work?
4. Do you have a preferred approach to this type of mediation or counseling? (Do you see each person separately, only together, or do you advise a combination of the two? Do you use some specific approach or philosophy?)
5. What kinds of information would you like to have from me at our first meeting? Or, how could I best prepare for this meeting to make the most of it?
6. How long do you think it will take to know whether we can all work effectively together?

7. How long have you been practicing? How long have you been licensed? (The two are not synonymous. You also may ask about any specific training or experience in this area.)
8. Are you a member of the American Association of Marriage and Family Therapists (or the American Psychological Association or other national or state recognized professional association)? Are you a member of the American Arbitration Association?
9. What is your usual fee? Is this due at each meeting?

QUESTIONS TO ASK THE LAWYER OR HIS SECRETARY ON THE PHONE

1. How do you prefer to work in divorce cases? (As an advisor, mediator, negotiator?)
2. How do you feel about couples who successfully negotiate between themselves and then bring their agreement to an attorney to put into the necessary legal form? (This legal format may or may not be necessary for local court.)
3. How do you feel about joint custody arrangements between parents? What has been your experience with such arrangements? (Many attorneys are unfamiliar with joint physical custody and/or the idea of two homes.)
4. Would you act as a mediator or as an arbitrator for a divorcing couple? If yes, is this common to your practice? Would you work with a counselor or therapist if indicated?
5. How long have you been practicing in this country?
6. How are fees charged? What types of billing procedures do you use—monthly payments, retainers, etc.?
7. Do you have any free time (fifteen minutes or so) in which a potential client can just drop in to talk? (This is not a period for legal advice but just for lawyer and potential client to get to know one another briefly.)
8. About what percentage of your cases are in family law? (You do not necessarily seek an attorney who does 100 percent of his or her work in family law, but instead one who has a substantial proportion of his practice in this area.)

QUESTIONS TO ASK THE LAWYER AT THE FIRST MEETING

1. What are my rights under the law regarding support, custody, and property?

2. Are there local fee schedules used by our own county courts on spousal and child support? (If yes, the attorney should show these to you at your first meeting.)
3. How do you feel about parents sharing responsibilities and authority after divorce? About legal and/or physical joint custody?
4. Then obtain the answers to the questions on *"Your Rights and the Law"* on page 152.

Negotiating Your Own Agreement

"Reasonable rights of visitation are awarded to the father." This phrase is common in legal agreements. But what does it mean? What is *reasonable*—does that mean three hours a week, a day, a month? Who decides what is reasonable—the father, the mother, a third party? How does visitation work—does it mean the father has full responsibility during the period the parent and child are together? Is the father to return the child to the mother if the child becomes ill? Can the mother have total authority over the time the child spends with the father? Can the father refuse to exercise his visitation rights?

The language is vague, open to many interpretations. People disagree on exactly how it works and the avenues are wide open for argument about what is "reasonable" and what is "visitation." Your own formal agreement should be the opposite of this. While you may privately agree to be far more flexible, an explicit formal agreement can provide a starting point for this later give and take. A formal agreement—explicit, detailed, and with teeth—saves many parents from later difficulties.

How to Be Explicit and Detailed

Parents who develop a working relationship don't agree on how everything will work. Far from it. But what they do learn is to agree on how to disagree. Sometimes they reach a compromise, sometimes they simply take turns. At other times, they may agree to take no action at all and allow the disagreements to stand as they are. Since most divorcing parents disagree with one another in some area—especially about each other's values or behavior—they need to acquire the art of learning how to share, divide, or ignore decisions and responsibilities for their offspring.

SHARE IT, DIVIDE IT, OR IGNORE IT   Any number of arrangements can work. Some parents want minimum contact. They want to make decisions that separate themselves in as many ways as possible. Such parents subdivide all the areas of child rearing, giving total authority to one parent in one area. When in charge, each parent is both kingpin and janitor. For example, a father may take over the area of sports and summer activities for his children even when they do not live with him. He might have all the choices, assume all the costs, and do all the chauffeuring back and forth to the games and practices. A mother might attend the activities, but they have decided that she has no authority to make decisions about where and when the kids enroll, for how long, or at what level. This mother might take over the children's education as her bailiwick. The father might attend school events, get copies of the report cards, and be listed on both emergency and registration cards, but Mom makes the choices of schools, teachers and after-school activities.

In other situations, parents share the major decisions about major medical coverage, hospitalizations, a long course of treatment, choice of schools, and ongoing psychotherapy. The minor decisions, such as treatment for the flu, overseeing homework, and routine doctor and dentist appointments, are left to the discretion of the parent in residence. When a father, for example, has his children living with him for two four-day periods a month, he has the opportunity, if this time overlaps on several school days, to look over their homework, bring the children to routine appointments, and even visit school and say hello to the teacher.

While some parents can attend school conferences together and frequently share feelings and impressions about a child's educational progress, others find such proximity too provoking. These people prefer their paths not to cross often. Still other parents make their decisions more traditionally. One parent will bear the costs and the other the responsibilities. Dad may pay for clarinet lessons but Mom will choose the teacher and get Junior to his lessons.

Your own Parenting Agreement can only be clear if you work to make it so. The clarity is your responsibility, not that of any counselor or attorney. You construct the definitions, make them clear to one another (and to your advisors), and *then put it in writing*. You will all have a better chance to live more happily with what happens in actual practice if you take this extra step of being specific and then writing it out.

Putting Teeth in the Agreement

What happens if a parent doesn't follow through with his or her part of the agreement? Dad might get the flu and not be able to take Junior on a weekend. Mom might start school and tell Dad she just can't drive Junior to his house every Tuesday and Thursday night as she had earlier agreed. Be flexible, but balanced. Find a way to substitute for yourselves. If Dad must miss a weekend, or Mom is unable to have the children back at the designated time, have an alternate game plan. Perhaps Dad, with Mom's permission, can take a make-up weekend within a month. Mom might bow out of the evening driving with Dad's permission, but pay him back with an extra day of time at Dad's house or driving the kids round-trip. Several parents have arranged for child support contributions to be at a high level when Dad can't take either of the children as agreed or make a substitute time. The contributions are at a far lower level when he can put in the time. Time is money to some parents and money is time. Substitution, however designed, is only fair. Some people say, "I can't put a price tag of time or money on my children." But other parents don't see the checks and balances as a price tag; they see it as a way to continue to work together without becoming resentful at the lopsided way the agreement is being honored.

For example, Marsha has three teenagers. She needs her one long weekend a month away from them just to regain her balance. When their father, Richard, needs to travel as a result of his business and cannot take the teenagers as he has agreed to, Marsha will have to cancel her plans and the children will be without their father. Marsha can easily become resentful as the father's schedule, even after divorce, takes precedence over hers. Richard might become anxious, because he feels he has little choice in the matter and is damned tired of being the bad guy in the scenario. Some built-in teeth or "what if's" would get both off the hot seat. Richard can increase his child support payment by a significant amount if he isn't able to have the children living with him at agreed times or hire a sitter at his house. Or Marsha can hire a sitter and get her time off by Richard paying the sitter's fee. Then Richard knows that while he's not seeing the kids, at least he's not cutting out on his financial responsibility. Or, both may agree that Richard's sister will have the kids for the weekend he has to travel, getting Dad's family more involved with the kids.

When one parent fails to follow through, it costs the other parent time, money, reduced mobility, and opportunities, not to mention the hurt and disappointment felt by the children. The financial burden becomes a forced form of unawarded spousal support. Written agreements on acceptable alternatives, substitutions, and compensations minimize these difficulties and the hard feelings that come with them. Forced payment of unawarded spousal support is *not* the way to build mutual respect.

Preparations for Negotiations

Checklist for Parents

1. Get the information about your rights as outlined on page 152.
2. Get the information on your state's custody laws.
3. Find out the route your private Parenting Agreement must take before it can be incorporated into your court order.
4. Obtain a sample paragraph or the advice of an attorney regarding the change of residence of one parent from one state to another.

5. Check your feelings. Cool off if necessary.

6. Check out attorneys and counselors so you will know how to get and use expert advice, consultation, mediation, or negotiations if the need arises.*

7. Reach an agreement regarding the use of third parties—either as mediators, negotiators, counselors, or consultants.

8. Take the time to look over the survey in Chapter 3. If your score shows too many hot spots, use a neutral third party from the beginning of your discussions, or delay your discussions until things improve.

9. Have you had at least two previous short-term agreements that have given you the experience of how the principles of discussion and negotiation work best for you? If you have, you are that much ahead.

10. Do your homework on money and the cost of raising children.

11. Review the guidelines for negotiations with the other parent outlined in Chapter 11.

12. Give yourself a brief refresher on the way to retreat from intimacy and develop a business relationship, as described in Chapters 8 and 9.

13. Make a "ready" and "not ready" list as described from the "Master List of Parenting Responsibilities and Rights."

14. Try to reach an agreement (at your first meetings) regarding the issues of children's vote, questions of fees, and interim matters.

Do the Children Vote?

The inclusion of your children in your discussions and decision-making process is a highly individual family decision. Should children be given the option to veto their parents' plans? Should children be able to tell their parents their preferences for a school-year residence? There are many degrees of involvement, and each family must make its own decision. Parents should give the children every opportunity to voice their preferences but children should not be forced to choose. Instead parents can say, "We want to know what you think will work best for you but we will make the final decision." This gives children a voice without the accompanying responsibility of making Mom and Dad's decisions for them. It also eases the internal conflict of loyalty that children so often feel when they think they have been asked to choose one parent over the other.

Issues of Money

The following issues are often ignored till the last minute. My advice is to attend to them as soon as possible.

* Some people prefer to hire an attorney from the beginning, telling him or her that they are working out custody themselves. They feel that an attorney familiar with the family can give better advice when it is asked for.

ATTORNEYS', COUNSELORS', AND MEDIATORS' FEES   Decide who will be responsible for the fees and put it in writing. Don't leave the question of who pays whose fees till the last, since this can become a major bone of contention. Realize that these professional fees may be a major item in a divorce budget and plan ahead for them.

PAYMENT OF ANY PAST-DUE CONTRIBUTIONS (SPOUSAL OR CHILD SUPPORT)   When parents have been divorced for a while and there are unpaid debts in the picture, the specter of the payment can cloud your negotiations or turn them upside down halfway through. If this becomes a hot issue, use a mediator or counselor to talk it out. You might as well get it off your chest at the onset.

INTERIM MATTERS (THE AMOUNT OF TEMPORARY CONTRIBUTION, SUPPORT)   From the time you separate to the time you finalize your agreement can be a confused and confusing period. When money passes hands with or without a written agreement, it is important that you take time to learn about your rights under the law and get some legal advice on such issues as how your interim payments might set a basis for your permanent payments, what the tax consequences of such payments might be, and what might happen if either one of you claims reimbursement for payment of joint debts.

Working Out an Agreement: An Example

Carole and James McKay, parents of ten-year-old Jesse and eight-year-old Carolee McKay are a composite couple, given fictitious names but typical of real histories. To prepare for their initial meeting, they follow the Guidelines for Negotiations with the Other Parent from the last chapter. They each feel they are now in control of their feelings and have as an objective the development of a working relationship and two homes for their children.

They have done a good deal of homework, but they still have a lot to do. They have negotiated two previous short-term agreements that have worked out more or less, and they have some ideas about their shortcomings at negotiating. They know that their previous not-ready lists contain some sore subjects that may require the help of a third party at some point.

By phone they discuss the pros and cons of the several professionals each has talked to and seen. They share the information they have received from their local conciliation court and Arbitration Association. They decide to choose a mediator and agree to share equally the payment of the fees for the service if they need it. They also agree to hold back on negotiating the property settlement until they have completed their Parenting Agreement. (More affluent couples may find this holding back unwise.) Each agrees to contact a separate attorney for continuing advice but not for negotiating *per se*. They set up their first meeting.

At the first thirty-minute session they compare their information on rights. Often parents find that the information they have received from different sources may be ambiguous, seem unfair, or even sound contradictory. Recognition of these inconsistencies sometimes helps people to appreciate better the need for private negotiations.

The McKays see that the questions of finance and child support may be the two biggest snags in their discussions and they agree to leave them till the end—possibly for meetings with the mediator, or if necessary, to be left to the attorneys.

Even if Carole and James decide to leave the money issue to the last, they should have done their homework on "Money: The Costs of Raising Children" and prepared their Ready and Not Ready lists from the Master List of Parenting Responsibilities and Rights from the last chapter. They will have to do this work even if their private negotiations break down and they end up using attorneys to bargain for them. This couple does not have any past-due monies between them, but they do need to think about how later fees for attorneys might come into their Parenting Agreement process through a back door.

Their second meeting, in person, can be strengthened by the assurance that they have already made some ground rules for their discussions and procedures. They have pooled their information. So far, of course, Carole and James have done nothing that they wouldn't have to do if they had attorneys handling the negotiations—except that they are saving on attorneys' fees.

Carole and James have to decide: "Should we bring the children into our discussions at any time?" They believe the children should know about their discussions, but are not in agreement about how they might be part of the negotiations. They shelve the question for the present. They also look at the question of custody and the way their state looks at joint custody. They decide to develop their Parenting Agreement and describe their situation as clearly as possible and to push their attorneys for the joint physical custody award if such legal terminology needs to be substituted for their own layman's language of "joint responsibility." Finally, they agree that if any temporary custody award will be made, it too will be "joint physical custody" and that they will not undermine their hope for two homes with a sole custody to one and visitation to the other in an initial court order.*

If their thirty minutes are up before they come to an agreement, they continue another time. A couple needs to stop talking before old feelings begin to grow too strong.

---

* Note that the McKays will use the equal status of joint physical custody but will divide the children's time between homes about one-third to two-thirds.

Once they begin discussing the children, they find their ready lists and the previous negotiations lend themselves to relatively easy early meetings. They ask themselves, "Do we divide it, share it, or ignore it?" For example, they agree on where their children should attend school, on the teachers, the location, and costs of the after-school day care.

The Master List of Parenting Responsibilities and Rights reads under Education: Choice of school, costs/supplies, homework, decisions, access to information/records, teacher conferences, report cards, activities, discussions. James—the recorder—writes down: "We agree that the children will continue to attend the ABC Schools in Port Swatterly, should continue with the same teachers." Then they ask themselves if they need to think about who would underwrite school costs, supplies, and if the area of homework would be an issue for a Parenting Agreement. They choose to ignore these items and not mention them at all. Next they look at "Teacher conferences, report cards, and activities." They decide to alternate teacher conferences, both receive copies of report cards, and both attend or remain active in school affairs. James writes: "We agree to attend teacher conferences on a rotating basis, to be active in school events as our schedules allow, and that both will have full access to information and records regarding our children's progress."

With each easy decision and area of agreement, following the basic rationale for the "easiest first, hardest last" rule, a sense of common interest and respect can grow. Yes, the McKays have their differences and their hurts—but they also have areas of agreement and such agreement builds strength to go on.

The real differences between Carole and James come out with the Not Ready lists. James can't see why the children need so many tennis lessons and special classes; Carole can't see why James is opposed to such advantages and seems to emphasize building life skills for the children. James thinks the children are overprotected; Carole thinks they are overstimulated. Here is where the "divide it" and "my territory, my philosophy" guidelines can help negotiations. If the couple adopts the principle of noninterference, Carole cannot dictate how James spends his time with the children, nor can James dictate Carole's parenting style. If James wants to educate his children in life skills, he has his own time to teach them about insurance, banking, about negotiations with salespersons and merchants, etc. Carole, on her time, and with her money, can arrange for the lessons she feels are important. But she may not arrange such lessons on James' time. (As you cut the pie together, remind yourself that you can neither have it all, nor tell the other parent how to eat his piece of it.)

Here is where the out-of-control emotions and the "see why I divorced" cry can come back into the negotiations. The money issue is central, even though it is now the last one on the table. James doesn't want his money supporting an activity he disapproves of. Carole doesn't want her parenting style dictated by James' withholding of monies. This couple needs an accounting of funds procedure. It won't stop Carole from providing those lessons if she can, but it can give James some proof that the money he contributes is being used for other things. Feelings can get hot over seemingly small things but these are the "pots the emotional divorce gets cooked in."

Although the McKays had agreed on dollar amounts *before separation,* each is now having second thoughts. Temporary agreements had set and continued their original levels of dollar exchange until this new, more permanent agreement could be worked out. James is willing to continue the present level of support, but needs to register his objections to the way he sees Carole spending the money. Here the best strategy will be a clear accounting of actual disbursements and eventual compromise that takes into account parental rights to individual parenting styles.

When parents reach no agreement in two meetings they should cool off for a few days and then get in touch with a mediator. The McKays were close to having their entire agreement negotiated by themselves but they needed an extra boost, so they met with a mediator. They explained that they needed help in this area only, that they planned to write up their own agreement from their already written notes and sentences. The mediator heard them out and after two sessions the McKays reached the same compromise that the noninterference rule suggests. Carole and James agree on an accounting of funds and to keep hands off the other parent's parenting style and activities.

It's common for a couple to near the end of their agreement process and get held up on a seemingly minor issue such as this. But the issue often is a symbol of that "old family feeling," of the reasons why they are divorcing, and a way to stall the final stage of the move away from intimacy. The value of the mediator was clear. It was easier for them to close off the discussions this way and get on with the other business of ending their marriage.

The McKays spent several weeks on their Parenting Agreement—drafting it, then revising some of the wording. Their document embodies the special feeling that closes one kind of life and begins another. They talk about the decisions with their children and ask them how they feel about them. The children have no serious problems with the agreement and everyone feels more satisfied with the results.* The McKays have the agreement typed in its final form and find a witness for their signing ceremony. They are now ready to present copies of the agreement to

---

* A different couple would have included their children's opinions from the beginning instead of waiting until the last minute.

each of their separate attorneys. They can then begin their property and financial discussions without further involving the child-rearing issues.

The Parenting Agreement

The McKays' agreement is unusually long because it contains many of the standardized forms and terminology of the two-home approach. But it can be used as a guide for your own words and statements. Provisions missing from this agreement are those of a technical nature— provisions for tax exemption, head of household assignment, and the out-of-state clause. You should consult an attorney and accountant for the best course for you and then see that these provisions are incorporated.

Parenting Agreement

FOREWORD

We, Carole McKay and James McKay, the parents of Jesse and Carolee McKay, enter into this agreement in order to better meet our parental responsibilities and to safeguard our children's future development. We both recognize that they wish to love and respect both of us, regardless of our marital status or our place of residence, and that their welfare can best be served by our mutual cooperation as partners in parenting and by each of us providing a home in which they are loved and to which they belong: their mother's house and father's house. We also jointly recognize that court proceedings regarding children and custody and visitation matters can be detrimental to children, and we therefore have decided to resolve these questions ourselves, using this Parenting Agreement.* Finally, we have chosen to avoid the traditional terminology surrounding divorce and children by using terms that more accurately describe the reorganization of our former family to two new one-parent families. Accordingly, we wish to instruct our respective attorneys, if necessary, to inform any courts involved in our dissolution that our desires are as follows regarding the custody and upbringing of our children.

1. *Terminology:* In order to reaffirm our commitment to our two-home status, we choose to use the terms "live with mother" and "live with father" in describing our arrangement, rather than the more traditional one-home, one-visitor terminology of "custody and visitation."

---

* This last sentence is used by just a few parents. Further, it might displease the judge asked to approve it.

2. *Responsibility for Jesse and Carolee:* Jesse and Carolee will be our joint responsibility.* Both of us recognize that each of our contributions toward our children's welfare is real and genuine, and we agree to co-operate with one another on establishing mutually acceptable guidelines and standards for development, education, and health. We agree further to discuss all major issues jointly and that day-to-day decisions for the children will be the responsibility of the parent in residence. Each of us will have equal access to all health and school records and unlimited phone contact with our children. Jesse and Carolee will live with their father every other Friday beginning at 6:00 P.M. through the following Monday at school time. The remainder of the time they will live with their mother. During the summer vacation they will live with their father the entire months of July and August. This schedule will continue through-out this year, unless their normal development seems impaired by this arrangement, in which case we will review and reassess the arrangement. Changes in scheduled times at either home will require immediate substi-tution of times of equal length and will be subject to our mutual approval. If an acceptable substitute is not found, the parent unable to be home with the children will hire a sitter or make arrangements with friends or relatives to care for the children during the period of his or her responsibility.

3. *Contributions:* Each parent will contribute time and energies on a daily basis toward the children's day-to-day care when they live with him or her. In addition, the father will contribute $225 per child (child sup-port) toward the expenses incurred in the mother's residence on or before the fifteenth of each month. During the summer months when the children live with the father, the contribution will be reduced to $200.†

The mother agrees to give the father a written simplified accounting of this contribution three times a year (every four months), on the first of January, May, and August.

4. *Medical and Dental:* It is agreed that the mother will carry and pay all the cost of the children's medical health insurance. The father agrees to pay 75 percent of all medical costs over and beyond that covered by in-surance. Dental costs will be paid by the mother.

We also agree that transportation to medical appointments will be the responsibility of the parent in residence.

We agree that although the parent in residence has final responsibility in making day-to-day medical decisions, the other parent is to be in-volved in all major discussions and decisions, and consulted and advised about illnesses or accidents.

5. *Education and Child Care:* Both parents agree that Jesse and

---

* Notice the word "custody" is omitted entirely. Your attorney may want to put it in, however. If this happens, be sure you understand the ramifications of the type of "custody" that he or she adds.

† Some people add a cost of living clause here.

Carolee will remain in their present schools and child-care arrangements will remain the same for this year. Tuition costs will be the responsibility of the father; child-care costs, the responsibility of the mother. We agree to attend teacher conferences on a rotating basis, to be active in school events as our schedules allow, and that we both will have full access to information and records regarding our children's progress.

6. *Holidays:* We both agree that the Thanksgiving holiday, beginning with the day before and ending the following Monday morning at school time, will be spent this year with the mother and next year with the father.

We further agree that for this year Jesse and Carolee will live with their father the first week of Christmas vacation through to the twenty-seventh of December, when the children will then be with their mother. Next year the situation will be reversed and the children will spend the Christmas period first with their mother. Other holidays, Memorial Day, school holidays, and Easter vacation will be negotiated between the parents.

7. *Children's Activities:* Summer activities will be the responsibility of the father and will also be undertaken at his discretion and expense. School-year activities are anticipated to be ballet and guitar for Carolee and Pony League Softball for Jesse. We agree to the continuance of these activities and will share the responsibilities for transportation, costs, and communications in the following manner: Jesse's Pony League activities will be supervised by his father, and all costs incurred will be met by him. Carolee's ballet and guitar lessons will be the responsibility of the mother, and all costs will be met by her. It is not anticipated that the ballet lessons will continue past June of this year. The father agrees to transporting Carolee during his times with her so that she can have her guitar lessons on some Saturdays.

8. *Respect for One Another's Parenting Style and Authority:* We agree to honor one another's parenting style, privacy, and authority. We will not interfere in the parenting style of the other parent nor will we make plans or arrangements that would impinge upon the other parent's authority or times with the children without the expressed agreement of the other parent. Furthermore, we agree to encourage our children to discuss their grievances with a parent directly with the parent in question. It is our intent to encourage a direct child-parent bond.

9. *Agreement Time Period and Renegotiations for New Agreement:* We both agree that this Parenting Agreement is to be in effect a minimum of two years and is automatically renewable if no revisions are sought. If revisions are sought after two years, we agree that this agreement will be considered binding until a new agreement is reached. If unusual circumstances arise before the end of the two-year period, all or part of this agreement will be renegotiated, either privately or with the aid of a third party, given thirty days' notice before either of us seeks modification

through the courts. We further agree that, should any serious dispute arise between us relating to our children's education, health, or other aspect of their welfare, before either of us seeks modification through the courts, we will first seek the services of an objective third party, such as a trained counselor or arbitrator.

_____   _____
Date   Signature

_____   _____
Date   Signature

_____   _____
Date   Witness*

Wording Your Agreement

Parents have used the sample Parenting Agreement paragraphs and vocabulary in several ways. Some use the examples just as they are and simply insert their own decisions in their own words. Others redesign paragraphs; still others build a total agreement from scratch. Many parents find the idea of a Parenting Agreement a good chance to write down their own joint philosophy on their commitment to their children, as well as their decisions.

I suggest that you consider your own Parenting Agreement in the same way that you might any other public document or ceremony, such as a ritual of confirmation, graduation exercise, or a wedding ceremony. This agreement is your chance to bring some kind of formal validation to your beliefs. It's an excellent opportunity to show yourself and your children that you and the other parent are working it out and that you have a plan for the children. Like writing the script for your own wedding ceremony, writing your own Parenting Agreement has important symbolic as well as realistic value to your peace of mind and to that of your children.

Make It an Agreement Your Children Can Read

The words you use will make all the difference in how effective the document can be, both practically and psychologically. The importance of value-laden words and what one parent called the "fear words" should not be overlooked. The new vocabulary changes the meaning as it clarifies the decisions. Having "joint and shared responsibility" feels better than having "joint custody."

* A witness is probably not necessary, but it does add a more formal tone to the procedure.

Here is a series of words you can use as you design your own agreement:

Beginning Vocabulary for Two-Home Legal Agreements

Try Saying:	Instead of Saying:
Parenting agreement	Custody agreement
Shared and joint responsibility	Sole custody or joint custody
Living with, live with	Visiting or visitation
Primary residence	Sole custody
Contribution	Child support*
Primary-home parent; parent in residence	Parent with custody
Second-home parent	Parent without custody

The Effect of the Parenting Agreement on the Children

Some parents have reported certain calming effects that the actual Parenting Agreement document had on their older children. "It was a pleasure to give it to my teenager to read. It's a positive, accurate document, and it showed her that we could agree on something." Another parent who had typed up a first draft of the Parenting Agreement at home said that her fourteen-year-old son looked over her shoulder as she was finishing the typing and asked what she was doing. She answered that it was the Parenting Agreement that itemized decisions about him and his sister. When he asked, "Can I read it?" the mother reported, "It felt so good to say, 'Of course,' and give it to him. He seemed somewhat calmed by reading it." If the son had been handed a traditionally worded legal document, he might not understand the legal terminology or know what the document was for. It may even have frightened him. The simplicity of an agreement written in everyday terms, with the intent and details of decisions clearly spelled out, helps children as well as parents to understand and to appreciate what to expect and what will be expected of them.

Since the document is about what will happen to your children, it stands to reason that these children should have the right to read it and understand what it means to them. In some cases, as we have already seen, older children can also be part of the agreement process, giving parents their opinions or choices on important things that directly affect them.

* The use of the phrase "child support" has many legal ramifications and your attorney may advise you to use it along with your newer term.

The New United Front: Your Written Agreements

The temporary two-month agreement on the refrigerator door is your first written example of the new united front you can present to your children. Despite your adult incompatibility and disagreements, it shows you can come to a meeting of the minds when it comes to the kids.

The Parenting Agreement establishes a more formal contract between yourselves and with your children. The agreement often reinforces your family solidarity, increases your children's and your own sense of security, and maintains a sense of family continuity. That agonizing period of indecision or changing positions is finally over and everyone can relax.

When parents go through the long and demanding process of thinking through their situation, they go through many steps. They have to take the time, effort, and thought to cover the series of questions about the children and themselves. All by itself this review leads to a sense of accomplishment. You need to gather the information whether you go a traditional attorney-negotiated route or that of a self-negotiated Parenting Agreement. When you have assumed responsibility for your own actions by your considered preparation, the final product will be reason for self-congratulation and hope. But when you go further and discuss and negotiate your own Parenting Agreement, you earn a well-deserved pat on the back and a sense of true satisfaction.

If I could, I would want somehow to reward all the good efforts of parents everywhere who steadfastly, sometimes grimly, persevere in their job of sorting out their personal feelings about one another from the issues of money, children, time, and energy. Their accomplishment is magnificent and worthy of high praise.

Your Private Agreement and the Court's Approval

A private agreement, negotiated by parents either alone or with a mediator or by attorneys, can become a legal stipulation. This stipulation is a signed document, the form of which is often open to the creativity of the attorney or parties themselves. The bottom line in a stipulation is that the parties have come to a mutually acceptable settlement of their rights, responsibilities, and differences.

When the bench is presented with a stipulation regarding the care and upbringing of children, it often gives a rubber-stamp approval. Many judges and attorneys have reported to me that the stipulations are infrequently reviewed by the bench, owing to time pressures and case backlog. The general consensus is that parents do know best, especially when they can agree on what best is and have a plan for how it will work. The courts usually honor this expertise, even though the bench holds the right to review such documents and the power to order a modification if it seems desirable. There are exceptions, however. Some courts will not approve *any* documents that deal with joint custody. Other courts have established a review process whereby a trained professional reads every agreement before it is submitted to the bench. Your attorney should be able to tell you what is customary in the court having jurisdiction in your case. Ordinarily a well-thought-out Parenting Agreement presents proof of parental ability to work together. Counselors, almost universally, approve and encourage parenting agreements, and all who have seen this one heartily approve it.

The attorneys may insert additional provisions to cover technical issues, but, for the most part, what you put in your Parenting Agreement to present as a stipulation is what you will come out with. The result is that your own private ordering of your own private lives, described in your own everyday language, can be approved by the court. There is a working relationship in Mom's house and Dad's house.

"It feels kind of sad," said one father as he looked at his final Parenting Agreement. "I didn't want the talks to end because it was a way for us to be together again, I guess. But if we had to end, then this is the best way I know to do it."

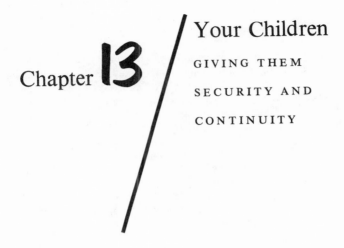

Chapter **13**

Your Children

GIVING THEM

SECURITY AND

CONTINUITY

Under the best of circumstances, raising children calls for self-confidence, patience, skill, and a sense of when to leave well enough alone. During a crisis period—like the transition process of divorce—the parents' emotional state can blind them to their basic parenting work. Crisis or not, parents are still parents. When parents understand how the dynamics of divorce affect their children and what can be done about it, their parenting job becomes far easier.

This chapter only summarizes some of the child-rearing issues that need attention when a marriage ends. What happens between parents and children who are undergoing drastic change is a complex subject, and the Notes at the end of the book will suggest further reading and resources. While you are reading, keep in mind the following important conclusions drawn from research on children and divorce. Children who seem to do best after their parents' separation are those whose parents spend time with them, who make them feel loved and wanted in each home, who keep the children out of the middle, and who allow the children independent relationships with each of them. When children do not have to worry that their relationship with a parent is dependent on how well the two parents are getting along, they can feel free to love them both without a conflict of loyalty, to have access to each of them without fear of losing either.

Changes for Your Child

In general, the fewer changes that first year the better. Parents should first ask themselves how many changes they are forcing their children to make. As suggested in Chapter 10, do your best to keep your children in the same house or at least in the same neighborhood for that first year. Unless the children were doing poorly in their school, the known rituals there, the familiar teachers, and the friends and activities they have combine to make a safe haven for children undergoing drastic changes at home.

Here are some examples of how this works for children:

Marilouise's parents separated six months ago. During the week she lives with Mom in the same place she has always lived, goes to the same school, has the same friends, and knows the same neighborhood. Her father took an apartment about a mile from the house, and Marilouise lives with him every other Thursday evening to Monday morning. She's made an additional batch of friends at Dad's house, and some of her school friends live near there. Her parents, by not asking for too many changes within too short a time, are allowing themselves and Marilouise a chance to get used to the *biggest* change of all, that the parents are now living apart in two homes. It is not easy for any of them, but it is working.

On the other hand, David and Ronnie's parents separated, immediately sold their house, and the boys and their mother went to live in another state while their father remained in the city where they had been raised. These children have massive changes to contend with—not only the loss of their father's presence on a daily basis, but the distance that will make it prohibitive for him to see them more than once every two or three months. Further, the boys have to adjust to a new climate, a new neighborhood, a new school, and have to seek new friends.

Parents can help children cope with massive change in many of the same ways they help themselves. Help your children build a sense of mastery over frightening or new circumstances by bolstering their sense of self-esteem, self-confidence. This means knowing how to reassure, how to be worthy of trust, how to listen, how to give simple but important information, how to set limits, how to let children express their feelings, their opinions, and their love. Most of all it means being there everyday—in person, in spirit, by phone, by letter.

Explaining Change to Children

Children need things to be tangible, seeable, touchable. They are concrete and practical, a "different kind of thinking machine," until they are about twelve years old. Abstract terms such as "love" and "loyalty" need to be spelled out in everyday terms. When children ask, "Will I have to move, change schools, change friends?" they need a concrete set of answers, not a sad and frightened "I don't know" from a distraught parent. They at least need answers that give possible alternatives: "We will stay here for at least one year and then perhaps move to Eighteenth street or maybe closer to Grandma's house."

Children's fears escalate during the tumult of the divorcing period, and they have their own sadness, grief, anger, and off-the-wall emotions. Children often worry that their mothers can't cope and that their fathers are lonely. "Is Dad lonesome?" "Can he really cook for himself?" "Is Mom scared—can she really make my big brother shape up without Dad?" Demystify the change. Provide the children with tangible evidence. Bring the children to the new place, let them see Dad cook, and Mom take a stand with big brother and make her own house rules.

Some parents who move out of the family home may stop seeing the children for a while. These parents often feel confusion and pain, but their unexplained absence can create serious problems for their children. Each parent is an essential source of love, security, and continuity for a child. Even though parents may feel powerless or inadequate, their children need to know that they are not gone forever and that they have not taken their love away from their children.

If you are separated by many miles, make contact frequent and tangible—a note sent in the mail is a thought made visible, touchable (and re-readable). An autumn leaf given as a token of a solitary walk is tangible evidence that the parent thought of the child when alone. The best contact is daily contact. When you can't make this contact in person, do it by phone, or letter.

"Who Is Reassuring Whom?"

Even the most conscientious parents can erroneously expect super-human behavior from their children during the crisis months. For example, some parents unconsciously don't want their children to display any painful feelings, especially those about the effects of the separation.

"I would cry from missing my Dad so much, but I had to go in the bathroom or hide somewhere," said one eleven-year-old girl. "Mom really gets mad at me when I cry anyway, and if she thinks it has anything to do with Daddy, she gets supermad." Many children hide their real feelings from parents. They feel this is what their parents need or want. Sometimes they fear censure, sometimes exposure or being misunderstood. Other times they are shy.

Other parents seek their children's approval or permission for the divorce. "I told my daughter I'd stay married to her father if she wanted me to," said one mother. "She told me she wouldn't blame me if I did divorce him." Such parents want adultlike support and reassurance from their children at a time when the children need exactly that from their parents.

It's easy for parents to lean on their children during crisis. They love you, they know you, and they deeply care. They are there when others may not be. But children are not your emotional equals, nor are they yet equipped for adult traumas. Yet listen to some parents talk about how the children are expected to take over when the adults fell apart. "Joanie takes care of me," said one young mother of a daughter aged eight. "She makes her own meals, she asks me how I feel, and she tells me not to cry. She is all I have now that her Dad is gone."

This role reversal is not healthy. Children need parents who act like parents. And despite the presence of children, parents need people their own age. If your moral support is coming primarily from your children, you may be expecting too much from them. Find someone your own age and size to lean on instead.

The Neighborhood, School, and Church

Parents sometimes forget that quite aside from the changes divorce brings to a family, it can also bring about changes in their children's sense of social status and of belonging. Children can feel like aliens. Even though divorce is part of the American way of life, our culture and its vocabulary are still basically programmed to serve, acknowledge, and value only the married home.

"My friend's mother said I couldn't play with my friend anymore," said a ten-year-old girl recounting a common experience among children. "She said it was because of too much homework, but my friend told me it was because my parents got divorced."

When this happens to children, it hurts. Sometimes children will tell their parents. Other times, especially if they sense their parents' pain and guilt about the divorce, they will silently keep their own pain to themselves. "I got into trouble at school and the teacher said it was because I came from a 'broken home.' I told her my home wasn't busted, it was just fine," said a ten-year-old boy, "but she didn't listen."

Such incidents can deeply wound a child. When any part of a social setting sees divorce as a tragedy, a stigma, or a failure, children of all ages undergo loss of self-esteem and confidence. They may hear gossip about them or their parents. If this happens, children need the warmth and support of a family circle that can act as a buffer to this outside world. Parents and friends need to reassure children that their family is perfectly acceptable and that they are acceptable as well.

Children's Basic Needs and Fears: What to Do About Them

Children, even sophisticated teenagers, need adults in order to survive in the world, and most of them know it. The family provides a place that says, "You are safe, you are loved, your needs are cared for."

When family life is changed by separation and divorce, the child's sense of security and continuity is shaken. Who will take care of me now? Will I still be loved? Where will I live, sleep? Where will I go to school? Will I still have a real home?

Children do not yet have adult size, strength, wisdom, or economic and social power. When divorce threatens their security, their impotence becomes a conscious reality; their vulnerability needs your care and some special measures of protection.

Children's fears are affected by the way the adults in their lives function. When the adults are not functioning well or are behaving out of character, children develop fears:

1. Being denied the basics of survival—food, shelter, clothing, sleep
2. Being abandoned or left, forgotten, or being unimportant
3. Being punished, or assaulted, hurt, being the object of hostility
4. Being unloved, having love taken away, or losing love

Imagine then how terrifying it can be for a child of any age to have the family change its composition, to have one parent suddenly gone from the house while the other parent is in alternating stages of numbness and shock, anger and hurt. Younger children may wonder, "Did Daddy leave because of something I did?" "Maybe Mommy left because I didn't clean my room. Am I being punished by losing her?" "Who will take care of me now?" Older children and teens can wonder, "How much does Dad love me to leave me like that?" "Will Dad desert me like my friend's dad deserted him?"

Some children are strong enough to think about these questions and settle them for themselves with an internal, "Naw, my mom wouldn't do that" or "I know it will be okay." But some children can't do that. Do reassure your child whether or not they ask such questions. But when they do ask these kinds of things, be aware that behind the questions may be a storehouse of anxiety and a need to confide that could mean professional help is in order.

Some children feel that the parent who moves out of the original family is also removing his or her love from the child. Other children conclude that the resident parent has forced the other parent to leave. As a result, anger is sometimes directed at the parent who stays, sometimes at the one who goes, and often at both. Instead of being shocked at such angry outbursts or being punitive with the children, parents can help with reassuring action and honest explanations. The children have their own need to mourn the end of their parents' marriage and anger is a legitimate part of the process. A final suggestion: Children, like adults, need to get away from it all sometimes. Let your children spend weekends and extra time with relatives and friends where things are stable and supportive. The time away may do everyone good.

Clarify What's Happening

One important way to calm children's fears is for parents to clarify briefly what's happening and take full responsibility for it. Just as security is built on trust, trust needs understanding. Try to have a short, true explanation and, if possible, one that is phrased in a positive way: "Your mom (dad) and I decided it is best for us to live apart" conveys a more reassuring message than "We simply can't stand to stay together any longer" or "We don't love each other enough to live together anymore." In particular do not give all the gory details of the fights you've had or how you feel betrayed by the other parent. Your children do not want to know—and they should not know—how you hurt each other. They need to be able to respect both of you, now more than ever. And most of all they need to know that it is all right for them to love the other parent even though *you* don't.

Explaining a situation simply, without embellishments or excuses, gives the children confirmation of your concern for them. "Mom and Dad know what they are doing. I don't have to guess the real truth and wonder how it concerns me." Remember, though, that too much information can be confusing and can end up being as useless as too little. Make it brief, make it simple.

It is usually easier for children to deal with the truth than to confront abrupt changes, whispered hostility, martyred silences, or those double messages in which your action or voice tone contradicts your words. If you are feeling sad and tell a child that "everything is fine," you are giving a double message. Better to admit "I'm sad right now," and then reassure the child, "but it's not about you and me, it's about 'grown-up' matters." A straight answer can calm your child's fears and release him from responsibility. But a double message can blow up small incidents to giant proportions. Demystification of events is very important.

A Checklist: Calming Your Children's Fears

Clarify What's Happening, Take Responsibility, and
Show Them Your Love

1. Reassure your children that you love them and will always take care of them and look after their needs, no matter what happens between you and their other parent. You will always be their parent and do what you feel is best for them.

2. Explain that the separation and, later, the divorce are grown-up business between Mom and Dad. Do not ever imply or state that your children had any responsibility for your fights or for the ending of your marriage, even if in your off-the-wall moments you may feel they did.

3. Tell your children they will now have two homes instead of one and begin to use words like "live with Mom or Dad" instead of "visit," as shown in Chapter 5. Tell them how your two homes will work and back it up with action.

4. Reassure your children that although there will be changes in your family life and that it will take time for all of you to get used to these new ways, after a time, things should turn out well. Explain to them that you may all have times when you feel confused, perhaps sad or angry, but that all of you will have happy times too.

5. Show by your actions that you and the other parent can cope, that you are the grown-ups and are in control of what is happening to your family. A regular routine and house and safety rules are important ways to restore order.

6. Listen to your children's opinions and whenever possible give them options. When children are consulted on family matters they seem happier, act more confident. You are responsible for the final decisions, but your children should be heard.

7. Be honest with your children; demystify the process with concrete information about the change that is simple, brief, and appropriate to their age.

8. Never threaten your children with abandonment, not even in hopes that it will make them obey you. It is dirty fighting on your part, unnecessarily frightening (they have already lost one parent, would they lose another, too?) and can lead them to disrespect you and your tactic.

9. Don't lead children to believe that you and the other parent will reconcile unless this is a strong possibility. Fostering false dreams of reuniting their parents in that original close family feeling is *not* a help to their readjustment to this new life.

10. Find comfortable ways to show affection for your children. Hold them on your lap, or hold their hands, touch them, give them spontaneous

happy hugs, have loving eye contact. Words are not enough; follow or accompany them with affection. This human warmth and comfort is a vital physical communication that brings its own special kind of reassurance for both of you.

11. Reconfirm your assurances frequently during the first year and even into the second year after separation. Such reassurances are part of their feelings of security—especially actions and affection that say you are glad to be their parent, that you love them, and that they will be taken care of.

12. Check yourself occasionally to see how heavily you may be leaning on your children for *their* support. While you have a right to your children's respect and love, they are not adults and do not have the same emotional resources or experiences that you do. Repeatedly ask yourself, "Who is reassuring whom?"

13. Don't outlaw crying or honest display of emotions for your children or yourself. Crying is natural and offers release when it is spontaneous and follows appropriately on hurts, frights, or spats.

14. Enjoy your children, have some family fun times. In the midst of all the do's and don'ts and new pressures, take time just to relax together or play together. Laughter is a great healer and it nearly always gives a new perspective. The years together will go by quickly enough and these fun times will be part of your treasure.

15. Trust yourself and your instincts. Trust in your children, have confidence in their ability to change and learn. You are the best judge of what is best for you and for your children. If you have restored order to your household, have done your two-home groundwork, and established safety rules and house rules, you have already gone a long way in demonstrating your love for your children and in caring for their needs.

Keep Children out of the Middle

Divided Loyalties: Whom Do You Love Best?

Your children love both of you. You are their parents, and we have seen how hard it is for them to understand what has happened to your love for each other. If we think of ourselves as part our mother and part our father, it may be easier to see how conflicting and frightening it can be to have one part inside of us hate the other part that is also inside. So if you ask your children to believe that you are the injured parent, or good guy, while the other one is the persecutor, or bad guy, you are asking the children to distrust and dislike another part of themselves. Children don't want to choose sides, any more than they want to have an internal battle.

Children usually pick up covert signals given by anxious, angry parents about who loves whom best. Overheard phone conversations are common channels for this information. "My daughter and I can be talking on the phone, laughing about her day," said one father, "and then, wham! Her attitude and tone of voice change right in the middle of a sentence. She becomes suddenly reserved and cool, acts like she is bored with our conversation. Then I find out that her mother has walked into the room during our conversation." This daughter is changing her attitude toward her father in midstream for her mother's benefit. Perhaps by acting bored she hopes that Mom won't ask any questions about Dad or become jealous that she is sharing her day with her Dad. The daughter is reassuring Mom.

Children often say and do what they think their parents need to hear and see. Children love their parents and they want to protect them, make them happy and keep their love, even at their own expense.

The Old Family Feeling and the Kids

Nature has equipped children with phenomenal powers of observation and mimicry, abilities that allow them to learn about life. They instinctively know what gets your goat, what pleases you, and what gives you (and them) a feeling of love, acceptance, and approval. They know the behaviors that will spark your deeper emotions and responses.

The old family feeling is one children may naturally attempt to re-create *after* the separation, even to their own detriment. Why? Because divorce makes many children feel alone and left out. The old family feeling is familiar to them, it feels like home, and most of all they know *how* it works. They may not yet know how a calmer, more positive atmosphere works in a two-home situation. They don't yet have a new family feeling. So, in an attempt to keep any kind of continuity, they may be instigators of friction between the parents—by carrying tales like: "Daddy says you drink too much," or "Mommy says she can't trust you." Or they may mimic the other parent's words, tone, and inflection.

Re-creating the *old* family feeling is common during the first two years and is often unconsciously encouraged by parents who put children in the middle. It's helpful to remember at these times that:

1. children want a family feeling and *until a new one is well established, they will often try to re-create the old one;*
2. children want both parents;
3. children may do things they feel will please each parent (such as information passing, hassling, or ignoring one parent);
4. children may feel responsible for their parents' behavior and may try to "help" by being mediators or catalysts.

One surefire way to maintain the *old* family feeling and to delay developing new family styles is to put the children in the middle. Parents can use children as messengers: "Tell your father that his support check is overdue." As tale carriers: "Mom said she thought you drank too much." As informants: "Is your mother's new boyfriend sleeping over at night?" And as accomplices in secrets: "Don't tell your father that we bought this new TV set." Many parents fall briefly into such behavior at one time or another. But these are bad habits for everyone, especially children.

Besides, a second-hand message is rarely delivered exactly as you intended nor received in the manner you hoped. On top of it all, the messenger (your child) usually gets the static. "Your mother is asking me for a support check already?" Dad may storm, glaring at Junior. "What does she think I am anyway, a money machine?"

If you have a worry about the other parent or a question, go directly to the source—the other parent. Don't involve your child in your worry by asking the child to get information for you.

The tendency to blame the other parent for the child's behavior appears in some family feelings, too. Such blame games can lead to disputes between parents when one believes the other is encouraging the children's absences. It can also lead to estrangements between the second-home parent and the child when perhaps each one accuses the other of being uncaring and insensitive or each withdraws in silent hurt and resentment. In such a situation the child can often get his way—he doesn't go to the second home, doesn't see the other parent, doesn't make other arrangements, and instead leans on the primary-home parent to make it up to him. When parents are overwhelmed with feelings of guilt and fears of losing their children's love, they may be afraid to discipline them or to be the cause of any disappointment. In such circumstances, children learn how to be manipulative.

"I Lost Respect for My Parents"

Regardless of the parents' marital status, children usually hate being in the middle. Some children describe solemnly to me how they have to say things for a parent because that's the way they are called "good." Other children seem initially to enjoy the power of the messenger position, but quickly learn that the middle position is a losing one and that they can be used unfairly. One teenager expressed it this way: "I love my parents, but I don't respect them and how they treat one another. They argue about things and they expect me to be part of that argument one way or another. At first, when I was younger, I felt important and needed. Now it's just obnoxious. They are always asking, 'What did your Mom say?' 'What did your Dad say?' It's just a hassle and I'm pulling out of it. But I worry that they'll be really mad at me if I do." This teenager has valid fears. Parents who need an audience for their disagreements or want the child in the middle are unhappy when a child refuses to act out their scripts as the middleman. Such parents rarely succeed in working out a two-home arrangement for their children.

Some present-day adults who were once children of divorce look back in revulsion over their parents' immature behavior and addiction to negative attachment. Several of these adults have described to me how they quietly but deliberately chose schools thousands of miles from home, took summer jobs that kept them away from parents, and eventually established their own marriages and family lives in places where they did not have to be near their own parents.

"I was so disgusted with them," said one man of his own childhood experiences with his divorced parents' battles, "that I just decided the hell with them. They will never again get close enough to me to use me like they did."

There are simple ways parents can keep their children out of the middle. These are the same guidelines that also aid people in settling the emotions of divorce.

1. *Don't badmouth the other parent in the children's presence or where they might overhear you.*

2. *Do not participate in your children's angry feelings about the other parent.* Let them blow off steam but don't add water to their boiler, even though at the moment you might want to.

3. *Encourage your children to speak about their difficulties with the other parent to the other parent, and decline to give them advice.* Suggest the names of close friends of the other parent if they need more "talking out" time. Children need adults who are safe to confide in.

4. *Go directly to the other parent for information or an answer.* Do not put your child in the middle, even if he or she wants to be there. Keep your communications direct.

5. *Do not ask your children about the other parent's life or circumstances. Give the other parent's motives the benefit of the doubt.* Review Chapters 8 and 9 for ways to proceed.

Garden-Variety Complaints

The Schedule

The schedule between Mom's house and Dad's house serves many purposes. It is a basic framework for making family plans, for ordering a week's time; it can lend a sense of security and continuity, of order, and symbolize the parents' new united front. So if all this can be true, why do some people hate schedules so much?

First, many people hate to be inconvenienced, uprooted, or regimented. They hate it most when they have no say in the matter. Divorce can force this situation on people and a schedule can symbolize it all. When people have little or no opportunity to help make decisions that will affect their lives, they can feel powerless, worthless, angry, and frustrated. When a court decision, for example, forces parents into visitation arrangements in which they have had no say, they sometimes declare, "They are my children, I'll see them whenever I want to!" Parents who make decisions about their children's lives without consulting them force their children to have many of these same feelings. One sixteen-year-old, left out of decision-making about his time at his mom's house, exploded, "She's my mother and I'll see her anytime I want to," adding, "and you can't stop me."

The moral of all this is if you want a schedule to be useful and positive—ask your children what *they want* and then ask them *how their plan would work*. Then, when it comes to making decisions about them, take as many of their needs and wishes into account as humanly possible. The teenager who exploded, once given the opportunity to say what he wanted and how it could work, described how he wanted to stop by Mom's house on his way to school in the morning, to call her anytime he wanted, to spend more (or less) time if he wanted. He didn't want absolute veto power as his parents had feared, just a chance to negotiate on his own behalf. His parents agreed to his requests in principle, but how would it work out in real life? Dad was willing to have his son phone Mom anytime he wanted, to stop by at her house, even to spend extra overnights, just as long as his son checked in with him when he wanted to stay past a certain hour. Mom now had to make plans with her son alone. But both parents insisted that when their son wanted to change weekend plans, they each be consulted with plenty of prior notice.

A successful schedule is often one that is adaptable. During the first two years, two-home ground rules and times at each home usually need to be clearly written. Everyone needs to know what they can count on, at minimum. But flexibility is also necessary. Seasoned two-home parents, long accustomed to negotiating changes in plans, often report that while they have a schedule, they may not always follow it. By mutual agreement, parents and children make changes as the need arises. But these parents also state that schedules and agreements are important bases for smooth changes and for their businesslike communications style. As one mother put it, "If things ever get tense again, we can fall back on the schedule as is. We know it's fair and it's safe."

Both children and parents need to feel they can have spontaneous, even daily contact with one another, whether or not they take advantage of it. One second-home father talked about how much he missed this unstructured time now. "When I was married, the kids and I would pass one another on the front walk, exchange comments, perhaps talk for a few minutes over a drink in the kitchen. When you don't live together full time, you can lose this." Frequent phone calls, brief stops before or after school or work, the opportunity to negotiate for more time together are all crucial factors that contribute to maintaining that special bond. Do not underestimate their importance to you or your child.

The problem with this unstructured contact is that it often happens during the other parent's time of responsibility or authority. While phone calls or dropping by Dad's or Mom's office after school are rarely unacceptable to the other parent, dropping by unannounced at the other home or picking up a child from school or the sitter without notice can cause problems—especially the first year. Parents need to agree on what is considered acceptable unstructured contact and what needs the other parent's say-so.

Finally, some extra words of caution: flexibility means that, by mutual agreement, plans can change. It does not mean that capricious cancellations or no-show behavior are acceptable. *If you are due to pick up your child at a specific time and you do not show up at all, you risk hurting your child deeply.* Too many times I've heard parents tell of watching their child sitting outside on the doorstep or by a window waiting for a parent who never came. The pain children bear and the rejection they suffer when this happens are devastating. If you say you are going to be there, or if it is on your schedule, please, *please* follow through. Be on time, be back on time, and if you are late or need to cancel, make substitute plans immediately, giving your child reasons for the change. The same principles hold true for both parents. A parent who forgets to have a child home in time for the other parent's arrival, or who cancels out at the last minute, or who sits on the fence about a proposed schedule change undercuts a child's trust and self-esteem. Children, especially during the first year of separation, need parents who follow through with plans. Your child's sense of trust, of security, and of being worthy of being loved is at stake.

"I Don't Want to Go to Mom's/Dad's House"

Children, especially teenagers, may say they are too busy or too involved to go to their second home. "I don't want to go," "There's nothing to do," "It's no fun there," or even "I don't *want* to be there."

Reluctance to go to the other home or unhappy returns from one home to the other are common the first year or so. Children go through their own emotional wounding and healing process and having to say hello to one parent and goodbye to another during all this is not easy for them. It reminds them that what they don't have is what they want most—both parents living together. Furthermore, since their parents' retreat from negative intimacy is not yet complete, children feel many feelings of guilt or disloyalty, somehow feeling responsible for their parents' behavior. It's hard for children to separate how they feel from what their parents feel, especially when parents are unhappy with one another. Yet, over the next few months and years, this separation will be an important and necessary accomplishment for them.

Tune into your children and see why they may not want to be with one parent or why they need to reassure the parent that they are leaving. Sometimes children feel anger, shame, or resentment toward their parents, embarrassed or disgusted about how they now live or act. A mother once good for giving advice may now seem more like a woman in need of advice herself. "I don't like the way my mother looks now." "Dad acts like he's a teenager instead of a father." Parents do change after divorce and children may resist adjusting to their parents' new routine, style of dressing, activities, or social circle. A new lover often upsets teenagers. "I'm not coming to your house as long as you have a woman there," a fourteen-year-old son might say to a father. Is the son upset with his father's new behavior? Or is he competing with him? Is he unable to watch his father with a woman who is not his mother? Is the son caught in that classic father-son tug-of-war often seen in the teen years? These are common questions posed during the first years of separation, and only the people involved can answer them. It also happens that children are sometimes reluctant to go to a parent's home because they will have to share him or her with a friend, a lover, or a job. It hurts to miss a parent when apart only to find that when together, someone or something else is playing the leading role.

Children do have their own lives, and the older they get, the more separate and independent they become. How many never-divorced parents have heard their teenagers say, "I don't want to go to Uncle or Aunt so-and-so's place for dinner—it's boring there." When parents live separately, the script is the same, but the object of complaint is now a parent, most often the one who especially needs to feel wanted, loved, and valued.

The second-home parent can be a sitting duck for an all-or-nothing reaction to the "I-don't-want-to-go" wail. When second-home parents tell about how their children refused to come and live with them during regularly scheduled time, they show feelings of anger, hurt, and rejection. Some are ready to retaliate with, "I don't want you, either." When primary-home parents tell of the child's reluctance or refusal to go to their other home, there is sometimes a tone of triumph in their voice when they say, "They just don't want to be with him/her. They want to stay with me." Sometimes they are bewildered. "Can I make her go to her father's if she doesn't want to?" Sometimes angry: "I planned a weekend with a new friend without children and now they won't go." It is as if some children say to their second-home parent, "Either make coming to your house worth my while, or I'll not come at all. If you force me to come, I'll be miserable and hard to handle and you will be sorry you didn't give me my way." Or, "you got a divorce, not me—this shifting around isn't for me at all. You pay the price."

When children are so out of control and angry, the second-home parent can admit to honest relief that the kid is *not* going to be there for three or four days. The "I-don't-want-to-go" power move is typical teenage behavior in any home, however.

The mother with the teenage son who says, "Mom, I can't go to Dad's house this weekend, I have a game," can hear him out for a minute and say, "Well, that's up to your Dad, not to me." If the son persists with "Dad won't listen to me, Mom," Mom can persist as well. "That's something you and your Dad have to work out, son. I can't speak for either you or your Dad—only you two can do that for one another." Son at this juncture may stomp out of the room saying, "Oh, forget it," and make that phone call himself to Dad or try a little guilt-induction with "You don't understand how awful it is for me" or any number of other maneuvers that are quite predictable. If that Mom runs interference for her son, she is putting herself back in the middle. No matter how much she may sympathize with her son's cry of "he doesn't understand me," she needs to remember that her objective is for the son to talk to the father directly. This is Dad's time and his decision. The son knows that, doesn't think Dad will cooperate with him, or just doesn't want to bother asking. Furthermore, to bring it up with Mom may offer him an edge in his particular rebellion, making Mom somehow responsible for (and guilty about) his behavior, his feelings, and his schedule. No matter how strongly the mother may inwardly agree with her son that the father's lack of tact, understanding, or ability to communicate (she did divorce him, after all), their arrangements fall outside her jurisdiction. Mother will not make the father perfect for the son, nor will the son make his eventual peace with his father's foibles or personality unless he puts out some effort. When he wants to put Mom in the middle, Mom should refuse.

The second-home parent must play a firm role when the child says, "I don't want to come to your house." Remember, the days that the child lives with you are *your* days of responsibility and authority. If your teenager wants to go surfing or off on a camping trip on your time together, it should be you who gives or withholds permission, not the other parent. If you say yes, you sign the emergency medical slips and you pick up at the bus stop. It is your time for supervision.

Maybe Dad doesn't want to share his son with a game or even with other family members. Perhaps he hasn't seen him in more than a month, misses him, and wants his company. He can say this simply and then stick to it. Perhaps the boy will be angry, disappointed, or even rebellious. Many a firm parent has found that a yelling, hurt teenager dissolved in tears and relief when that parent cared enough to stand his ground.

Parents need to clear up for themselves and for their children what part of the time together is negotiable and what is not. "Matthew is sixteen, he has his own life," said his father. "He can negotiate with me for Saturday nights out, using the car, and staying overnight with friends. He doesn't have any choice about whether or not this weekend is with me or not, though. He knows it is our time, even if sometimes I hardly see him." Matthew knows what to expect. He has the safety and comfort of his father's attention and authority, even if it's in that unconscious way that comes from sleeping in the same home for a few nights.

Second-home parents sometimes fear losing their children's love. They also miss them and are far more willing to respond to their requests than they might have been when they all lived together as a married family every day. Flexibility and support for a child's plans can be an especially rewarding way for parent and child to begin to get reacquainted and renegotiate their new relationship. But such accommodations should not be entered into out of fear of losing their love. If you are a second-home parent and your teenager lives a full and busy life that competes with your time together on weekends, don't always settle for the "convenient" thing and arrange for him to stay at his other house. You will miss the breakfast chatter and the surprise secret revealed while you exchange car keys. "He's never here, anyway," is not the point, Dad or Mom. *He* doesn't need to be home, *you* do. Those weekends when you hardly see your kid are still precious because that child is yours and if you are not sleeping under the same roof, you'll miss some opportunity, that brief glance or hug that means home and caring.

When a child is able to call all the shots about where he spends his time, many things can deteriorate over a period of time. The children, even teenagers, must learn how to check their plans with the appropriate parent as automatically as they put on a pair of shoes. This strengthens their relationship and teaches them the benefits of going directly to the source and, if necessary, how to compromise.

In many ways, parenting after divorce is the same as never-divorced parenting. Children seek limits, question standards, test and retest their elders, and absorb values regardless of their parents' marital status. And during a family's history there are normal stages of growth for both the children and parents regardless of family circumstances. Children grow up and parents grow older. This is the same process for everyone.

Differences between divorced and never-divorced parenting do exist. But the first question a parent should ask when difficulties arise is, "Does this type of thing happen in never-divorced families, too?" Often the answer will be "yes." Some never-divorced parents say, "I have a hard time controlling my preschooler." Other never-divorced parents say, "I feel awkward trying to talk to my children about the facts of life." Such situations are common and have little to do with whether Mom and Dad are married, single, or remarried. So, when a problem arises concerning the children, don't automatically assume that it is caused solely by the divorce. Instead, first ask yourself these questions:

1. Does this type of thing happen in never-divorced families, too?
2. What part of the situation may be due to our personalities and our unique family style?
3. What part of the difficulty may be due to outside influences—friends, school, TV, the neighborhood?

After you have looked at those possibilities, then ask yourself:

4. What part of the problem may be due to the changes brought about by the divorce (or remarriage)?
5. What part of the problem may be due to the way we parents are relating to each other or putting our children in the middle?

There may be problems that will need a professional consultation. Don't wait for problems to become serious before you act. A social worker, psychologist, or counselor can advise you on what steps you can take to ease your situation for the better.

Many everyday problems with children respond to genuine love and common sense. Trust yourself and your instincts and . . . enjoy your children.

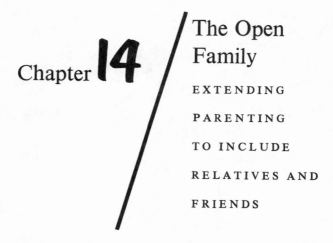

Chapter 14

The Open Family

EXTENDING

PARENTING

TO INCLUDE

RELATIVES AND

FRIENDS

"I had to fill out one of those emergency cards for David at nursery school today," one father told me with unconcealed pleasure. "When I came to those three lines where you list people to call in case you can't be reached, it really hit me how my life has changed since the days I was married. Then I would have had to really search around wondering whom I could 'impose on' for my son. Maybe there'd be each of the grandparents and the lady up the street. But now, after four years as a single parent, I can list at least twelve families I know who would be there for David if he needed them. Now, that's a real community."

David's father had a closed-family system when he was married. Now that he is divorced he has chosen to develop an open-family system. An open family is a network of people who know one another, give and get things from one another, spend time together, and in general act toward each other as the social beings they are. Friends, neighbors, associates, and other families are involved with David's family, and his family is involved in their lives as well.

An open family can be limited to a circle of people such as neighbors who are not necessarily close friends in the usual sense of the word but who support one another in material, emergency, and child-rearing tasks. The open family can also be close knit and intimate like an extended family. Five, six, or more families interweave their lives, tasks, and activities around one another redefining and maintaining standards, providing interpretations to everyday events, and in general providing a buffer to the outside world.

Our links to others can be made up of co-workers, old and new friends, relatives, and neighbors. The network can be formal, informal, of long or short duration. But the significance of the network cannot be underestimated. When a person can call out in time of personal need and be assured of assistance in the form of funds, emotional or practical aid, help or advice with the kids, or perhaps the daily demands of living, a sense of security and well-being can't help but be enhanced.

The more supportive a network is to a parent, the more confident that person will feel as a parent. To the extent that a person's sense of competence as a parent affects how he or she behaves toward the children, it also follows that the kind of people Mom or Dad has as friends affects the children's personal adjustment. Studies and common sense both show that when parents feel good about themselves and their lives they usually have children who feel competent and self-assured as well. It's no accident that many single parents who seek counseling two or three years after their divorce is final are frequently parents who have closed families.

Over the course of history people have always banded together to give each other mutual support or protection. This process can be especially crucial when a big life change such as ending a marriage disrupts or fragments close relationships or a way of life. While old bonds can be strengthened, it is also likely that new ones can form. New standards need definition. The open family provides the validation for these new and necessary standards. Your new friends, along with some trusted old standbys, can be the soundingboards you need.

Common Barriers to Open Families

The idea of an open-family style often delights and enchants people. But when they ask "How is it done?" or "What do people do?" some find that certain attitudes and past beliefs stand in their way. Here are some of the most common barriers:

MAKING IT ALONE This is a traditional do-it-yourself approach. The original ideal of family includes only mother, father, the children, and maybe—but only maybe—a grandparent or one uncle or aunt. For this making-it-alone view of the family, the fewer people a tight nuclear family unit depends on the better. Ideally, those rugged individuals are so strong and independent that they never have to say to anyone but a mate or child, "Help" or "I need a friend." In this version they only need one another. For those who want to remain ruggedly independent, uneasy feelings are associated with being a joiner or being part of a group. "I don't want a person to tell me his troubles," people say, "I've got enough of my own."

The difficulty with this closed system is that families have many personal needs, many responsibilities, and too little time for fun and for enjoying one another. For some families it becomes a merciless cycle where there are too many needs and too few people to meet them. If such isolation continues over a very long time, family members become afraid to deal at all with the outside world, victims of excessive internal dependency. Sometimes quarrels become extreme and physical violence a way of life.

A family's closed ranks may be a healthy response to the challenge to new and sometimes threatening situations. But, later, as the family settles down, it can relax and open itself to the advantages of the outside world.

What sometimes happens, however, is that the family members are unaware of the ways and means available to them to establish an open-family style. "I've been in a closed-ranks position so long," said one father, "I've forgotten how to be any other way." A closed system may have its disadvantages, but it is familiar and he knows exactly what to expect. An open-family style, on the other hand, may be one that he will have to teach himself to develop.

THE ONE-HOME-ONE-AUTHORITY BELIEF   How often this one-home-one-authority belief surfaces! In this case, it takes form in the idea that not only should parents present a united front, but that the child should not have any other significant influence in his or her life. "I don't want anyone's ideals to influence my child except my own," some parents say.

Such an attitude pretends the child is under a bell jar, untouched by the outside world and other people. The parents expect to provide everything the child needs. While an actualized control over a child's environment and influences is rare, the feeling that a parent *should* have such total control is surprisingly common. Sometimes, the bell jar is seen as providing an environment where the parent is the total executive orchestrating the child's world. The parent-executive usually feels totally responsible for the child's relationships, behaviors, and development. This parent is often prey to feelings of guilt and of a sense of parental failure that are hard to share with other parents.

Fear of Imposing upon Others

Old habits of reserve can be very powerful deterrents to building an open family. I've heard many horror stories told by parents faced with accidents, serious illness, or sudden calamity who had no one to turn to. These parents were unwilling to impose on neighbors or acquaintances, so they struggled through endless hours of aloneness, fear, and even danger. But their isolation and lack of help were usually avoidable. Louise, for example, told a workshop group of the time her young son had required hospitalization in the middle of the night because of a serious asthma attack. She left her two other children, aged two and four, alone asleep and rushed her son to the hospital emergency room. Ada, an acquaintance who lived two blocks away from Louise and also a member of the group said, "You should have called me. I would have stayed with the babies." Louise replied that she didn't want to impose on Ada in the middle of the night. When I asked Louise if she would call Ada tonight if the same thing happened again, Louise answered honestly that she would still be reluctant to disturb Ada's sleep to help her and her children out even in an emergency.

Mr. Right and Ms. Wonderful

To many newly divorced parents, the search for new social relations is limited to a search for a new mate. Every new person they meet is evaluated as to whether or not he or she is a potential lover or can help in the search for a new lover. But building a network or friendship circle is not an adolescent dating situation. If you are constantly asking yourself whether this new person is a potential mate every time you meet someone new, you will not be able to see the other qualities the person has. Standards for a mate are usually high, often too complicated for friendship. "Too young," "too old," "he's a doctor and I'm a programmer," "she's too plain," "he's too macho" are quick judgments made by some singles when identifying the mate potential in another. But are these same standards realistic when considering a new acquaintance or friend? Just because a person is not attractive as a mate does not mean he or she is not companionable, sensitive, helpful, or fun-loving. To build an open family, you need to shift your emphasis from finding a lover to connecting with new acquaintances. Don't let the search for Mr. Right or Ms. Wonderful keep you from building your own circle of good friends.

Discouragement, the First Year

Building an acquaintance or open family takes time, a commodity always in short supply; it is especially scarce during the first year after separation. Some single parents reported that while they often made three good friends that first year, others came more slowly. The time and effort you spend will often seem one-sided. "I seem to be making all the efforts," some people complain. Laments about time, work, fatigue, and the absence of baby-sitters are common. These words often mask inner reservations. What many parents really mean is: "What guarantee do I have if I make the effort? The risk is high; what if I'm rejected? I don't want to be disappointed. I don't want to cope with other people's problems, and besides, I feel guilty about leaving my children. Yet I want friends."

If this could be you, just try to remember that the time and effort you do spend during that first year will most probably pay off in a year or two, three, or four.

Your Own Needs and Personal Style

An open family with friends and relatives is not just for the kids' bene-fit, it's for the grown-ups. Sometimes the people who become close to your children are your close friends too, but they can also be acquaintances whom you know and trust but with whom you are not close.

Take a look at the following questions. First, answer them for your-self, then go back and answer them for *each* of your children.

A Self-Survey

A. Whom Do You (Parent) Count On?

1. If some calamity such as a severe auto accident were to befall you, whom would your family immediately call on to help out while you were out of commission?
2. How many other families could your children stay with if you suddenly had to go out of town tomorrow for three days? Would there be more places for the children to stay if you could give two weeks' notice?
3. Who besides yourself could talk to your children like an aunt or an uncle if you needed some adult support with a problem at school or in the neighborhood?

B. What Is Your Personal Style? (Parent)

1. When you are lonely and feeling blue, do you have a friend or set of friends to talk with? Do you want to be by yourself or participate in some activity to take your mind off of your troubles?
2. If you want to relax and have fun, with whom do you share this time? With your children, your friends, other family, neighbors, or usually alone or with one other person?
3. Who shares your holidays, such as the Fourth of July or birthdays?

Look at your answers to A. Ideally, you could have some immediate family and some other family friends or acquaintances who could step in in an emergency or who could (and would) feel comfortable with your children over a weekend period. Furthermore, to have other adults your child can trust and confide in is also a healthy expansion of a child's world. If you have such options you probably already have (or have the makings of) an open family. If you do not have such alternatives, you may have a more closed-family system.

In B, when it comes to your own feelings and private life, do you de-pend on yourself, perhaps on one other person and your children for support or fellowship? If so, yours may be a closed-family system, but you may also be a person who prefers to live quietly and privately.

What was your human-income score back in Chapter 6? Was it well over 100 or was it hovering around 90 or 80 or even lower? If you had a high score, was it high because you had people you could count on? Your answers can give you another indication of your open or closed style.

If you feel you have an open family now that you can reinforce and enrich, the next few pages will seem old hat to you. But if you do not feel you have an open family but are interested in exploring what this might mean to you and your children, you will find some simple ways to begin.

How to Begin the Acquaintance and Neighborhood Network

An acquaintance network is essentially low voltage, requiring no emotional disclosure. Asking for information is very different from asking for time or effort, and most people are glad to share. Requesting the name of a good family doctor is not exactly an emotional overture, yet it makes a liaison that establishes you in the fellowship of neighbors, particularly if you call later and report a successful contact.

Take a look at the following lists and picture yourself asking nearly everyone you meet or know at least one of the following questions, each beginning with, 'Whom would you recommend as a _____?" For example, "Whom would you recommend as a good foreign car mechanic?" "Could you recommend an exercise class?" "Could you recommend any of the neighborhood groceries for fresh mushrooms?"

"Whom could you recommend as—
1. A doctor, a dentist, an attorney, a tutor? (the professionals)
2. A dance studio, sports leagues, discussion groups, classes? (activities that can make life more pleasurable)
3. Schools, teachers, supplies, clothing, day care, baby-sitters, public transportation, etc.? (children's needs)
4. A good mechanic, a good place to shop for groceries, dry goods, children's clothes, etc.? (the nitty-gritty of daily life)
   Also ask about
5. The "neighborhood watch," issues that affect everyone on the block, emergency procedures?
6. Referrals re: jobs, discussions, feedback, etc.? (the work world)

After trying this approach for several months some people say, "I didn't realize that I didn't have to tell anyone my private business in order to develop a network and a sense of belonging."

When the exchange of information and request for recommendations lead to casual conversations, acquaintanceship can sometimes blossom to friendship. Giving an acquaintance a lift home from the car repair shop, picking up his package at the post office while you get some stamps for yourself, sharing names of doctors, dentists, and places to shop all build trust and caring.

An acquaintanceship expands to friendship, spontaneous pot-luck suppers or birthday parties appear, often drawing in more new acquaintances. Your children meet. Perhaps they play together for longer and longer periods of time. Then they ask to sleep over. All these steps happen naturally enough.

Some of the Many Ways Open Families and Acquaintance Networks Begin

Once parents begin thinking about their connections with other people in families, they find connections all around. It's like finding a four-leaf clover. When you find one, you're in the middle of a patch.

"I started thinking about this open-family business," said Frank, father of two teenage sons. "After I took stock of whom I could count on, I realized that we have a ready-made one now because of our soccer league parents. We met one another naturally at games and the boys really got on well. You know how kids are. Pretty soon one or the other of their soccer buddies is coming along on a weekend we go out of town, or they are invited to go somewhere with another family. When I started counting, I found three other families the boys could spend three days with on ten minutes' notice."

Frank had not become good friends with the other parents over the last two years of the soccer league, but he did trust them with his sons. One of the fathers had some business in common with Frank, and they sometimes had lunch, but the open family was one the boys had built themselves. I asked Frank if any of the parents provided a confidential ear for his sons. He answered, "I honestly don't know. If they do, I'm for it because they are really fine folks. But I never even thought to think about it." When I asked Frank about his own circle of friends, he answered, "I kept most of my friends from the marriage. I have a lot of people I have known for many years, but they aren't especially interested in children."

Some people say their open families began because their neighborhood was so friendly. Others talk about some neighborhood crisis that brought them together. In a neighborhood, the least people can do for one another is to look out for one another's safety and interest. For some areas, "neighborhood watch" refers to property, but when you have children, it should refer first to caring about the kids.

In one community, a small group of single mothers canvassed their five-block area to count the other single parents. They found thirty! Were they interested in forming a twenty-four-hour emergency service so that those who needed help would know the names of neighbors close by?

Most of the parents agreed willingly. Many had found that living alone and without friends had made it almost impossible to deal with emergency situations.

Caring About Other People's Children: How to Give What You Get

"Carla came bounding in from the Datterleys' house saying Mrs. D was going to teach her how to sew if it was all right with me," reported Carla's mother, a mother of five. "It was fine with me. The more people loving and caring for my kids the better I like it. Furthermore, the Datterleys are a blended family and Carla can see firsthand what happens in some families after remarriage. I bless the day those people moved in down the street because they are showing my kids graphically that there are other stages beyond the divorce stage that we're in now." Children such as Carla are getting new points of reference, an added sense of security, and another instance of how continuity in families can be maintained. Families such as the Datterleys are generous people. They share their lives with other people and other people's children. They don't see time with other people's children as a duty, a favor, or a baby-sitting. Mrs. D genuinely related to Carla, who glowed from her warmth. Children are fortunate when they find such an adult friend.

Have You Hugged a Kid Today?

You can duplicate this kindness with your friends' children and be a friend for a child. This relationship is not baby-sitting but has its own intrinsic value. Welcoming your friend's child while you play, relax, or work is a traditional way adults have transmitted skills to children while enjoying the human interchange. Both generations have their worlds expanded and sometimes, as trust grows, children will disclose parts of themselves to you—their adult friend—away from the day-to-day interaction of their homes. You need not meddle or give advice. Instead, be a good ear or judiciously share your own experiences. Many parents have recounted how a small friend has given them insight into their own situation. Here's an example of how it works for some parents.

"My little friend John came over to help me polish my car," said a father about an eight-year-old neighbor child. "As he worked alongside me, I found myself far more patient with him than I was with my own children. He began to show up more often after that, for about an hour or so at a time. Eventually he asked me why daddies sometimes go away and don't phone or call children. I knew his dad had not dropped out, and I didn't at first know what to say. I did tell him that I had a time a while back when I didn't call my children because I was so sad and lonely. I wondered why he hadn't asked his own father but didn't want to meddle. Then, I began to wonder why my children had never asked me that question. I initiated conversations with my own kids after that about how they had felt. I found that there were still some unfinished feelings."

Sometimes parents are suspicious of adults who befriend their children. This is often just a normal protective reaction and usually fades away as soon as the adults meet and get to know something about one another. It is wise to keep this reaction in mind, however, and not rush things along. Being an adult friend for a child is not grounds for surrogate parenting, nor should it be a challenge to the natural parent's role or authority.

Many children who have adult friends do not share private feelings or thoughts with them. Instead, times together may be to show off a new skill, to ask for a drink of water, or just a quiet time of occasional companionship while the adult washes a window or waters the lawn. Later, if the relationship between you and the family develops further, you might become part of one another's acquaintance network, or even join an open-family network. You might even become closer to your young friend, gradually becoming an adopted uncle or aunt. Each relationship with a child can have its own special qualities. Many parents speak of brief contacts over a week's time with other people's children who come in for hugs and affection, youngsters who want physical contact with a safe and warm adult. The need, hope, and thirst for human affection run deep. Children have much to teach adults about directness, spontaneity, and a sense of wonder. When we limit our involvements to children who call us Mom or Dad, we limit ourselves.

When There Is No Other Parent

Doris and Harry are the names I've given to describe two common types of parents whose former spouses have totally dropped out. These are parents who are going it alone.

Doris had hoped that since the children's father did at least make contact with them on their birthdays and was faithful in sending the support checks that she would eventually be able to develop a working relationship with him. She had taken many of the steps necessary to develop a working relationship.* Doris's efforts had brought her a release from her former anger and resentment, but they had not brought back the children's father. Despite her good efforts and some eased tensions, the children's father did not choose to become reinvolved with the children. She finally said, "Dead or alive, he's gone."

Doris began to turn her energies toward reinforcing her already func-

* These steps are described in more detail in Appendix I.

tioning open-family system and to beginning a shared parenting relationship with a close woman friend, Alice.

Doris and Alice took several steps. They first agreed to be second mothers or "aunts" to each other's children, even though both sets of children have at least three other homes open to them. Alice (now Aunt Alice) insisted that she have a clear understanding with Doris regarding what she would and would not do as an aunt. She did not want Doris to interfere in her relationship with her children. Alice said, "I want the principles of two-home parenting to apply to our situation. What she does with her kids on her time, in her house, is her business. We will be sharing information with one another," she said, "but we won't be puppets for one another." Each mother wanted her own direct relationship with the other children. In return, they wanted their own children to have the same experience. The two women settled their few basic rules and jotted them down. They were on their way to another form of cooperative parenting.

The situation Harry typifies was somewhat similar to Doris's in that his son's mother had dropped out four years ago and he had never received any communications from her. Harry had no hopes that his former wife would ever again re-enter his son's life. In contrast to Doris's more gregarious personal style and her relish for an open-family system, Harry was a loner and probably would continue to be so. His approach toward an open family was to give his son the opportunity to develop a network as Frank's sons had. Harry made the opportunity available for his son while maintaining his own personal quiet style.

"I was surprised to see how I had insulated myself from others," said Harry. "I wanted to be by myself when I felt punk, I totally relied on Jay's grandmother for anything unusual that happened. I shared my birthdays with her, my son Jay, and Betsy, the woman I'm going with. I either went places alone or with Betsy." Harry's world suited him, but it wasn't especially helpful to his son or to him as a parent. Betsy was pleasant enough but not particularly interested in Jay. Harry was her focus. Grandma kept good contact with her grandson, but lived on the other side of town. Jay needed more places where he could stay over if an occasion arose, more people to give him a hug now and then, perhaps an uncle he could look up to and feel safe with.

Harry, for example, can give Jay the opportunity to meet other families by joining a father-son activity like Little League or some club like those found at Boys' Clubs or the YMCA. These are easy and fun ways for someone with Harry's more private life-style to meet other parents and children on safe, nondemanding terms. The schedules are structured, the activity supervised by other adults, and parents and children alike can make as much or as little of this focus as they wish. Jay can meet the kids and their parents with his father's blessing and scrutiny. Harry's initial presence is his stamp of approval that encourages his son. Once Jay gets started in such activities and becomes friends with some of the others, Harry's presence will be far less necessary. If Harry helps Jay make contacts with his new friends *outside* of the activity after a few meetings, he will be launching Jay on his own open circle of friends.

Solo parenting—where you are quite alone because the other parent has seemingly dropped off the face of the earth—is a common occurrence. Nevertheless, the children need education, affection, emotional and physical security, standards, and limits. The parents' needs are similar. Basic human needs are the same, whether there is one involved parent or two. All parents —married, single, remarried—can give their children second and third homes by developing a working relationship with a relative or close friend. The tie doesn't matter, the love and caring do.

Chapter 15

Long-Distance Parenting

HOW TO FEEL

CLOSE WHEN YOU

ARE FAR APART

"She's taking the kids to Michigan," cried Phil, a forty-four-year-old engineer, in fury and in fear, "she's taking them away from me! She knows damned well I can't hop a plane every other weekend or fly them out here to California. She's crazy to do this to the kids and me."

Phil knew about two homes. He had been a second-home parent for three years while he and the boys' mother had been living in the same city. He was shocked at the prospect of being separated from his sons by more than 2,500 miles, and he didn't know how he could continue his relationship over such a long distance. Perhaps even more threatening was his realization that his legal agreement had neglected to make his permission necessary for the other parent's out-of-state moves with the children. He had no formal or legal authority to block his former mate's decision to move with the boys to another state. He was angry, hurt, and frightened.

The First Big Move Away

Any major geographic change by one parent is going to affect the other parent, as well as the children. The change of residence brings a flashback to the uneven emotions of the original divorce, and can undermine any settled two-home arrangement and good working relationship. The same themes and behaviors that plagued the family at the time of the separation reignite. When one parent fears being denied rights to be with the children by a long-distance move, the flashback can be furious.

The following example of Nancy and Phil is a composite. It was designed to highlight the patterns of actions and reactions typical of families in such situations who successfully negotiated a two-home plan across many miles despite their fears and difficulties.

Phil's former wife Nancy had received a promising job offer. Accepting this offer meant a considerable advancement and she wanted very much to take it. But she had not warned Phil of the possible change in plans, nor reassured him of his continued role with the children. Her secretiveness had intensified his fears and distrust and he was frantic.

Although Nancy had been insensitive to Phil's vulnerability and possible reaction, she could now, by working out a new arrangement with Phil, reassure him of his role with his sons and of her good intentions. Nancy was sincere in her desire to continue the two-home arrangements for her sons and was willing to make changes and concessions to that end. But Phil was off-the-wall and Nancy was scared.

Air Feelings Safely

While Nancy and Phil have a series of important decisions and considerations, they first have to pay attention to their strong feelings if they hope to salvage a two-home arrangement over many miles. Wisely, this couple had placed a mandatory counseling clause in their legal parenting agreement for any issues in which they could reach no compromise alone, or for when things got out of hand. The family came into my office for their first appointment, fearful and filled with feelings ready to spill over into a family feud at any moment. The first set of meetings were reserved for feelings that need safe and structured expression. The practical decisions would be of little use when the emotional charge from the flashback phenomenon was so powerful. The parents—and for at least one meeting, the children—expressed their feelings about the impending move.

"You are the one who wants to move, so move yourself," said Phil. "Leave the boys with me. They have lived here all their lives and they feel secure here." Nancy expressed her apprehension about her move away from her home state and the rigors of a new job, but she also pointed out her need to advance her professional status. She had only been in the work world a few years, and at forty had had a late start. She couldn't pass this opportunity by. When Phil pressed her hard to stay in California, she countered with, "I don't have to answer to you to move to Michigan. I have every legal right to do this, with or without your cooperation."

Nancy had a tendency to pull out a trump card when she didn't know how to stop Phil's accusations and demands. She didn't really intend to pull a fast one on Phil nor to deny the children their father and a second home. She just didn't want to feel any more guilty than she already did.

But flashback emotions made dirty tricks seem very plausible. Once this flashback pitfall came out and was dealt with, both Nancy and Phil began to relax. They could now begin to review the many alternatives available in order to make two homes across many miles a reality.

Once the air cleared, Nancy could reassure Phil that she had no intention of torpedoing his second home and would be willing to have a supplementary legal agreement drawn up in Michigan that would assure him of that. Phil was able to reassure Nancy that he had no intentions of brainwashing the children into wanting to stay with him in their old home town. But he did want her to remember that they had an agreement that in a few years—regardless of where they lived—the boys would be living with him during the school years. Nancy responded by saying that it was because of this eventuality that she wanted the boys with her the school years ahead. Finally they began to get down to the actual practicalities of such a big change—the setting up of two homes over that long a distance.

Decisions for Parents

Parents like Nancy and Phil have to decide on some tough issues to cope with the circumstances of two homes divided by many miles.

1. Where will the children live:
   During the school year
   During the summer
   For long holidays?
2. Who will pay for travel:
   Both parents? In what proportions? What about rising costs? What priority will travel money have in family budgets? What happens if somebody fails to come through? Will older children contribute? Will certain money-conserving measures be written into the renegotiated agreement to ensure the lowest fares?
3. How long is too long for parent and child to be separated?
4. How will communications be handled:
   Between each parent and each child?
   Between parents?
5. Who will arbitrate disagreements over money or time, and how?

Following the easy ones first, hardest last rule, Nancy and Phil made several decisions during a short half-hour conference that began the second set of meetings set aside for negotiations. Costs of travel between the two homes would be first priority on both budgets, not to be changed short of major surgery or other specified emergencies. They looked at ways the second-home parent could communicate with the children (ways that are described later in this chapter) and agreed to continue giving one another total access to the children's school and health records. They further agreed that if one parent had the children during the school year, the other parent would have the entire summer and several weeks during the school year when there was Easter or spring vacation. Christmas holidays would be shared. They ended their first discussion with three solid decisions, specifically itemized. Before their next meeting, they would individually investigate travel costs between California and Michigan, and Nancy would have more information about the demands of her new job during the first six months.

The accomplishments of the first meeting usually help to calm things, and the next encounters are often surprisingly easy. Nancy had found that her job would be very demanding the first several months. She did want the boys to finish the school year at their old school, and she could use some free time to find new housing and to get adjusted. The boys, aged eleven and twelve, could live with their father then from early April till mid-August, when they would come to their mother in Michigan. Phil began to feel much better. The parents settled the hardest question of time division far more easily than the initial outbursts had suggested. The boys would go to Michigan for a two-week period as soon as school was out so they could see their mother, their new home, their neighborhood, and then return to Dad's house.

Nancy explained to Phil that since her sons would be living with their father in a few years, she cherished those years she had left of sharing day-to-day routines. The father could now better appreciate her feelings as a mother.

The Bottom Lines of Long Distances

There are two bottom lines to big geographic separations. First, distance feels final, and gives tangible proof that the parents are separated. If one member of the family has harbored, however unconsciously, a sense that the old family feeling or the old marriage was not finished, long distance will bring that hope painfully to the surface. Second, the physical separation hurts. Many miles means no way to hug, to brush back a forelock of hair, to drop in on football practice, or to watch a first book report being written. The parent separated from the child feels this pain and so does the child. Some children, veterans of this experience, can describe how it feels and they know about the money problems, painfully.

"It was not too bad when my dad lived in Seattle," said Robert, aged thirteen, who lived the school year with his mother. "That was only five hundred miles away. Now he's moved to Houston and I feel lonely." He touched his solar plexis. "Do you know about those lonely feelings?"

I nodded my head, touching my own place of knowing emptiness.

"Two of my children are 2,500 miles away, too."

"Then you know how it is. Right about two months since you've seen them last you get to miss them like crazy but you can't do anything," adding, "My dad and I are close, even though we don't see each other in the usual ways," he said.

When children separated by many miles from a parent show signs of strain, I ask them, "When will you see your mother (or father) next?" If they answer, "I don't know," I ask "What about letters?" Often they answer, "Sometimes I get a letter. I don't write much, and phone calls cost too much. Mom (or Dad) doesn't have much money."

Children can be adrift on their lonely feelings, not knowing when they will have that all-important contact with Mom or Dad. Parents can save their children unnecessary pain by staying in touch, by giving their children some idea when they will next talk on the phone or be together. Some parents do an excellent job of explaining why they are moving away and the place the children will have in the new house. But these same parents may not say *when* or *how* parents and children might reunite. The absence of even a tentative timetable can hurt.

Both parents and children need factual clarity during such times. A flexible but well-understood master plan and a set of parental priorities to make this plan work are basic to successful long-distance parenting. Even so, separation hurts, the wail of children on the telephone sobbing, "You are so far away and I can't hug you." The strain of such times can be balanced by a parent's ability to keep in touch during long stretches of separation. And parents can learn to express more openly their deep appreciation of shared times.

When the link holds, parents talk about breakthrough periods when, as one father put it, "You know inside that it's working out okay for everyone."

A Checklist: For the Parent Separated by Many Miles

1. Review Chapters 7 and 16 on the emotions of divorce. The move may cause a flashback bringing reminders and emotions of past difficulties.

2. Review Chapter 13 on children's fears and on needs during big changes. They need your reassurance as well as your permission to go with the other parent.

3. Tell your child when you will see him or her next (approximately), when you will talk to him, and how you will be in touch. Children need this continuity.

4. Explain why this move is happening.

5. Give your child immediate, tangible proof of your connection with

him or her—the phone call on arrival at the new place, the new phone installed in the child's room.

6. Make contact with the child's school; it is a way for you to know a little and care a lot about his world.

7. Brace yourself for possible reactions from your children. Remember that children past the age of eleven may have a harder time adjusting to new areas than those still in elementary school.

8. Plan from the beginning on the dollar costs and allocate enough money to make travel plans work.

9. Be conscious of how long is too long for parent and child to be separated.

The School-Year Parent

"In many ways, the move to Michigan was difficult," said Nancy, six months after her arrival. "I felt anxious, unbearably lonely at first. I missed the boys far more than I expected. But I also felt a tremendous surge of excitement, and it wasn't all the new job, either. I was relieved to start over again somewhere without the reminders of the past staring at me in that little California town. I loved the time alone and savored it, but was happy when the boys settled in for the school year with me."

Nancy's story reflects the common patterns parents experience after they replant themselves far away from the other parent and old surroundings. It feels like a fresh start. "No one knows about your past; they only know your present. It feels great," said one father.

"What I wasn't prepared for was how much the children would miss their old neighborhood, their father, and their old school," said Nancy. "It was exasperating. Some of their obstreperous behavior during the early weeks of the separation seemed to come back. The youngest became withdrawn and the oldest picked fights at school. I tried to remember that they were really feeling a huge change in their lives and that this would pass, but it was hard. And there was no Dad on the scene to help me out when the going got rough. It was day-in-day-out parenting without a break. I began to wonder what I had let myself in for. Then I became furious with their father. He must have put them up to this resistance so they would agitate to go back to the old hometown. I was back in the off-the-wall distrustful place of three years before."

Such experiences are common to many parents who make the move away with the children—the excitement, the newness, the delight, the release, and relief; and the stark reality of the children's see-saw behavior, happy one day, miserable the next, all without a day off.

The Summertime Parent: Communications—the Key

No matter who moves away, the parent separated by five hundred or five thousand miles cannot watch the children grow and develop day by day, nor be there to share those spontaneous moments that proximity allows. This absence is felt by both parent and child, so that frequent communications with phone calls, letters, snapshots, and tapes become especially important.

If you are parenting long distance, try *not* to dwell on the time you're *apart*. Obviously, the only solution is to find new ways to relate, to use time and communication avenues wisely and well, so that your children can know that you really *do* feel like their parent and that you are still a family.

THE MAILS   Short letters (with self-addressed stamped return envelopes) are an unbeatable bargain for continuity and contact with children. Many parents write letters laced with travelogs and weather reports, as well as impressions and feelings. The subjects need not relate directly to the parent-child relationship. It is enough to share some of your day-in, day-out life with them. Content of the letters depends on the ages of your children. Small children can't read, but they know when something comes that is *for* them, *from* you, whether it is a leaf, a picture cut from a magazine, or a drawing signed with your symbol or name, and the XXXs and OOOs of kisses and hugs.

I'm convinced that when children don't answer letters it's often because of the work of addressing and stamping envelopes. Enclose a stamped, addressed envelope with all your correspondence or, better yet, send them in batches. Small children love the independence that comes with putting a scrap of paper with their mark on it in your envelope and mailing it themselves! Then the child can answer your letter easily and independently without the cooperation of the other parent. Your relationship with your child is not the responsibility of the other parent, who should not have to provide nagging and postal service.

MAILS AND THE SCHOOLS   The same technique you use to establish communication with your children also succeeds with their school. Some parents initially wonder what good all this information can do when they are hundreds, even thousands, of miles away. First, you know what's happening and can ask intelligent questions of your child concerning events, school, and the like. Second, your child knows that you know and that you care enough to know. This is most important for his or her sense of your caring and of your continuing relationship. But what if one of your children begins to fail in school and bad reports arrive in the mail? Your involvement is already part of the solution. Even though long-distance parenting does bring a sense of helplessness about your child's day-to-day events, nevertheless your knowledge and attention, even from a distance, can be most reassuring to both your child and to the other parent.

THE THINKING BOX OR JOURNAL   When we tell our children who are far away that we are thinking of them, and that even though we are far away they have a home with us, we should back up our assurances with concrete proof.

In long-distance parenting, the phone and the mails are very important, but a journal and/or a "thinking box" are additional and natural ways to add physical proof. The thinking box is a collection of little things that show where your heart is. Extra postcards bought on a trip; samples of leaves from the tree in front of a particularly colorful place; a small piece of driftwood; a book; an idea you had, dated with time and place, put in a special box or container, awaiting the child's presence.

Some parents keep a journal, putting in written entries for the child now and then: "I saw a sixteen-year-old girl who looked like you. I wondered if in four years you would have your hair as long as she did. Did you know our Aunt Jane wore her hair like that—long and silken—until about a year ago?" A journal is a concrete way of imparting belonging, talking with your child, of keeping your child part of your daily life.

Parents who have been denied total access to their children can collect these treasures for the day when they will be united with their children. When the reunion comes, and it most often does, even if it is years later, these dated mementos stand as testimony of the parent's steadfastness and love and provide both parents and child with a vehicle for making up part of their lost time together.

TAPES, CASSETTES   A surprising number of children own tape cassette recorders. Making tapes and receiving them can be a lot of fun, and their friends can play, too. It's a bit more costly than the letters, and your children need to have access to a cassette tape recorder, but it works.

One child's lonely feelings were eased considerably when he decided to use his friend's tape recorder to make an hour's contact with his father. He even recorded interviews with his friends. His father was delighted with the tape, and a better communications system began to grow between them. The children's responses on the tapes are occasionally so raucous that parents are amazed that their children's antics could be so sophisticated. "It sounds like 'Laugh-In'!" said one parent. Some parents read their children bedtime stories, others read them the classics. One mother found that the sound of the absent father's voice on a tape made for their two-year-old was especially soothing for the child.

Long-Distance Sharing, Projects

When child and parent separated by miles make a date to watch the same TV programs, read the same article or newspaper, root for the same baseball team, these sentimental and spontaneous links give double pleasure. You can discuss them in letters, compare notes briefly on the phone, and use them as bridges when you first get together again.

More extended projects generate even more concrete evidence of family solidarity. I, for instance, have my daughter Amy's fish in my care, following her telephone instructions about new snails, food, and what to do with baby guppies.

People can communicate over long distance in as many ways as they can imagine and put into action. Parents and older teenagers, influenced by the instant travel on television and movie screens, sometimes assume that distance won't bother them or their missing family members. "I can't do anything about it anyhow," marks the attempts to be brave or to stay cool. These long-distance sharing projects can't beat a hug or a pat, but they can take on their own vitality and—what is most important— stand as concrete, retouchable, rereadable evidence of caring.

A Checklist: Long-Distance Communications

1. Continually reassure the child of your love, but do it in simple terms and gestures. The key here is to show *and* tell.
2. Call at least weekly, and if possible more often. Consider a private phone in the child's room just for your calls.
3. Set up a telephone signal so the child can let you know if he needs to talk to you.
4. Provide the child with stamped, self-addressed envelopes.
5. Use cassette tapes for correspondence, reading bedtime stories, etc. Mail pictures of your life and environment.
6. Use manila envelopes to collect things that remind you of the child.
7. Start a "Thinking of you" box—dated items, unmailed letters to give the child when reunited, if you're out of touch with him at present.
8. Make connections with the child's school and if possible with doctors and coaches.

Re-entry

Home for the Summer

"I stood waiting for them to get off that plane from New York," said the father of two teenagers, "thinking 'My God, I'm shaking with pure excitement. It's been six months since we've been together and finally, at long last, here we are.'"

The feelings of reunion are sweet. Those of parting again at the end of the summer, with another long expected absence, are wrenching. But as one mother put it, "What's the alternative? I won't go without seeing them. They are my family. It hurts, but we take the hurt of separation as part of what we have to put up with. It doesn't keep us from coming together again."

The practicalities of reunion need attention. Sheer nervous energy and the fatigue that follow the trip, if there has been a change in time zone, add to the physical strain. "The kids need a lot of rest those first few days," say parents; keep this in mind. Then, gradually, the reality of being with the other parent sinks in, and within a week or two they settle into the old routine. A word to the parent putting the child on the plane, train, or bus to the other home: Try to see that the child has had plenty of sleep and rest before the trip. The child's energy and excitement often mount before the trip, making the re-entry period more fatiguing. Transition anxiety need not be a negative thing, and does respond to rest and calming schedules rather than late hours and excess activities.

Re-read those parts about safety rules and house rules, and take the time to walk the neighborhood again with your children (Chapter 10). All these things make everyone feel at home and relaxed again.

Parting at summer's end can be hard. As one child said somberly, "The day you think will never happen is here." The hard reality of saying good-bye again for another two, three, or six months can be softened with phone calls on arrival and more frequent talks during the transition period of the next week.

Home for the School Year

The school-year parent has the routine and home-base of school. For the children, it's time to find out what other kids have been doing over the summer, and the child who has been away for the summer takes center-stage for a while. The traditional routine makes re-entry much easier for everyone. But even so, children will show signs of missing the other parent, signs of withdrawal or of sadness.

"It takes about two weeks," said Cindy confidently, describing her own experience, "for me to get past some of those missing feelings and some of the weird feelings of being in two places at once. Then it's okay." Many children feel that the first year of separation is the hardest, since they must cope with the unknown, the differences between houses, plus missing the other parent and other family members. But school's demands and the excitement make up for a good deal of the emptiness and sense of strangeness.

Younger children do not re-enter as easily as school-age children. They, after all, had concrete expectations of life, and if one parent's routine is rigid while the other's is hang-loose, relocation is a time of bewilderment.

For all parents: Have patience with your children's behavior when they re-enter. Remember they no longer have access to both homes and both parents within one week as they may have had when you all lived in the same city. Long distances between their homes, sometimes with drastically different climates and time zone changes, can disorient them.

Children must face again and again the fact that their parents live very far apart. When they say good-bye to one and hello to the other, they know they may be separated from the other parent for a long time. This is hard for children, but they can handle it. "The only option is not seeing my dad at all," said sixteen-year-old Craig of his situation, in which one parent lived in England and the other in Ohio, "and that is no option at all. I have a Mom and a Dad and that's that." The inconveniences and the discomforts of travel and readjustments are far better than having one parent unavailable altogether or only on a very limited basis.

If you have been communicating regularly with your child while at the other house, re-entry troubles will be smaller for everybody. The more the two homes have been connected by good communications, the less difficult the transition will be.

The concept of two homes is a growing one. As both children and parents adjust and expand to the different circumstances of their lives and the experiences of two homes, many reactions emerge. Children have said such things as, "It hardly bothers me now. I've gotten so used to it, I don't even think about it anymore." "It's neat having two homes so far apart." "I missed my dad at first when I was at school at Mom's house, but he has been seeing me more this year and it's easier."

"I do it because they are my parents and I haven't much choice if I want to be with them," said one twelve-year-old girl. "But I'd like it better if they lived only twenty miles apart instead of two thousand." When I asked her to describe an ideal two-home situation, she and her friend, also with widely separated parents, described homes within easy driving distance where they could be with each parent no less than once a month. "After a month, I get to feeling bad and sad inside and I either have to call my mom or write her a letter before I feel better."

Other children describe a merciful amnesia that blocks out their need for physical contact with the other parent. "I got to missing Dad so much that I was crying a lot and then all of a sudden it was over and I never thought about him anymore—I couldn't even remember what he looked like. Then when I got off the plane and saw him, I cried a lot." For some children the distance continues to be painful, something they have to learn how to live with. Absence cannot continually make the heart grow fonder and more sensitive. Children have few choices when parents move away and they must cope as best they can with the consequences that accompany their parents' decisions.

Both parents and children will meet new experiences, new friends, new ties that can all enrich the child's sense of family and home. Children have an opportunity to become more flexible, to be totally immersed in one life-style when with one parent, without having to give up forever the other parent. Older children often report a growing sense of independence. "You have to be more independent," said one teenager. "There's no hopping on a bus so you can drop by Dad's office and talk a problem over with him at a moment's notice."

Parents report varying degrees of satisfaction with the two-home arrangement. "I don't like it. I'm the one separated from the kids the most. I put up with it and make the best of it, but I don't like it," said thirty-two-year-old Bill. "No matter what anyone says, the parent who has the kid for the school year is the parent who exerts the biggest influence on the child's life. I know that sounds competitive and it probably is, but that's how I feel."

"I like it very much," said thirty-seven-year-old Carole. "I don't have to look at my ex-husband's presence three or four times a month when he comes to pick up the children. In fact, I never have to see him at all. The kids are the ones who have made all the adjustments. I knew they would have to make the biggest sacrifices, and they have, but I think it's the best way for us. We have a better two-home arrangement than we did before because we don't need any personal contact at all."

"I like it." "I don't like it." "It's not what I expected of parenthood, but it is parenthood, nevertheless." There are no easy answers. As with so many of the choices that follow the reorganization of a family, you must consider all the alternatives and choose the best for all of you.

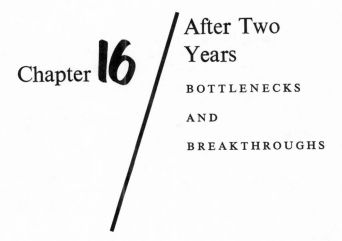

Chapter **16**

After Two Years

BOTTLENECKS

AND

BREAKTHROUGHS

"My divorce had been over and done with for more than two years, what a shock it was to find myself feeling depressed again! On top of it, I now feel hopeless, too. I had made so many changes and had done so well with my life, I don't understand this." The speaker was Sondra, a woman in her thirties, talking openly to a group of women who had come to a "Seasoned Single Parent Seminar" I was holding at a family agency. Other women nodded their heads; more than half of the women present had experienced the same type of feeling. Just when they should be feeling good about the fact that they have made it, they didn't feel good at all.

The Second Wave: Flashbacks

Over the years of working with families, the phenomenon of flashback periods triggered by certain circumstances and events became so predictable that I christened it the second wave. Each flashback contained many of the same feelings and behaviors that had been problematic during the time right after the separation. If parents had yelling sprees during this initial period, they might be tempted to do a repeat performance during a flashback period. If a child was a bedwetter those months after the separation, during a flashback period he may regress to the same behavior.

"How Far Have I Come?"

The second wave of feelings, thoughts, and circumstances has been described by people as a more sophisticated confrontation with the changes that the divorce has brought about. One woman described it this way: "I know I'm surviving and coping now. That's been established. I'm calmer, I'm thinking more clearly, and the intensity of my emotions has finally wound down. Now—without all that extra energy—now I can take a longer look at what's happened and where it's going to take me."

The pace of this second, more measured re-evaluation differs with each individual. Some say this second-wave experience hits them just about the time they get over the crisis months and survival is assured. Others have no clue that this is connected with their divorce at all and attach their feelings to a current situation with their child or with the job. If the counselor asks about the divorce, they dismiss it with, "It was two years ago," or "I'm over all of that." Children too, seem to have these second-wave experiences—sometimes more like delayed reactions to the new adjustments, realizations, awarenesses of how changed their lives have been and may be in the future.

"I'll never again be able to wrap my arms around both my parents at the same time," said twelve-year-old Beth. The true dimensions of the change divorce has brought about are beginning to sink in.

For everyone in the family, the second wave means finally having to face the fact that the parents probably aren't going to reunite. Some hearty optimists hold onto this hope for many years. One teenager, her parents divorced for six years, burst into tears when her father announced his coming marriage to his long-time steady. When her father gently and privately asked her about her feelings, she replied that she liked her intended stepmother, but she had kept hoping secretly that she would have him and her mother again under one roof.

For others, the flash of the singles scene and the promise of new horizons has not worked out as they had hoped. The hours at the job are longer than they realized, advancement slower, and available single companions hard to find. The single life has ended up looking just as complicated as the married life they left. "I've gone through all that hell of the divorce just to get to this," said one angry and hurt woman. "It wasn't worth it."

What Are the Triggers?

Sondra was describing only one of eight or more possible flashback situations. As she talked further, Sondra revealed two more flashbacks happening simultaneously: Her former husband was now making twice as much money as when they were married and he was now seriously dating another woman. The result was not just one flashback, but three. No wonder she felt so depressed!

Here We Go Again: Flashbacks and What Triggers Them

1. A more measured evaluation of the past two or three years, a "What have I done?"
2. The remating or marriage of the other parent.
3. Another child born from the other parent's new union.
4. A change in residence—by either parent—that makes easy access to the children difficult or inconvenient.
5. A change (or threatened change) in where the children will live the majority of the year.
6. Any other major life change—serious illness, job loss, income loss, or even increase, etc.
7. Another divorce or the ending of a major relationship.
8. The reinvolvement of a dropout or pushed-out parent (see Appendix I).

One at a Time or All at Once

The flashbacks often come in sequence. The first flashback may come two or three years after the separation, followed in a year or two by a remarriage and, even later, by a change in residence. But sometimes, these changes come together as they did for Sondra. A common combination of flashbacks is that of a thoughtful re-evaluation produced by the news that the other parent is going to get married again and now wants to have the children for the school year. "Josh's mother said to me, 'I'm getting married and I want Josh to come and live with us for the school year,' " reported Josh's father, Sam. "I couldn't believe how bad I felt. I was scared, angry, hurt, and now I'm depressed. What's wrong with me? I don't want to remarry her and I'm not against Josh living there for the school year." Sam has a heavier task of re-evaluation than Sondra—the remarriage of the former mate is one of the most demanding of the flashbacks.

How Long Does It Last?

Some people take a long weekend and do their re-evaluation in a few days' time. Others never look back and never think about it. The remarriage of a mate means a month-long case of the blues for one person and a good excuse to get loaded for another. The longer you were married, the more children you had together, the longer lasting the different flashbacks seem to be and the more intense the old feeling.

When a person is living a satisfying family and intimate life, a serious relapse into depression or difficulty is less likely. The flashback can often be short-lived, even informative and enriching. But, if the working relationship with the other parent is shaky or nonexistent, if your personal life doesn't meet your hopes, the second wave can rekindle and intensify many of the same problems that proved difficult earlier. Any crisis may bring back old habits, feelings, and fears.

Treatments for Flashbacks

The treatments for the flashback periods are simple: the same ones you used during the first months of separation. Don't be misled by a four- or five-year period of a reasonably peaceful and cordial working relationship. Recurring negative intimacy must be treated by a return to an acquaintance/business relationship.

"But he is such a sneak," a woman might say. "He's been so civil and cordial for five years, and now that he's married he's being sarcastic and snotty. He never changed at all." The dialogue and the intensity of feelings put the two parents back in a form of negative intimacy.

Any friendship with the other parent that may have developed over the quiet years is suspect or discounted during flashback periods. This may be an unfair appraisal. Perhaps after a cooling-off period, parents can regain a more cordial working relationship; during flashbacks, they should strive for business as usual, nothing more.

A Checklist for the Flashback Periods

1. *Your feelings:* You may be going through the same stages of the wounding and healing process as you did at first. The treatments are the same.

2. *Your working relationship with the other parent:* A renewed sense of dislike, hurt, or resentment can flare. Return to the business guidelines.

3. *Communications:* When tales and dubious information from children and friends increase, go back to a scrupulously direct and neutral style.

4. *Your own human needs:* During a flashback, just as during the initial crisis, you need to increase your human income.

5. *That old skeleton notebook:* If you have one from the initial period, take it out and reread your notes to remind you of troublesome, repeating behaviors and feelings.

6. *Your open family:* During flashback periods, friends and close loved ones can restore your equilibrium.

7. *Your old family feeling:* The old family feeling may be resurging. Children may put themselves in the middle; parents may want them there. A sense of the old family comes back. Reach out for your new family feeling for strength.

8. *Taking stock of your life so far:* Use the sprint of energy a flashback can bring to make some changes or bolster up some old ones.

9. *Flashbacks are short:* With the exception of responses to the other parent's remarriage or some drastic residential shift, flashback periods are short. If a flashback period lasts more than one or two weeks, or is particularly intense, then seek some professional consultation. The flashback may be telling you more than you yet know.

10. *Flashbacks recur:* Be alert to how you go through these periods and maybe take notes. You may have them again, and knowing your own reactions and what works best for you is found treasure.

The Second Wave: Bottlenecks and Breakthroughs

Which Values for Your Children?

The second wave can highlight the paradox for parents: Which values do they perpetuate with their children, those of their married days or the new ones of their single period? Many parents become comfortable with the new values concerning their own relationships, sex life, and commitments, but retain former married views for their children. This double standard is difficult for parents and gives children double messages. It says, "Do as I say, not as I do." The double standard often shows up in sexual rules. They hope their children will have dating experiences (without sexual experimentation), court, marry, and never divorce! "I date and have sex," said one mother. "I'm very discreet about it for two reasons. One, I don't want to confuse my children with different partners, but also, I really don't want my children to follow in my footsteps. I want them to get married and live happily ever after, something that I didn't and am not doing." The double standard, single for Mom or Dad and married for the kids, fools no one. If your children marry, they too will face the possibility of divorce. Do you really want them to look at the threat of their own divorces as failed ideals, dreams turned nightmare? Isn't it an important part of your job as a parent to update your own view of family life to include your divorce and your new integrity, one you feel is worthy to pass on to your children? Most parents want to spare their children the pain of divorce. But maintaining a married sexual morality in name only may not be the insurance policy they seek. Instead, their good example of reorganizing their family life, developing their new identity and establishing new family standards can be their children's legacy for their own adult lives with or without a divorce.

Remarriage: Your Own or the Other Parent's

Remarriage, your own or that of the other parent, nearly always unbalances your old working relationships and sets off a flashback period where you eventually reach a new perspective, a new equilibrium.

Remarriage: Yours

Remarriage adds new complexities: yet another family history, family feeling, and as Chapters 2 and 4 explained, a string of expectations for a happy ending, dreams of instant love between stepparents and stepchildren, and a longing to get back to normal.

Your remarriage is not a step back to your old family history, but a step forward to a newer version with its own unique values, customs, and ways. This new family can thrive with a good working relationship or be sabotaged by spiteful former mates and misguided children.

Your remarried family life is different from the single or never-divorced parents in certain important ways. The biological parent and children have had their own long history together, their ways of doing things. When a new mate comes into this picture, standards for personal territory, discipline, chores, and personal attention change. How will they be now? Whose closet space will be reduced, who decides on discipline, who sets the final house rules, who does the dishes, the lawn? Logistically, if both adults have children, there will be times with his, hers, and even their children, and additions to the open family, with new cousins, aunts and uncles, friends, and grandparents. Finances are often tight.

Parenting styles of the newlyweds may be surprisingly different once the couple lives together. A dad with kids in college may now find himself stepdad to a sixth grader. The new spouse may feel guilty that he or she is now spending more time with stepchildren with whom there has been no shared history and no legal responsibility than with his or her own children. The stepparent's role is ambiguous, fraught with old stereotypes, and often dependent on how much authority and autonomy the biological parent will allow.

The kids may wonder: Will the new mate pull his weight, throw it around, compete with them for the parent's affection? Will the new mate become part of the old group or will a whole new grouping emerge?

Most of all, the children fear the threat a new mate poses to their other parent in their second home. Is this new spouse a replacement parent, one who will shut out their other parent? An additional parent, a special adult friend or relative? Loyalty to the other biological parent is evident and new mates who attempt to usurp this bond, instead of forming their own, are often in for a well-deserved rough time.

The biological parents have their share of flack from the kids, too. They must watch while the children may yell at the stepparent, "I don't have to, you're not the boss of me, you're not my real mother (or father)." The children may constantly point out the shortcomings of the new mate, some heartily relishing the character assassination.

Direct communication principles are lost while a child gives Mom or Dad an earful of the new mate's latest transgression, or a new spouse storms about what rotten thing the parent's kid has just done. When distrust gets out of hand the first year, a new family's history can be anything but blissful.

Your remarriage brings on flashbacks for everyone; you, your children, your stepchildren, and the other parents. Everyone may feel a renewed burst of old fears, myths, and feelings. The myths of the evil stepmother, stepfather, and stepchildren can be handy scapegoats for such feelings. Like the broken home, the all-or-nothing trap or the one-home-one-authority myths described in Chapter 2, the malevolent "step" (or second-home parent) can be a conduit for the strong feelings of a reopened, off-the-wall stage. Your two-home arrangement can be endangered and so can your new marriage.

If this sounds depressing, take heart. Your remating can also mean a new family, one that reorganizes itself for your present life, not for your past. Your new family can nurture constructive and creative ways of communicating with one another, of cooperating, and of solving family problems. Even though you may not begin with a long history of shared experiences, you will develop them eventually. "How we always did things" can change to "How will we do them now?" The absence of old shared patterns can mean the emergence of new ones that you now share. Review Chapter 10. Remember the suggestions for groundwork for house and safety rules, for chores? Remember Chapter 13 on easing children's fears, on communications? These can work for you again in your new family.

Your relationship with the other parent is a critical one. To understand this better, read on.

Remarriage: The Other Parent's

The remarriage of the former mate may be one of the most painful and longest-lasting flashbacks of the second wave. You may not want to remarry the former mate, you may not even like him or her very much, but remarriage closes a door on the past in a way that says you have been replaced and your former option to return is gone.

Even when one spouse has been married happily for some time, the news about the remaining spouse's impending marriage brings about surprising inward reactions. "I'd bëen happily married for four years," said a father of two teenagers. "I wanted to be rid of the alimony payments and I wanted the children's mother to be happy. I felt a little guilty that she was alone and I was not. But I didn't expect my reaction when I heard the news of her coming marriage. I didn't like it, and I hated the idea of the children calling anyone but me Dad."

Some people have no conscious reaction to the new marriage, but they catch the flu or are short-tempered for a few days. Other people feel sad, still others are surprised that they have any feelings at all left over for that former lover. Still others find themselves in a full-blown, off-the-wall state, angry, suspicious, hurt, and ready to do battle. This is a bad time to make decisions but the temptation often seems too great to resist.

The idea that remarriage mends the broken home, that the family is now back to normal, the view of one home with all the authority often re-emerges.

"The first one married can get dibs on the kids" is not too far from the truth if the issue were left to some courts of law. One parent may see this as an advantage in the arguments about who should now have the primary residence.

As before, fears about the wicked stepmother/stepfather, or of losing custody or easy access to the children bob up. Worries about changes in agreement and in financial dealings are common. Suspicions arise as the validating blanket of tradition settles on the other parent's married household. The worry about losing the children's love, affection, and loyalty sometimes surfaces. Someone has indeed taken your old places. How complete will this substitution be? Will the children want to be in a traditional home again instead of in your single home? When the parent is unmarried, doubts can arise bringing questions. "Is there something wrong with me because I'm still single?"

The list can be long if the flashback is severe, and an off-the-wall former mate can sometimes successfully sabotage the new union. Conversely, a clever about-to-be-married mate or parent can push old buttons, saying again, "The only thing wrong with the kids is you."

Remarriage can also bring about a shift in the time the newly married couple wants to spend with children. Some never-before-married spouses do not want to spend their weekend time with children who are not their own flesh and blood. While the ethics of such behavior are debatable, when the new spouse says "me or the kids" at a strategic point in time, the two-home arrangement can go into temporary (or permanent) limbo.

Fears around remarriage can be subtle and hidden, but everyone, even the new bride and groom, has them. The danger is that these anxieties will be pinned on the two-home arrangement as a scapegoat instead of tied to the reality of remarriage.

Custody and Money

The months surrounding one parent's remarriage are sometimes punctuated by one or both parents consulting attorneys about protection of rights, changes in custody, child support, and alimony.

Child support payments can become a bone of contention. If the payment is late or not made, the interruption may be blamed on the second-home parent's increased expenses or the new mate's undue influence. Or, if it's the primary-home parent who has remarried, the other parent can be late or absent with payments because of not wanting to contribute to the support of a nonrelated adult. "They bought a new camper with my money," spouted one irate father. "That money isn't going to the kids, it's going into that family pot. I resent it and I'm not sending another dime! Furthermore, I'm not taking the kids to be their baby-sitter anymore either! See how their sweet little love nest thrives on that!" This father calmed down when he and the children's mother adopted the accounting procedure suggested in Chapter 11.

Sometimes parents find that their Parenting Agreement has to be renegotiated. In other cases, entirely new financial arrangements must be worked out. If the question of accountability for child contribution funds becomes a problem, perhaps it needs addressing in a more specific and formal way. When issues of custody and money arise, remember that this is a common flashback reaction to remarriage. Reread the checklist on page 218, review Chapters 7, 8, and 9, and if need be get some outside help. Don't let the flashback emotions get the upper hand. Stick to your business relationship instead.

"What Do I Call You?"

Mom and Dad are magical words, a symbol of honor with a special connotation. Some natural parents do not want to share their titles of "mom" or "dad" with stepparents, and some stepparents don't want to be called by these titles either. In other families, however, the situation is reversed. Children, sensitive to their parents' and stepparents' needs, can call stepparents by either their first names, special nicknames, or Mom or Dad. No one rule will suit everybody.

If you can let your children choose their names for their stepparents (including the title of Mom or Dad) it will be a relief for them. Children seem to find their own names for stepparents more easily if they don't think they have to protect your feelings as a parent or stepparent.

Beware of using the title Mom or Dad as a weapon against the other parent. "I want you to meet the children's new father," said one insensitive mother to her former husband. The natural father told this tale with fresh pain and fear months later. This woman not only hurt her former husband unnecessarily, but put him on the defensive to the point where he considered seriously having their sons live primarily with him lest the stepfather usurp his parental relationship.

Another remarried woman admitted that in her renewed flashback anger after the subsequent remarriage of the other parent she insisted that her children call their stepfather Dad and their natural father by his given name. "I reasoned that 'Daddy' should be reserved for the person who lived with the kids." Fortunately, her resolve was as short-lived as her flashback, and she averted any disastrous consequence.

Finally, children's usage has a good deal to do with their age. Teenagers who see their mother's new mate as a special adult or as a stepfather may call him both Dad and Larry, while little ones will probably stick to Dad or Daddy because, as one stepfather said, "That's what men my size are called."

The Cardinal Guidelines—A Review

You may have one home, but your child has two. Remarriage or re-mating can replace a spouse, but it does not replace a natural parent for the child. Regardless of how pleased and secure the child may be with the in-house stepparent, the child still knows he or she has a natural parent living somewhere else.

A strong two-home arrangement reduces doubts and fears during flashback times. The new stepparent is seen as an additional parent, not as a replacement or a competitor.

A Checklist for Remarriage

1. This time can be a full-blown crisis or it can be just a brief squall. Take good care of yourself in either case and go over (1) the earlier checklists on flashbacks in this chapter. Then, as a protective measure, (2) retake the self-surveys in Chapters 3, 6, 8, and 9. *You may have to take another step away from reborn negative intimacy.* If you do, look at it as a way to further personal growth, not as failure.

2. *Expect issues of custody, support, and authority to be either discussed or reopened.* New discussions and perhaps agreements may be needed and Chapters 7, 8, 9, 10, 11, and 12 should be reviewed.

3. *Reach out and give the other biological parent some reassurances*

that you want the working relationship to continue; that he or she will not be replaced or shut out; that any change can be taken care of in a business-like manner. *Don't take him or her for granted.*

4. *The new mate can help by being sensitive and open with the former spouse.* Listening, comprehending, and staying *off* the defensive and *on* an acquaintance level can save a lot of later misunderstanding.

5. *The new mate can adopt a neutral position with the parents' on-going working relationship.* If you aren't going to help, don't meddle or hinder. Let the two parents make their own arrangements.

6. *Let the stepparents and the biological parents develop their own relationship at their own pace without interference from either other adults or the children.* Let stepparents and children do likewise. It's not uncommon for the mother and stepmother to develop a solid working relationship by themselves—and when it works, it is a true bonus.

7. *Similarly, let stepparents and stepchildren develop their own relationship at their own pace without interference from either the natural parents or other children. This is most important.*

8. *Newlyweds, take time to be alone as a couple.* Try to get at least one weekend alone each month. Sounds impossible? Well, that's where the children's time at their second home comes in. If that doesn't work now, then make it a priority to make other arrangements. You need time alone, not just sometimes, but regularly.

9. *If you are now going through the other parent's remarriage, take time to have your own good times.* The other parent's remarriage is often an inevitable part of the life cycle. Use the energy from this flashback period for your own continued growth.

Another Divorce, Another Ending

What if marriage number two hasn't worked out? When that lover leaves, or a quick-replacement marriage ends, the combined effects of the original divorce and the new separation can be devastating. The second blow may fall on a wound that never healed properly the first time around. The survivor now may have two unfinished endings to deal with—an incredible double whammy of strong feelings, old skeletons, memories, and self-doubts.

"This relationship was going to be the one that was going to last forever," said one woman about her second marriage. "When it began to come apart, I asked, 'How could this be happening to me again?' I hadn't done my review work the first time around. I had tiptoed around my feelings and plunged headlong into this quick-replacement marriage. I dismissed the end of my first marriage as incompatibility, but secretly blamed it all on him. Now a two-time loser, I feel like a total failure. Maybe I

was to blame for the first marriage's failure." This woman's original resistance to dealing with her unfinished emotional business from her first
marriage before remarrying undermined her next relationship and has
caused her present emotional turmoil. Now she has the job of cleaning up
two relationships.

The process of setting the past in order demands its due when important relationships end. If the job is ignored or minimized, it continues
to poke and prod until attention is properly paid, and the wound finally
cleansed of its most major debris.

Some people have few symptoms of the wounding and healing process
of divorce the first time around, but find themselves incapacitated by
the end of their first meaningful love affair. "Breaking up with Ron was
far more difficult than separating from my husband," said one mother of
three teenagers. "I couldn't believe my feelings; they were strong and I
was so hurt and angry." The feelings she had stored up from her original
separation finally came out disguised as sorrow over the end of the second
relationship.

Despite the comfort and companionship of a quick-replacement marriage, such a union has a lot of strikes against it, as the unfinished business from the past can spill over to the new relationship. "I couldn't sleep
on one side of the bed because his former wife had slept there," said one
quick-replacement wife. "He really didn't see or know me, he only knew
what his former wife had been and he didn't want me to be the same. It
was confining, discouraging; even the way I held a coffee cup bugged him."

Many people are attracted to others who have the same characteristics
as former partners, whether in appearance, manners, or bearing. But often
the likeness is more hidden. People are attracted to the same type, and
when the layers of social amenities peel off and the inevitable disagreements arise, it's surprising how the new lover displays the same old dis-
agreeable traits!

By the time a person has experienced a divorce and the ending of an
important love affair, the reaction may be to pull back and be alone for
a while. The desire for companionship may be countered by the still
fresh memory and pain of those past relationships. Consequently, when a
likely acquaintance shows promising signs for a relationship, the reaction
may be one of aversion instead of attraction. "If my marriage had all that
promise and commitment and ended in so much pain, what is to keep
this new relationship from ending up the same way?" If you feel this
way, you might want to look to your open family and your friends for
companionship, forget about romance for a while, and let nature take its
healing course.

A Change in the School-Year Residence

Changes in jobs, health, and personal circumstances often bring about a necessary change in where a child will go to school. When a child changes a primary residence in order to be in one school during a year, a flashback often occurs. This flashback can be short-lived, as seen in Chapter 15, or it can be a full-blown crisis. For example, when a mother's last child at home goes to live the school year with his father, she faces both the life stage adjustment of the empty nest and the flashback legacy of her divorce. This combination can be heavy going.

When a two-home arrangement has been in operation for some time, a parent can switch to the second-home role more easily. The shift feels natural. It is the other parent's turn. "It's Dad's turn" or "Mom's turn" describes the happiest shifts. The change need not become a tragedy or crisis. Even if financial difficulties or a child's behavior initiate a parent's decision to have one or all of the children live with the other parent, don't overemphasize these reasons. Most important, the children have two homes; taking turns is part of the process. When Mom is in debt and temporarily unable to raise a family alone and Dad takes over, calling it "Dad's turn" is still a good idea. Too much focus on the parenting burden makes a child feel like an albatross, whereas a turn is easily understood. Fair is fair.

One of the most successful arrangements sounds strange, but it works. The parents exchange residences and the children (and their schools and friendships) stay put. For example, Mom has had the primary residence for three years, but Dad is going to take over for an indefinite period while Mom sets up a second home for the children. Dad moves in the primary family home with his furniture and things, the children's things stay put, and Mom finds her own place. If Dad brings in his furniture, kitchen equipment, pictures, and memorabilia, it will be his home. Like the children in Chapter 13, parents need personal belongings to bolster their sense of territory. The logistics of these moves hassle the adults, but as one child remarked, "Hooray! We get to stay put while you all do the moving around!" In other cases, the exchange is more traditional and the new second-home parent starts fresh from the ground up.

When a two-home approach is already established, such residence changes do not seem to bring children the old fears of losing one parent while gaining another. If a joint custody arrangement with a satisfactory parenting agreement has been working well, one parent has less fears of being cut out while the other takes over. But because of the soap-opera legacy, a shift like this can raise old myths about one parent abandoning responsibilities. Casual acquaintances and even family members may raise eyebrows, perhaps looking for causes of failure within the parent who is now becoming the second-home parent. Forget them. Your children have two homes and two parents who love and care for them. What more could children ask for in this new world?

"I CAN'T HANDLE HIM, YOU TAKE HIM"   One reason frequently cited when children take a turn at the other parent's house is: "I can't handle him, you take him." Or, "Send her to me, I'll straighten her out." This situation can spell failure for both parent and child.

If this is happening to you and a change in homes for the school year seems the best answer, take a look at your language and the attitude it connotes. "Send him" or "bring him" is not appropriate when a child already has two homes. "I give up, you take him/her" or "You obviously are not effective, let me take over" are all win-lose phrases. Sending a child to a parent's home implies exile, banishment, and failure for both the resident parent doing the sending and the child being sent. Avoid the temptation to wipe your hands of the whole situation. A mother of a six-foot-two-inch son now living with his father still has her second-home responsibilities to her son. Her relationship will go on, and anger, resentment, and fear left over from their stormy past together will not make it less of a relationship. The problems won't dissolve with just the passage of time alone.

TEENAGERS AND DADS   Most parents, married or single, disclose feelings of frustration and inadequacy when discussing teenage behavior. Many teenagers seem to need a close relationship with their father during these years. There are, again, no standard rules on this. "I want to live with Daddy," said a fourteen-year-old girl. "I was five years old when he and Mom were divorced, and I want to see what it's like to wake up a lot of mornings in a row and know that he will be there."

Young teenage boys seem to especially need their fathers, the girls their mothers. Those who feel the separation acutely might even agitate at school or get in trouble trying unconsciously to bring a separated parent more into their lives.

A father responding to a child's need has a special role here. There may have been some extenuating circumstances, such as unruly behavior, that have resulted in the change of residence. But, if there are any leftover emotions of divorce, here is where they can surface. A father might say, "I had to admit I was feeling some secret delight that their mother couldn't handle our son (or daughter) anymore. I knew it would happen sooner or later. You see, he doesn't dare act that way with me. She's always been a pushover." There it is. The new primary-home parent has the old blame game all set up to play again. The other parent failed; he, of course, will succeed. Children know how to play blame games with each parent. Often teenagers will set up perfectly capable mothers to be failures by getting into trouble in order to involve the father. Far too many parents have been labeled as failures who were nothing of the sort. More accurately, these parents were sacrificed by a child who desperately needed his *other* parent.

If you do a change of school-year residence with your child, remember, resist temptation to compete over who is the better parent.

When the emphasis remains on the fact that each parent gets a turn, and that turn-taking is a natural part of life, life can go on as before. Under such forthright conditions, blame games are hard to play and nobody can easily evade responsibilities as a parent or as a child.

Graduations, Weddings, Family Fiestas

Family gatherings are times when an intense, often short-lived flashback may occur. Be prepared for a poignant tug at your heart. A son's wedding or a daughter's graduation are traditional rites of passage. We are all reminded of how quickly life passes, how soon we grow older, how vulnerable our children still seem. Flashbacks from the divorce are quite common at such times, and may add to your deep feelings. Experience the feelings that properly belong to the traditional event. Ignore the past. The child's rite of passage is what should captivate your heart.

"WE WERE ALL THERE—THE OTHER FAMILY, MY FAMILY, THE KIDS, EVERYONE . . ." The rewards of a solid working relationship, or even one that is shaky but resolute, appear concretely at family gatherings such as a child's wedding or graduation. A history of a good working relationship between parents can mean a relaxed and rewarding family celebration together. Or, at the least, a civil containment of tensions enables the child to have the day without the parents' soap opera intruding.

Regardless of how the child's time has been divided over the years of school and summers, the child usually wants both parents there at the grand event, *behaving themselves*. Such events should never be a showcase for parents' unfinished personal business.

Graduation, for example, can include both sets of grandparents, new grandparents from second and third marriages, aunts and uncles, cousins, neighbors, and members of the open families from both Mom's house and Dad's house. The tone of the day is set by the parents' respect for one another and their separate relationships with the children. This mutual respect will give guests and friends a sense of security and guide their own behavior.

When a working relationship has a few years behind it, this respect, no matter if periodically shaken, does grow. The positive changes in the children's behavior and attitudes are usually proof enough for parents that their independent relationships with the children and hands-off policy with the other parent's parenting style and personal life have worked as a sensible solution to parenting after divorce.

This allows parents, when they must, to co-exist at a family fiesta. It even allows the two families to share the planning, the work, and the cost. Some parents spend a few private minutes together sharing the feelings that come with their child's growing up and going out into the world. Some cry together for a few minutes, others speak only in generalities. Whatever works in their ongoing parenting relationship can also be a guide for the party. Some flashback feelings will arise and may be painful. Don't let them spoil either your day or your child's event.

OTHERS TAKE THEIR CUE FROM YOU   Despite the ups and downs of a working relationship, when children are confident enough of their parents' relationship, and proud enough of their two-home life, they often insist on both their parents' active involvement in important occasions. "About four years after Paul and I had developed a working relationship, our son announced he was getting married," said a mother of three. "Paul and I talked about wedding plans the same way we talked about other things in the children's lives. As is our habit, we talk infrequently, come to decisions quickly, and then go our separate ways. We did the wedding the same way. What I didn't expect at all was how delighted all our relatives and old friends were to have a reason to be together again in one place with no sides to take. His parents and my uncle were talking away like old times; old friends were chatting.

"People came up to me and said things like, 'This is wonderful' first with one of us, then with the other. At first I didn't understand what they meant. I came to understand that while Paul and I took our working relationship for granted, there were others who had not. They took their cue from our behavior and relaxed. Our children loved it all, moving between their two families easily. I never expected that the wedding would bring such an unexpected bonus. We all saw how we had healed."

When a set of families survives a shared family event without serious repercussions, an additional dimension of confidence and respect is added to the parents' working relationship and to the children's sense of security. But when a family thrives in it, as this set of families has done, it is an indication of a job well done and a special blessing.

And Thanks for the Memory . . .

Some flashbacks are momentary and unexpected. They are poignant and purgative moments when history demands its due. "I was cleaning out the closet the other day," said Betty, happily remarried for two years, "when out tumbled an old baseball cap of my first husband's. I just found it falling in my hand. I don't know why it was there after six years. I started to cry, cry hard, and think, 'Why couldn't it have worked out?' I don't want to remarry him. I'm very happy in my present marriage. It was just those years together, the kids. I finally said, 'Oh damn,' and then it was over."

Countless times I have heard people tell of such brief but deeply touching flashbacks, bringing a sense of love, of sadness, and of loss. Sometimes it's an outpouring of feelings never before expressed, or of difficulties never admitted. Most people regain their balance within a few minutes and their normal perspective on life in an hour. But the impression lingers, reminding you that you did have a history together.

Such families, and each person in them, know that life's changes can season and strengthen them. Like many people who survive the end of a marriage, they have found that pain is bearable after all.

As one mother said, "I now know from my experience that I can choose to learn from life. I discovered that it was what I learned since the end of my marriage that determined what I did—not other people's opinions, not my memories. I'm not a statistic, I'm a mother, we are a family. If I'm anything, I'm a new-age pioneer."

With parents like this and their families beside them, the American home is not in danger of extinction. These families have not in any way been broken. They have been reorganized, reassessed, and revitalized.

The marriages ended.

The families, and the parents and children in them, continue.

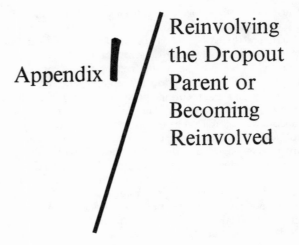

Appendix I / Reinvolving the Dropout Parent or Becoming Reinvolved

"My wife was so unreasonable and possessive that I just gave up trying to see the kids. I figured it was easier on everyone." A number of parents have a deep concern and love for their children but feel they hurt themselves and their offspring by being in the family picture. Some read innumerable articles seeking ways to become again, someday, active parents. For other parents, a parental amnesia appears to block out their children, many making no effort to see their offspring for years at a time.

"My 'ex' has faded away. He pays child support, but he never sees the kids. The children miss him, ask about him. I never made it difficult for him to see the children. I encouraged visitation; he just wouldn't respond." The solo parent often makes statements like this about the other parent's behavior. The only reason seems to be that the absent parent doesn't care. A deep resentment can grow when a mother survives the rapids of parenting alone, holding afloat children suffering the loss of a parent. She finally gets her life together only to have the dropout parent call, announce his new marriage, and expect instant reinvolvement with the children as if nothing had happened. I've heard such mothers say: "Fat chance that ———— has of seeing these kids." "Where does he get off thinking he can use them like some kind of yo-yo's?" (Of course the male is not always the missing parent, and some parents have been pushed out or left behind by a virtual kidnap when Mom or Dad takes off with the kids.)

The reinvolvement process is often a complicated one deserving at least several volumes by itself. It nearly always requires some professional consultation or advice. Commonly there are unsettled issues between the mother and father—often debts around property or child support, bad feelings, and old frozen ways of looking at each other. The complexity weaves itself with anger and hurt resulting from the imbalance and injustice both parties feel. Even parents who say "what is the use" often admit that their apathy overlays anger, hurt, and feelings of revenge.

Custody

The crux of the problem is often the initial award of sole custody. Most often custody has been awarded to the mother. However reasonable she may be, her sole authority has in no way guaranteed the father's relationship with the children. In the end he may feel stripped, defeated. Or he may feel he can parent only at the pleasure (or whim) of the mother. The mother, often unaware of the psychological power of her position, may find that sole custody award a silly reason for his withholding behavior. "I'll give him more authority," she may say. Or even the classic, "All he has to do is ask." The latter is the Captain-May-I? position; you must ask the custodial parent permission for everything, nothing is in your realm of authority. While some see no reason for anyone to be so bullied by laws when it comes to parent-child relationships, the truth is that the loss of legal status is often at the root of the dropout parents' feelings of invalidation, defensiveness, or sense of powerlessness. In my experiences, parents with solid joint custody arrangements don't seem to fade away in the same numbers as do sole custody/visitation parents. It is clear that the more involved parent demands a more equal legal status, but it is also clear that when the law took an all-or-nothing view of authority after divorce, many involved and caring parents were given no options for shared parenting at all.

"The Feelings Can Eat You Alive"

A lopsided custody arrangement is rarely viewed as the root cause of dropout or overburdened parenthood. Instead, the situation is seen more as a personal affront between the parents rather than as a confrontation with the system of values that sets parents up for this all-or-nothing standoff. Consequently, each parent feels a deep injustice that is funneled out as anger toward the other parent. The result is that each parent can have a load of hurt and anger that seems unending. Yet this load must be dumped for good. "The anger and resentment will eat you alive if you don't watch out," said one mother of four teenagers whose father had dropped out. "I have good reason to be angry—no child support, no father for the kids, and no help from the authorities on any count. But you can't let these feelings become a part of you. They will destroy you."

This mother, like countless others whose children have a dropout parent, has gone through the toughest knothole. She knows that she must change her situation for herself and her children regardless of what the law or the other parent does. If this effort results eventually in the re-involvement of that other parent, fine, but if it doesn't, she has still liberated herself from the insidious poison of pervasive bitterness. She can go on to build an open family for herself and her children, one that may include a second home for the kids with a friend or relative.

The sequence of progress should be:

- *First:* Move away from negative intimacy, in your mind, in your heart, and in your actions. Take your children *out* of the middle.
- *Second:* If and when you have dealings with the other parent, make them businesslike.
- *Third:* If he or she doesn't respond within a reasonable amount of time, shift your attention to other good people in your life who will be open and caring about you and the children. You can build two homes with a relative or friend.
- *Fourth:* If the other parent later comes back into the picture, keep an open mind but keep your open family. Your children might end up with it all—the other parent, extra homes with relatives and friends, and an open family!

Where Are You Now?

THE LAUNDRY LIST   Take a careful look at your situation now. Answers to the following questions can be helpful to your self-assessment.

1. What is your overall score on the self-survey in Chapter 3?
2. Look at your individual answers in all the sections in the self-survey in Chapter 3, especially your hot spots.
3. Are you and the other parent free from negative intimacy? (Chapter 8)
4. Do you (or did you) have a businesslike way of dealing with one another and coming to agreements? (Chapters 9 and 11)
5. Is (or was) your communication direct? (Chapter 9)
6. Are (or were) your children kept out of the middle? (Chapters 3, 9, 10, 13)
7. Are (or were) each of you as parents finished with the off-the-wall stage of ending the marriage (Chapter 7) or free from a flashback period? (Chapter 16)
8. Are family and friends avoiding blame games or taking sides? (Chapters 2, 7, 15)
9. Could you identify the hidden agendas of your difficulty with the other parent? (Chapters 3, 8, 9, 12)

What Your Answers Show

Each no answer is an indication that you could reread the chapters given above. You can get some idea as to how and what might be needed to eventually free yourself from the potentially harmful effects of long-term hostilities or neglect.

If you have at least four no answers that need review work, you may need to think seriously of talking to a counselor or therapist about the way the other parent's behavior is affecting your life. A counselor can't pay you child support, but he or she might very well help you find a better way to deal with it. The more answers that suggest reviewing chapters, the more chances you have of being tied into the other parent because of past injustices or negative intimacy. When strong feelings are present, I do not recommend that involvement or reinvolvement be managed alone. It's usually too complex for one person and yields better to a team approach, so see a counselor.

Checklist for Parents

The first steps, your own preparation:

1. Using your laundry list as a guide, reread the suggested chapters.

2. If you are the outside parent, think about the ways you could build a second home. *List ways that don't include the other parent.* Work on your attitude and your rights as a real parent and family. Focus on your home, your decisions alone.

3. If you are the inside parent, think about how you can continue to solidify your own life-style, the new family feeling, and your own family life.

4. If you are the parent with sole custody, ask yourself, would you be willing to give up some of your authority to the other parent? In which areas would you share or divide authority? (Chapters 11 and 12 can be useful here.)

5. If you are the parent with sole custody, seriously consider sending letters to your school, the children's doctors, the clubs your children belong to, or at least talking personally to the professionals there, and give them your permission to give the other parent information and courtesy about the children's progress.

The granting of equal-information privileges by the custodial parent to the other parent is simple (Chapters 10 and 12). It does not give the other parent the right to make decisions for the children, but it does give him or her the right to *know* about the children. The custodial parent has lost nothing, but the other parent can gain a good deal of respect and status as a result. Remember that under most state laws the parent with sole custody usually has total and unquestioned authority in nearly all situations including access to information.

The Big Step—Investigate Joint Custody and Shared Authority

The next step for the parent with custody is to ask yourself how willing you are to give your former mate the title of a joint legal custodial parent instead of a visitor. What would this change really mean to you? Titles are status. A visitor is a person who doesn't belong, who must obey the rules. Being a joint custodian—even if that word "legal" modifies its clout in the real world—is better than and different from being a "visitor."

You might consider joint custody from many angles. You could offer to go all the way to a modification of your previous court order; you could offer it as a sincere gesture of seeking a more balanced scale of power as parents. You could offer and give information, access, and status, but still retain all the legal authority. The more you can give (hoping to work out your shared authority), the greater the risk and the potential benefits.

Often, the inside parent who seeks the other parent's reinvolvement is more than willing to share authority. But the outside parent may not be willing, at least at first. "I'm giving you joint legal custody and I'll put it in writing, too," said one mother. "What do I have to do?" growled the father. "Nothing," she replied, "it's just there if you ever choose to be more involved than you are now." A year later this father returned from his fading status and became a two-home parent. This change was not without the usual ups and downs of a working relationship, but it may never have happened if Mom had not opened the door. Please note that this Mom didn't open the door just to reinvolve Dad. She confessed she wanted to feel that she had done all she could. "If he decides not to take the option, no one can blame me."

The Re-Entry Parent and the Children

Parents who want to re-enter their children's lives need to first contact the parent the children are living with and make an initial attempt at a civil and businesslike conversation. Even if the initial attempt is unsuccessful, a follow-up letter, stating your intent and desire to become an active parent can be sent. Persistence and a show of good faith on your part are important.

Once the first hurdle with the other parent has been passed, you can more safely begin increased contact with the children by phone and letters. If you haven't seen them in years, this should be a gradual process. If your separation has been a matter of months, then your timing will be different. A simple, "I was thinking of you" when contacting the children often suffices. No long explanations are needed at the beginning unless you have had an especially close relationship with the children before and they are able and willing to question you about your absence right away.

Once the children and the other parent have had a chance to get used to more frequent contacts, the actual "visitation" can resume. Sometimes parents religiously stick to the original court order's specifications of designed time. This is a known quantity, a beginning framework. Even if the old agreement was a troublemaker before, it's something that might temporarily work while another short-term schedule is discussed.

Concurrently, the once outside parent can begin to establish the second home. The ground work, house safety rules, and house rules discussed in Chapter 10 need to be done or at least renegotiated. Often just purchasing a sleeping bag and some clothes for the children breaks the logjam of the parents' defeatist attitudes.

There may be tension and distrust. "Is this just a false display of interest? Will my custody be challenged?" a mother might think. "Is my relationship with the children going to be cut off? Will the children be persuaded not to come with me?" a father might wonder.

The first four or five months of a trial period are a time when trust is being re-established, and little by little, pieces of the old puzzle of those past events may fall into place. "Why did you stop calling me?" a child might ask of a parent after four months' absence. Parents need to answer questions for their children, and a review of Chapter 13 can help.

Most children want both parents involved in their lives. The dropout parent who re-enters the picture after several years of silence can often become an active parent again despite the other parent's disbelief and possible resentment. If the former dropout is willing to start from the ground up and rebuild trust and respect with the children, he or she can, in time, establish a second home. If the resentment of the other parent is a continual barrier, perhaps professional counseling can point the ways to a trial parenting agreement. The unfinished business of the past should be put to rest for all concerned. The change, when it works, is worth the time and the effort.

Reactions

When reinvolvement does become a reality, the wonder of watching the past right itself and old wounds heal feels like a miracle. The healing, however, also shows how deep the hurt. There are often unexpected reactions from one or more members of the family. Knowing about what these reactions may be and where they may appear is useful.

The skepticism of friends and family may show itself in distrust or hostility. "I'd just wait and see if he really means it this time." "Where does she get off acting as if nothing happened all those years when she denied him seeing his children?" "I'd never forgive a woman like that." "I'd make him pay dearly for what he's done." Or, "I'm surprised at him even wanting to have her back in the children's lives after all she's done."

Others do not understand the complexities of the inside history. Not even the people directly affected by such a situation understand it completely. A father can feel real guilt when he sees how his children have suffered because of his absence. A mother can feel real remorse when she sees that her behavior denied her children their father. These honest feelings need not take over the show, however; they are there, they can be felt, and you can then get on with a better plan. If you find you have a series of amends to make, perhaps you could begin by saying simply, "I'm sorry it all happened the way it did. What can I do to help make it up?"

The Price of Re-entry—For Both Parents

Part of reinvolvement means paying a re-entry price. This may mean that at some juncture you have to admit that you were wrong. You may see that some of your old behavior or decisions were not wise or generous or benign. You may have badly hurt people, especially your children. You may have yelled "I never want to see you again," and meant it five years ago. But you don't mean it now. One day at a time. One meeting at a time. Reinvolvement usually takes time and happens gradually over months, even years. As one mother said when her children's father became reinvolved in their lives after a two-year absence, "It became clear to me that the natural relationship between the children and their father was just not canceled by the emotions that I had been through with him. The kids needed him, he needed them. I began to see how he needed to feel in order to be a real father. I hadn't given him a chance. I had taken the kids out of state. Why should he support them so far away from him?" When the mother described the end of their first two weeks together in three years, she said, "When I saw John and Lisa with their father it was so clear to me how important they were to one another. It was easier to forget all those times when I needed him to be their father and he wasn't there. I thought, there is another person who is just as responsible as I am for these children. I didn't feel so alone." A year later she said, "Seeing my son with his father is so revealing. They look and act so much alike. I recognize the same dynamics of personality. Now I'm not threatened by the thought that he may want to live with his father some day."

A year later, when the son went to live with his father, the father was delighted. The mother did not see it as an insult to her.

When Reinvolvement Does Not Work: Two Homes
with Friends and Relatives

Not all parents who seek reinvolvement will get it, and not all parents who investigate it will want it. Some mothers with sole custody awards have initially sought consultations for the express purpose of reinvolving the father and then changed their minds when they began to explore what this would actually mean. A few said, "I don't want him to have any authority at all. He should just see them like the agreement says." A few admitted that the baby-sitting was their prime concern. A few more tasted the implications of reinvolvement and decided to think about it more before they made any changes.

On the other side of the coin, fathers who sought reinvolvement were also of various minds. Some had romantic fantasies of freshly scrubbed cherubs who would complete their lives with their love and childlike wonder. These fathers didn't want the children when they were ill, poorly behaved, or cranky. They wanted a form of joint custody that gave them fully one-half of the child's time but wouldn't hire a baby-sitter or make arrangements for after-school care if they were successful. Some still called the other parent their "wife" and still expected that their "wife" would act like their executive secretary.

Like other counterparts in the mother's group, such fathers often were stubbornly competitive and suspicious about any items of authority regarding the children's up-bringing. Often they would say they wouldn't be tied down to any kind of regular schedule for the times the children would be living with them. "I'm not a baby-sitter."

On the surface, such parents do not appear to be candidates for a two-home arrangement. This doesn't mean that a little history behind them or a change of heart wouldn't put them in a more favorable frame of mind, but as of now, the timing is not right and perhaps may never be so.

"If you try hard enough, it will happen" may be a dandy motivator for some things in life, but it doesn't always hold true in building two homes. At some point a parent may simply stop and evaluate the progress to date and conclude that the two-home situation is not going to work. Not now, at least, and maybe not ever.

If two homes—one with you, one with the other biological parent—are not going to work out because of personality, attitude, or other circumstances, turn your attention to the possibilities of a second home with another family, a relative, a friend. Instead of Mom's House, Dad's House, you can eventually build, as Chapter 14 shows, a Mom's House and Aunt Ellen's House or Dad's House and Joan's and Harry's House.

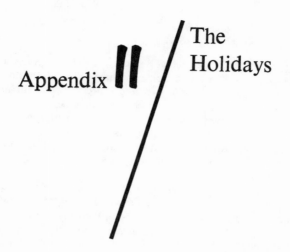

Appendix **11** / The Holidays

Before you talk things over with the other parent, get some idea of what you want yourself, set up alternatives to that plan, and then prepare to be reasonable and flexible. Some parents have details about holidays in their legal agreement, others work plans out every year in personal conversations. In any case, detailed planning is important.

Some Practical Planning Suggestions

1. Consider your hopes for this holiday season—the times with the children, the times without the children. Have several versions, all acceptable to you.

2. Present these alternatives to the other parent. (If you don't communicate well, use the mails.) Give the other parent time to think about your proposals and respond.

3. Try to plan your holiday times well ahead. Two months' notice is not too much.

4. If you talk in person or by phone, follow up your understanding of the conversation with a brief and informal note of confirmation. When emotionally laden post-divorce holidays tangle with practical matters such as dates, plans, expenses, and responsibilities, written confirmation is essential.

5. Be very specific when making plans. Which parent will have the children, which day? For how long? Who will do the transportation? What about transportation costs, etc.? Remember the holiday season is the

perfect time to fan the anger and resentments from the past, to reignite unfinished emotional business.

Sharing the Holidays: Tips from Parents

MOM, DAD, AND THE KIDS ALL UNDER ONE ROOF JUST LIKE OLD TIMES Use this alternative with caution. It is only for the very brave, since parents report that pretending they are reunited again *for the children* often becomes too painful for the adults and a dirty trick on children who harbor hopes for a reconciliation . . . and most children do.

ONE CHILD WITH MOM, THE OTHER WITH DAD   This arrangement also has many drawbacks. Obvious problems of favoritism and rejection surround who chooses which child to be with them. There is also the poignant reality that on the holiday, not only does a family member get to miss the other parent *or* the children, but when the children are split up like this everyone can miss everyone else! Use this option with caution.

ALTERNATING HOLIDAYS   Alternating holidays, where all the children are with Mom for the day (or a week or even more) and then with Dad for the other part of the holiday period, need to be predetermined.

Other parents have a more one-sided arrangement and alternate years. Thanksgiving Day with Dad, Christmas with Mom this year, then reverse for the next year. The children remain perhaps only two days with one parent, and the remaining two weeks of the holiday with the other parent. Still other parents split the day of the holiday: half of the day with Mom, the other half with Dad. There are no hard-and-fast rules. But usually, what one parent is allotted one year, the other parent has the next year.

If your children are old enough to participate in the planning stages, by all means make them part of your discussions and give them a voice in the decision. As in other matters, final responsibility for holiday decisions rests on the adults. Expecting children to make heavy decisions does not produce happy holidays.

Two of Everything

Whatever your decisions on time divisions, update your holiday calendar as well. Consider two Christmases, two Thanksgivings, even two ways to celebrate Chanukah. In short, if it's not your year to have the children with you on Christmas Day, think about celebrating it with all the trimmings on the twenty-first, or on Christmas Eve day. The kids love having two celebrations; it concretely proves they have two homes and helps everyone cement your new family rituals and holiday customs. Few parents are honestly fearful that children will be irreparably spoiled with two celebrations. Usually, they are delighted with the double ritual. Your new family feeling can include a new family calendar to serve your reorganized family, and a new set of family customs updated and blended with your old ones.

Once you have established plans with and without the children, here are some final but important suggestions for you personally.

THE USUAL HOLIDAY QUESTIONS PLUS   After divorce, the slice of children's time and affection is cut thinner than before. "My mother always did dislike the idea that holidays had to be shared with my husband's family as well. Now that we are divorced, she sees even less reason for sharing and I get more flack from her than ever." But even with families where grandparents, uncles, and aunts are more understanding, the slice of time is still smaller. This is one of the prices of divorce.

FEELINGS IN THE PIT OF YOUR STOMACH   When you attend gatherings of friends and family, with or without your children, be prepared for a surprising resurgence of old memories and some wistfulness of feelings. "I was having a mellow time," said Peter, "until I saw my brother lean over and whisper something in his wife's ear and I thought I was going to break down and cry right then and there." A gesture of tenderness between a couple, a child's tugging at a parent's sleeve, just about anything can bring back an old memory at a holiday time.

Being with other couples, families, and friends brings many warm and good feelings. There are exchanges of camaraderie and that sense of continuity so welcome and nourishing at holiday time. But many parents find that it's just too difficult to be around married families, especially when it's their turn to be without the children. Weigh the alternatives and consider having an alternate plan for the day if you fear the togetherness at the relatives' house. Perhaps you can plan something in the evening that is more in the single life-style.

YOUR TURN WITHOUT THE CHILDREN   If you don't want to be or can't be with other relatives or friends on the holiday itself, avoid being completely alone.

Special interest trips for adults only might be just the ticket for you— ski trips, motor trips, sightseeing, something different, a reward for all your hard work. "After all those hectic years of paying bills and punching the clock," said a forty-five-year-old father, "I promised myself a ten-day skiing vacation by myself in December. It was my gift to me and I loved it!"

UNPLANNED VISITS TO THE OTHER HOME   Please don't "surprise" the other parent or the kids. If you are thinking of dropping in on the kids and the other parent, unannounced and uninvited, even if you appear in costume as a Halloween ghost, or Santa Claus bearing gifts, rewrap that thought and put it on the shelf for a couple of years. Your time with the children is your own, and your children's time with the other parent is equally private.

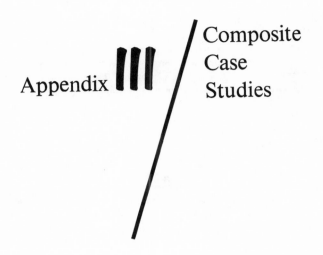

Appendix III / Composite Case Studies

A WORKING RELATIONSHIP WITH FEW PROBLEMS Walter and Selma began with important assets. They had gone through a year of marriage counseling before separation; they were convinced their marriage was finished. Legally, Selma had temporary sole custody of their ten-year-old daughter, Kelly, but she had never interfered with any plans Walter suggested for his and Kelly's time together. Three months after separation, Walter, bewildered and lost, came to a workshop trying to resolve his own feelings of uselessness. He heard other parents without custody talk about humiliation, about their feelings that "the family doesn't need me anymore." He heard them talk about children who yelled at them: "I hate you! Go away!" By contrast, his situation seemed hopeful for the first time.

As Walter explored the two-home approach, he saw things he had done to sabotage himself, his parenthood, and his new life. He realized he had been expecting Selma to design Kelly's (and his) second home instead of taking this on himself. When he began to act and think like a second-home parent, he and Kelly settled into a positive part-time family life that filled Kelly's needs to spend more time with her dad and improved Walter's confidence in his own ability as a parent.

He next turned his attention to the custody and authority questions. He had not questioned the temporary custody order that gave Selma sole custody and Walter visitation rights. He began discussing the two-home idea with Selma. He wanted a joint custody arrangement and some authority with Kelly's schools and music training, shared rights in major decisions, and a long uninterrupted stretch of time with her during the summer. Selma agreed, but wanted Kelly with her during the school year.

The parents negotiated a Parenting Agreement to formalize their shared parenting. When practical, they included Kelly in their talks. Then Walter and Selma gave the final agreement to their attorneys as a stipulated agreement on custody and visitation. They privately decided to review and revise their personal Parenting Agreement each year. (Some parents want such negotiation rights written into the agreement and, in many situations, that is a wise precaution.)

The path was relatively smooth for Walter and Selma, but many parents can't arrive at a working relationship so directly.

ROUGH BEGINNING, SMOOTHER ROAD AHEAD When personal antagonisms between parents remain high, attempts at the establishment of two autonomous households sounds like a wild dream. Both parents may be telling their friends: "Sounds great, but that woman [man] will never agree." When one takes up the idea, the other may back off. The two may never have thought about how to relate as parents after divorce. In such cases, the interested parent doesn't wait, but explores the principles of the new way, adopting new behaviors that increase self-confidence and strengthen family life. Often, when one starts, the other becomes more reasonable after the groundwork is laid. Attitudes change, new respect grows, and a working relationship takes form.

Although Ann and Jerry had been divorced for a year when Ann first came to a seminar about the two-home approach, their three small sons had yet to spend a night with Jerry. Jerry said he loved his sons, but saw them infrequently, mostly only on holidays. Jerry made a comfortable salary, but paid little child support. Ann's full-time job as a secretary provided a marginal existence for the family. At first, Ann assumed that Jerry would be a total loss as a second-home parent.

Like Walter, Ann heard parents without custody talk about how they felt, she began to wonder if Jerry shared their feelings. Did he, like them, feel hurt and humiliated as he waited for his visiting hours with his sons, in the forbidden territory of his former home?

She heard parents say: "I have no parental clout without custody, no dignity, no future, no autonomy." "I'm just a baby-sitter and a source of funds." "Talk about taxation without representation," said one father. "When you don't think you can overthrow the government, you either revolt or get out." Other parents told about staying away in protest or in pain, blaming the other parent for their exile. They rarely telephoned the children or had them spend the night. Ann realized that she and Jerry had never talked openly about the children. Neither had suggested that Jerry take the boys for a weekend. Jerry hadn't offered more money; Ann hadn't asked for it. They were caught in a typical stand-off, with each assuming this was the only way. Underneath, both Ann and Jerry were furious.

Jerry was angry at being a visitor with no rights. He didn't know how to be a nontraditional father. Ann saw his behavior as insensitive, equally insensitive to his sons' need for new shoes and for love.

Ann took a cool look at herself and at the way she was communicating with Jerry. She admitted that she always used bad words about him, out loud and in her head. She had seen him only as the source of needed dollars to pay basic expenses. She had seen him as not caring about his boys. The problems in her approach might be coloring Jerry's behavior and actions. Maybe if she softened her language and her approach, Jerry might act differently. So Ann took a chance. She began to talk with Jerry, even offering to put some tentative agreements in writing "if that will help." She said she thought the boys were old enough to stay overnight with their dad on some regular schedule. Jerry would have full responsibility and authority when the boys were with him. She knew the boys loved and missed him and that he loved them. They still needed their father.

Jerry responded more positively than Ann had expected. He made plans right away to have the boys stay overnight, at first only once every three weeks. After a while, the overnights became weekends, then long weekends of three nights. Jerry became a second-home father more slowly than Walter, but now, three years later, the boys spend their entire summer with Jerry. In a year or two, they may spend the school year with him while Ann takes a turn as a second-home parent.

Over a period of three years, Ann and Jerry changed from being distant and hostile to being coordinate parents, distinguishing parenting from mating. Their children progressed from whining, unhappy boys to sturdy youngsters back on normal growth patterns.

ROAD BLOCKED: WHERE ONE PERSEVERES   The road was far bumpier for Melinda and Bob,* whose hurt and acrimony from the dissolving marriage spilled over into a custody battle involving five lawyers in two states. In a fit of anger, Bob kidnapped their son, took him East, and was charged with child stealing. Six months later, Melinda still had not seen her son. More than twenty thousand dollars in legal fees later, Melinda came to one of my lectures. An exceptionally intelligent woman, she came up to me afterward and asked for everything I had written on the two-home concept. "I've never heard of this before," she said, "but it makes a lot of sense. Maybe Bob would listen."

Mutual friends reached Bob by telephone. He refused to talk, but since Melinda hadn't seen her son for six months, she persisted. Finally, Melinda did talk to Bob. He didn't trust her, didn't think she was sincere about shared parenting and joint custody. Melinda kept trying. She sent him copies of the materials she had obtained from me. She made copies for the attorneys. For eight months, Bob and Melinda talked on the

---

* The case of Melinda and Bob is not a composite and represents a single family situation. Names have been changed.

phone and several times in person. A few times they talked alone, without counselors or lawyers. Little by little they worked out agreements, first about joint custody, then about where their son would live during the school year. From time to time Melinda called me to report progress.

About a year and a half after Melinda first heard of the two-home approach, she and Bob went to court to legalize a joint physical custody arrangement they had decided upon. At first the judge denied their request, not because of any remaining problems between Bob and Melinda, but because the judge had simply never heard of such a working relationship between parents, let alone one in which sex roles seemed to be reversed. Melinda became the parent in residence during summers and all school holidays, while Bob became the school-year parent.

For Melinda and Bob and their son, the ending was, and still is, four years later, a happy one. The son has two real parents who have developed their own style of communication and of adjusting to necessary changes. Recently, Melinda told me: "It has worked out extremely well. I never think about the troubles now. They're so far back in the past."

WORKING RELATIONSHIPS WITH FRIENDS AND FAMILY   All parents—married, single, remarried—can give their children second and third homes by developing a parenting relationship with a relative, close friend, or a friend who is also a single parent.

Denise had three teenagers living with her. Their father had ignored the divorce decree's provisions that the children live with him during the summer and at least one weekend a month and had found a way to reduce his child-support payments to fifty dollars a month. She came to a parents' seminar.

Fathers like Walter would listen wide-eyed when Denise and other women parenting alone talked about the exhaustion of eighteen-hour days, of full-time employment at inadequate pay levels, of inadequate child-support with rarely enough money to meet more than the very basic survival needs. The idea of any help with the housework by domestic workers was out of the reach of all but top-paid professionals (most often male parents with custody). Three jobs in twenty-four hours—child-rearing, a job, running a household—was overwhelming, and statements like "there is no one else but me for the children" were common. Walter had others thought, "Maybe my 'ex' has this situation, too."

Using some of the methods described in this book, Denise began to identify her needs and her resources. Even though she wanted the children's father to take on his responsibility as a father, she first had to take a look at what was sapping her energies in her own life and what could and could not be changed. Denise was dangerously overburdened, but while she knew that she could set the stage for two homes, she could not guarantee by her actions alone that it would actually come about. Denise did have a series of changes she could make totally on her own that would increase her own strength, stabilize her new family life, and release her from feelings of guilt and anger that so sapped her energies and demoralized her and the children. These would also help build two homes. She sought counseling during part of this process.

She, like the other parents, examined her legal agreement and analyzed how she communicated with the other parent, what her feelings were, and how the children responded. She made a series of other self-investigations that gave her important information for her private life as well as for her role as a mother and head of a family. She learned how to keep her cool with the children's father, stopped the drain on her hopes and energies that his irresponsibility had caused, and left the door open for the father's greater involvement. Don did not choose to respond. When a parent gets to this stage of personal development, the communications with the other parent have usually improved, talks have begun, and the children are sensing a new respect in the air between the parents. When a parent feels stronger, the children feel more secure, relaxed. The stage had been set for Don to become an autonomous second-home parent. But he never made his entrance. Denise saw this as his loss.

Denise had done what she could. It had not led to the father's involvement, but it had released her from her overburdened and exhausting life. It was time to turn her energies in other directions. The teenagers could see that their father's absence was his own idea and their loyalties were no longer divided now that their mother's disparaging daily commentary about their dad had stopped. Their· Mom wasn't asking them to choose to pass on demands, and Dad was not there to ask anything.

Families need not be denied the safety and closeness of having extra homes. While this is different from a working relationship between the natural parents, shared parenting with friends or relatives takes thought, effort, and know-how too. Many, if not most of the basic two-home principles apply in these situations as well. When people are willing to experiment and learn, they can set up their own two-home plan, perhaps a Mom's house and Grandpa's house or a Dad's house and Steve and Katie's house. Chapter 14 on the open family describes how solo parents can create this for their own family.

Appendix **IV** / Information for Schools

ANNUALLY

BY PARENTS

This is a form that *all* parents—married, divorced or remarried—can use with their children's schools. It can eliminate guesswork on "who to call" or "who makes decisions" and can encourage more home and school cooperation.

---

1. Please write in the names and phone numbers of the adults who will have dealings with this school this year.

   Natural mother   Name _____ Phone _____
   Natural father   Name _____ Phone _____
   Stepfather   Name _____ Phone _____
   Stepmother   Name _____ Phone _____
   Adult friend   Name _____ Phone _____
   Relative   Name _____ Phone _____
   Guardian   Name _____ Phone _____
   Other   Name _____ Phone _____

2. Please indicate how these adults may be involved with the school by writing their names next to the activity listed below.

   A. The adults below have the following rights and responsibilities with the child:

      Teacher-parent conferences: 1. Name _____
                                           2. Name _____
      Classroom visitations or observations: 1. Name _____
                                           2. Name _____

Emergency release to this adult from the school grounds

1. Name _____
2. Name _____

Adult to contact regarding discipline

1. Name _____
2. Name _____

Adult to contact regarding placement and education matters

1. Name _____
2. Name _____

3. What is your own legal status or relationship to the child you are registering?

Please mark all that apply:

___ I have sole legal custody ___ I have joint legal custody ___ I have joint physical custody

___ I have educational rights specified in my divorce agreement

___ I have a private agreement with the other parent

___ I am a stepparent   ___ I am a legal guardian   ___ I am the natural parent

___ I am the adult the child is now living with

4. Which adult that you have listed can the school release the child to in case of an emergency?

Name _____ Phone _____
Name _____ Phone _____
Name _____ Phone _____

Which adult listed above should be called first if you cannot be reached?

Name _____

Your name _____ Child's name _____

Your address and phone _____ Grade _____

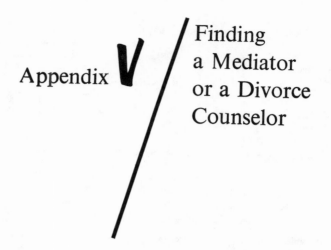

Appendix **V** / Finding
a Mediator
or a Divorce
Counselor

You may write to the following organizations and ask them for members who list mediation or divorce counseling as their specialty or who hold group or workshops for divorcing people.

- American Association of Marriage and Family Therapy, 924 West 9th Street, Upland, California 91786.
- National Organization for Women: Your local chapter may have some divorce counseling services.
- Your county Department of Family and Child Services or conciliation court: They may have some groups you can join or brief counseling services. Increasingly, mediation services are being offered as well in matters of custody or visitation.
- Your nearest junior college, community college, or university may have a continuing education department or an extension division that will run workshops, seminars, or low-cost divorce adjustment groups.
- Your nearest Family Service Agency: There may be groups you can join and brief and long-term counseling services.
- East Coast: Write to the National Institute for Professional Training in Divorce Counseling, 1295 Lenox Circle, N.E., Atlanta, Georgia 30306. Their graduates may be holding groups and workshops in your area.
- West Coast: Write to Center for Legal Psychiatry, 2424 Wilshire Boulevard, Santa Monica, California 90403 for divorce and custody counseling.

- West Coast: Write to Isolina Ricci, The Family Center, 210 Cailfornia Avenue, Suite G, Palo Alto, California 94306, for counseling, mediation, parent groups, and professional training.
- East Coast: Write to the Family Mediation Association, 2380 S.W. 34th Way, Fort Lauderdale, Florida 33312, for the names of trained mediators in your area.
- Call your own county or parish family court. Ask if a local family mediation center exists in your area or if they have a Conciliation Court service.

You may also look in your telephone directory *Yellow Pages* for divorce counselors and mediation services. The American Arbitration Association has branches throughout the United States and can provide names of qualified mediators for domestic matters.

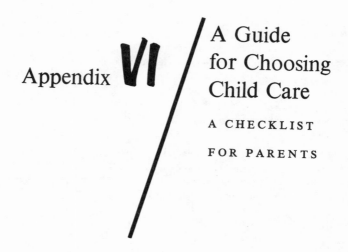

Appendix **VI** / A Guide for Choosing Child Care

The checklist below has been adapted from the San Francisco Child Care Switchboard guides and from my own workshop checklists.

1. *Don't delegate this job.* Visit the day care center, the home of the day-care family, or the home of the sitter who may be coming to your house. Ask yourself one question only: How comfortable do I feel in this setting, with this person? Deep down, do I feel welcome and at home?

2. *Spend at least two to three hours two or three times at the center or home that has made your "finals."* Just stay there with your child(ren) or have the sitter take charge in your home while you are around. Observe:

   a. *The physical setting:* Is it clean, pleasant, with adequate bathrooms, fire exits, safety fixtures? Does it provide good places to play and nap, even in bad weather?

   b. *The program:* Would your child enjoy the activities, learn from them? Notice the basic approach, educational and social. Which takes precedence?

   c. *Meals and snacks:* Are they appealing and healthy? What happens if a child wants something different? More? How much variety is planned?

   d. *Interaction of adults and children:* Do the children seem happy? How does the staff handle discipline? How are children (and parents) greeted?

   e. *Fees and parent participation:* How much? Are there any discounts, any hidden costs? Do you have to pay for absences due to illness or family vacation?

f. *What kind of extended time arrangements have been made for parents* who (regularly or occasionally) will be working past regular closing time? How expensive is this service, and what is expected of your child and you?

g. *Emergency procedures:* What provisions are made for the emergency needs of children?

3. *Ask yourself:*

a. Would my child fit in in this group?

b. Would my child's emotional, social, and learning needs be recognized and developed here?

c. Do I feel comfortable with the style, methods, and philosophy?

d. Will my child be physically safe and comfortable here?

e. Finally, what do my instincts tell me about this place?

For Sitters Who Will Come to Your Home

1. Ask for references and check them out before you spend time talking to any prospective sitter.

2. Ask for information regarding the sitter's emergency procedure if you cannot be reached. (This is especially important if the sitter is a teenager.)

ONCE YOU HAVE MADE YOUR CHOICE

1. Drop in unexpectedly a few times. Do you like what you see and feel?

2. Watch your children. Watch their reactions: their reluctance to go in the morning or a joyful anticipation of the day to come is an important indicator of what is happening during the day while you are away.

3. If problems do develop, don't hesitate to change arrangements. Your kids are worth the time and trouble.

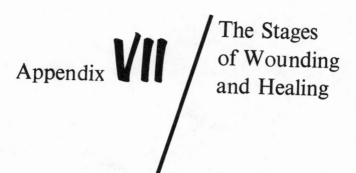

Appendix **VII** / The Stages of Wounding and Healing

ONE: Preseparation	TWO: Separation	Barrier to Three

Future of marriage in doubt
  Uncertainty
  Disappointment
  Anger
  Disbelief
  Anxiety
  Depression
  Hurt
Decision period
  Increased symptoms for person left
  Leaver may feel relief and guilt
	Shock
	Relief
	Denial
	Numbness
		Denial
		Numbness
		Depression
		Apathy
		Guilt
		Shame
		(possibly acting like a lid on strong feelings)

THREE: Off the Wall	**FOUR:** Adult Adolescence	**FIVE:** The Mature Identity and Life-Style
Roller coaster of raw feelings	Reshaping one's identity	Retreat from intimacy complete
Anger	Beginning again as a single	Evaluation of old way complete
Revenge	Changing life-style	Comfort in life-style
Distrust	New friends and social circle	Security and comfort with changes
Resentment		
Disappointment	New parenting style	High self-esteem
Sadness		
Regret	Staking out new territory and status	Settled friendship circle
Balming		
Bitterness		Comfort in parenting style
Competition		
Relief		
Euphoria		
Tenderness		
Integrating old ways with new reality		
Longing		
Taking blame		
Sorrow		
Hopes for reconciliation		

Major Symptoms:

Review work

Strong feelings

Denial (that relationship, way of life or married parenting are over)

Stress

Physical symptoms

Danger Signals:

Accident proneness

Poor judgment

Lowered resistance to illness

Denial of strong emotions

Persistent depression, hopelessness, thoughts of suicide

Persistent thoughts of revenge or violence

Temptation to think the courts can settle feelings

Temptation to make a quick-replacement marriage

Junkie danger, getting hooked on anger, depression, guilt, blame games

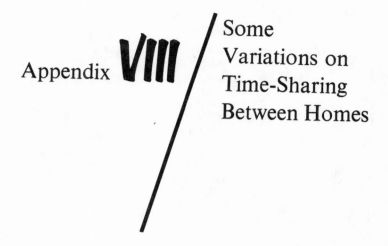

Appendix **VIII** / Some
Variations on
Time-Sharing
Between Homes

1. One primary home where children stay for the school year, with scheduled times to live at the second home during month, (e.g., every weekend, every other weekend). Long stretch of unbroken time (two weeks or more) during the summer spent with the second-home parent.
2. School year at one home, all vacations and holidays at the other home. Works best for parents separated by many miles and where weekend times together during the year are impossible because of distance.
3. Alternating years, with one home as primary residence for one year, and the other home as primary residence for the next year. Parent whose turn it is to be "second-home" parent takes weekends, vacations, and long stretches of unbroken time in the summer—two or three weeks or more—with the children.
4. Alternating six months and six months. Works like the alternating years arrangement above. This can be reduced even to three months and three months. Special "overnights."
5. One month in one home, one month in the other home. At least one weekend with other parent during the time children are in one home.
6. Two weeks and two weeks, one week and one week. Vacation periods are decided by mutual agreement.
7. Three days, four days alternating between homes. Parents decide how weekends will be split between them.
8. Children remain in one home, parents move in and out of the house according to a schedule that works best for the parents.
9. Time between homes is open and children make the decisions as to where they want to be and when. Their decision is up to them and the parent they want to live with next.

Notes

The following works are helpful reviews of the literature. A complete bibliography on the important work done by Judith Wallerstein and Joan B. Kelly (University of California, Berkeley) and by Mavis Heatherington (University of Virginia) can be found in each of the reviews.

Kimboko, Priscilla. "The Impact of Divorce on Children and Their Parents: A Bibliography." Portland State University, National Criminal Justice Educational Development Project, 1978.

Schlesinger, Benjamin. "Children and Divorce: A Selected Review." *Counciliation Courts Review*, September 1977.

Camara, Kathleen; Baker, Octave; and Dayton, Charles. "The Impact of Separation, Divorce and Remarriage on Youth and Families: A Literature Review." American Institute for Research, P.O. Box 1113, Palo Alto, CA 94302, June 1979.

Wallerstein, Judith S., and Kelly, Joan B. "Children and Divorce: A Review." *Social Work* 24:468–475, November 1979.

Heatherington, Mavis. "Divorce, A Child's Perspective." *American Psychologist* October 1979.

For an up-to-date annotated bibliography of ongoing research on divorce, write to Dr. Randal Day, Department of Child Development and Family Relations, South Dakota State University, Brookings, South Dakota 57007.

PREFACE

Most of the conceptual and educational/clinical models presented in this book were developed over the period from 1971 to 1976. Between 1974 and 1977 approximately 1500 parents who attended seminars, workshops, and counseling sessions provided many opportunities to examine the usefulness of these frameworks.

Since 1977, refinements and additions to these models have been made as a result of both the changing needs of parents and families and continuing program evaluation. Parents attending these workshops came voluntarily and are not representative of a cross section of the population.

CHAPTER 1

The first series of structures in the two-home approach is described in "Dispelling the Stereotype of the 'Broken Home' " by Isolina Ricci (1976). The article was adapted from a lecture given at the Los Angeles Conciliation Court in February of 1975. It includes, along with the two-home model, the three-phase chronological view of the divorce process (first two years; the coping years; the mature years); the different types of one-parent families; the critical psychological factors; and the stresses and strengths of families.

Research findings that support the benefits of close and continuing contact of both parents with their children after divorce have been summarized in Heatherington (1979), Camara, Baker, Dayton (1979), and Wallerstein (1979). The study done at Stanford University by Robert D. Hess and Kathleen Camara on preadolescent children (1979) states the following points: "The relationship of the child with each parent appears to be as important in mediating the effects of divorce as the level of conflict between the two parents. . . . After divorce the child's relationship with the father is as important for the child's adjustment as the continuing relationship with the mother. . . . The frequency and amount of contact, however, does not seem to be as important as the nature of the time they spend together. The most successful relationships appear to be those where the father's home is seen as a second residence and where the child is treated as part of the father's family rather than a guest. . . . The children who deal with divorce most easily are those who believe that their parents each continue to love them and who are free to maintain close contact with each parent without becoming involved in the relationship that the parents have with one another." Also see Jacobson (1978), Keshet and Rosenthal (1978), and Jones (1977).

CHAPTER 2

Despite the prevalence of new family structures and forms, a family's reorganization and sense of wholeness is complicated by feelings of incompleteness, guilt, or failure promoted by stereotypes and traditional biases. Perhaps when divorced and remarried families take positive, political stances that identify them as a strong interest group, the new family will obtain a stronger sense of validation. Roman and Haddad (1979), Ricci (1976), Gettleman and Markowitz (1974) discuss some of the stereotypes accompanying divorce and custody, as do Wooley (1979), Folberg and Graham (1979), Bane (1976), Brandwein, Brown, Fox (1974), Eisler (1977), Stack (1976), Bohannan (1970).

CHAPTER 3

I am indebted to Ann Metcalf, Ph.D., who so patiently and expertly made the technical changes in the layout and scoring of this survey so that a reader, unaided by an interviewer or counselor, could wend his way more easily through the seven sections. This self-survey has been used in workshops and private counseling sessions to indicate where parents stand, at one point in time, on a shared parenting arrangement. However, I want to stress that this survey is not a standardized instrument and should not be used as such. It is best used as an impressionistic self-survey and as an interview schedule administered by a professional who seeks to help his client identify strengths and "hot spots."

CHAPTER 4

The diagram "The Houses: From One Home to Two Homes" was rendered by artist Theresa Abramian. It was initially published in Ricci (1976) and was designed by this author to give visual parameters to the characteristics of a family's new reorganizational tasks before, during, and after separation. As with the Ericsonian and Piagetian models of development, successful completion of the tasks of one stage is expected to facilitate satisfactory completion or entrance into later ones. This seven-stage model has been used to organize the other frameworks (as described in later chapters), and has helped provide structure, direction, and a sense of validation. Traditional family life-cycle theory is task oriented, and divorce is usually seen as a disruption of the traditional family cycle. Bohannan (1970) had his seven stages of divorce organized around psychological/social/economic tasks. Also see Chapters 6 and 7 for additional references.

CHAPTER 5

This chapter first appeared in the *Single Parent News* (now called the *Journal of the One Parent Family Community*) as a series of articles begun in December of 1975 under the titles, "Noah Webster, Where Are You Now That We Need You?"; "Some Adults Should Have Their Mouths Washed Out With Soap"; and "Stinkweeds and Roses," later reprinted under the title "A New Language."

CHAPTER 6

The "Human Income" self-survey was originally intended as a supplement to the traditional intake, or initial client interview, process. It has proved useful in discovering coping styles and situational tension generators. When clients are asked to explain each rating it becomes diagnostically useful in designing treatment plans. As a self-help, it can heighten personal awareness of stress or "income" points and suggest behavior. Since 1977 it has been used by an increasing number of counseling or social welfare agencies and private practitioners as part of their intake procedure. For further readings on the subject of stress, see Holmes and Rahe, "The Social Readjustment Rating Scale," *Journal of Psychosomatic Research* 11:213–218, 1967; and McQuade and Aikman (1974) for a general resource text suitable for both parents and professionals. The "Ten Basic Rules" were compiled by this author in response to requests for simple-to-use reminders for maintaining balance and perspective during rapid and drastic change.

CHAPTER 7

The initial framework for this model was developed in collaboration with Lorraine Sanchez, RN, MN, during the years 1969 to 1973 and was based on the literature on loss and crisis intervention. It was first used with private groups of women undergoing multiple role changes and in individual counseling sessions. This model was called "the dynamics of loss," then "the divorce virus" (in an attempt to identify for the client a metaphor that promised stages and recovery), and finally "the emotions of divorce," with an attendant metaphor of a wound that needs cleaning, care, and attention in order to heal properly. The "adult adolescence" concept was first presented at a lecture series on Human Development at Pacific Oaks College in the fall of 1973. The use of the metaphor has been especially important in working with parents, in that past known experiences generalize more easily to the unknown of the present when a metaphoric parallel identifies the familiar structural components contained in the new, often normless, circumstance. Hence the use of familiar terms such as "junkie," "off-the-wall," and "adult adolescence."

The grief and mourning framework devised by Mel Krantzler (1973) was an important supportive influence. Other adaptations of the loss model by clinicians can be found in Levine (1974) and Wiseman (1975). For a recent review of the literature, including citations on the classic works such as Parad and Caplan, Lindemann, and Kübler-Ross, see Rosenbaum and Beebe (1975). For an in-depth look at marital separation see Weiss (1975), and for a survey of therapists' views on the process of divorce, see Dressel and Deutsch (1977).

CHAPTER 8

The first model on human relationships was developed by the author in 1975 after direct observation in clinical and educational settings. This observation showed that (1) parents often lacked the simplest information on differences in relationships, especially role boundaries after separation, and (2) parents who achieved relatively workable visitation and negotiation arrangements had different interaction patterns from those who did not. The model on human relationships served three purposes. It identified simple role boundaries for individual and interactional behavior; it allowed for the "retreat" concept, which incorporated the observed behavior of successful relationships after divorce; and it gave a label to ongoing hostile behavior, identifying it as intimacy and attachment. The full model is more complicated than the one illustrated in this volume. The business relationship concept grew out of the relationship model and has been steadily refined and re-evaluated over the past five years. The self-survey, "Move Away from Intimacy" was designed as a self-teaching tool, but it has proved useful in intake procedures and in designing treatment plans.

CHAPTER 9

The principles of an effective business relationship which can apply to a parental working relationship are more complex than those represented here. However, a clinician or educator can use the simplified material in Chapters 8, 9, and 10 as a foundation for group discussions on contrasts and comparisons between "business" and "parent business" where stakes are very high.

The concept of separate territories, independence, and autonomy was one of the earliest of the two-home ground rules, and its continual ability to ease tensions and foster respect encouraged a closer look at the components of the independent parent-child relationship. Initially, parental noninterference was part of the "second-home" section of our workshops and included other aspects of how to set up the "second-home" (see Chapter 11). The communication principles isolated for this chapter were selected because of the often appalling misinformation that contaminates parent-child, parent-parent, and parent-professional communications after divorce. For a general resource on communication for parents and professionals see Wahlroos, cited in the notes for Chapter 13.

CHAPTER 10

George Holland, Ph.D., gave the first workshop address at UCLA Extension for fathers without custody in 1974 and continued through 1976. He coined the term "second-home parent" and developed many of the basic concepts dealing with the differences between parents with custody, notably the "dropout" and the "visitor."

Division of time between homes is also discussed in Wooley (1979) and Galper (1978). Contact with other adults in your child's life at school is further described in Ricci (1979, 1980). Appendix IV has a form parents can use with the school. Also, the National Committee for Citizens in Education is completing a study on single parents and the schools. For more information write to Phyllis L. Clay, Suite 410, Wilde Lake Village Green, Columbia, Maryland 21044.

Some schools are instituting peer group meetings for children who have experienced divorce or some serious loss. If the group is sensitively led by an experienced professional and is focused on life changes, of which divorce is one, it can be extremely helpful for children and teens experiencing the discontinuity and ambiguity that divorce often brings to their family life.

CHAPTER 11

The material in this chapter was developed by the author as an aid in mediation of parenting agreements (see Chapter 12) and was later adapted and enlarged as formats and instructions for teaching parents how to negotiate their own agreements. At present, these techniques are being taught to parents after the basic series of models has been presented.

CHAPTER 12

I am grateful to attorneys Michael Flicker of Palo Alto, California, and Harry Peck of Milwaukee, Wisconsin, for their review of and suggestions for this chapter. The first parenting agreement was drafted in 1975 and profited from the suggestions of Los Angeles attorney Barbara Warner Blehr. It was she who first used the terms "primary residence" and "secondary residence" along with joint custody terms. The preamble to the parenting agreement was the result of a lengthy discussion with my UCLA graduate class for professionals in the fall of 1975 and owes much to the contribution of Meyer Elkin, then Director of the Los Angeles Conciliation Court. This same class provided the nucleus for the charter of the Los Angeles Council for Families in Transition and included lawyers; church leaders; social workers; members of the Los Angeles and Santa Monica Conciliation Courts, YMCA, and YWCA; and community leaders.

A comprehensive review of the issues in joint custody can be found in Folberg and Graham (1979). Also see Elkin (1978), Foster and Freed (1978), and Roman (1978). The legal view of private bargaining between parents can be found in Mnookin (1979). Meehan (1980) provides information on the child's view of a custody dispute.

CHAPTER 13

Parents can choose a series of articles or books on the subject of children and divorce. The following is only a partial list of what is available.

Gardner, Richard A. *The Boys and Girls Book About Divorce.* New York: Bantam Books, 1970. (For children.)

Gardner, Richard A. *The Parents' Book About Divorce.* New York: Doubleday, 1977.

LeShan, Eda. *What's Going to Happen to Me: When Parents Separate or Divorce.* New York: Four Winds Press, 1978. (For children.)

Ricci, Isolina. *Divorce and Remarried Parenting.* YMCA Communications Skill Center, 3248 Alpine Road, Menlo Park, CA 94025. (For parents and teens.)

Richards, Arlene, and Willis, Irene. *How to Get It Together When Your Parents Are Coming Apart.* New York: McKay Company, 1976. (For teens.)

Salk, Dr. Lee. *What Every Child Would Like Parents to Know About Divorce.*
New York: Harper and Row, 1978. (For parents.)

Wahlroos, Sven. *Family Communication: 20 Rules to Improve Communications and Make Your Relationships More Loving, Supportive, Enlightening.*
New York: Macmillan, 1974 and Signet, 1976 (For parents and teens.)

CHAPTER 14

From the beginning of our classes and workshops a major objective has been to promote supportive groups among parents and children. This belief in social networks came about as a result of my work with the grass-roots groups of the Christian Family movement (1960 to 1970), my research on marriage (Ricci-Firstman, 1968) and later research and observation work on role changes during divorce (1969 to 1973). A UCLA Extension series, "The One Parent Family Community" (1976) focused specifically on this objective, as did *The Single Parent News,* edited by Art Herman. Mr. Herman was successful in creating a network of people concerned about the impact of divorce on children, adults, and the community at large. He was also a member of the U.C.L.A. workshop and seminar faculty. Over the past four years anthropologist Ann Metcalf, Ph.D., has conducted research on social networks in extended families in 1979, 1980. This chapter was greatly enhanced by her suggestions and contributions. She can be reached at The Institute For Scientific Analysis, 1940 B Bonita Street, Berkeley, CA 94707.

CHAPTER 15

This material grew out of the "second-home" module and rapidly became a special area unto itself, involving, as it does, many of the heavily charged emotional aspects of the original feelings in divorce and the need for rigorous communications between parent and child separated by many miles. The first parental reaction to long distances had some defensive elements, e.g., how to make the best of a bad situation. This quickly yielded to a more positive and action-oriented view of what seems to be an increasingly prevalent family life style.

CHAPTER 16

The "flashback" phenomenon of the second wave of emotions was observed in 1975 and incorporated into the teaching and clinical models in 1976. The subsequent refinement of the second-wave theory has been a most useful conceptual framework for educating parents and professionals on the consequences and subsequent emotional responses that can threaten previously settled relationships or agreements.

For further readings on step-parenting and remarriage see Visher and Visher (1979), *The Stepfamily Bulletin,* Jackson Hill Road, Chittenango, New York 13037. You can also write to the Consumer Information Center, Dept. 111H, Pueblo CO 81009 for their booklet "Yours, Mine and Ours," ($1.30).

Bibliography

Ahrons, Constance. "The Co-Parental Divorce; Preliminary Research Findings and Policy Implications." Unpublished paper presented at the annual meeting of the National Council on Family Relations, Philadelphia, Pennsylvania, October 1978.

Bane, Mary Jo. "Marital Disruption and the Lives of Children." *Journal of Social Issues* 32(1):103–118, 1976.

Bane, Mary Jo. *Here to Stay: American Families in the Twentieth Century.* New York: Basic Books, 1976.

Bohannan, Paul (ed.). *Divorce and After.* New York: Doubleday, 1970.

Brandwein, Ruth A.; Brown, Carole; and Fox, Elizabeth M. "Women and Children Last: The Social Situation of Divorced Mothers and Their Families." *Journal of Marriage and the Family* 36: 498–515.

Burch, Carole. "Making Visitation Work: Dual Parenting Orders. *Family Advocate* 1: 22, 1978.

Dressel, K., and Deutsch, M. "Divorce Therapy: An In-depth Survey of Therapists' Views." *Family Process,* December 1977.

Eisler, Riane Tennenhais. *Dissolution: No-Fault Divorce, Marriage and the Future of Women.* New York: McGraw-Hill, 1977.

Elkin, Meyer. "Reflections on Joint Custody and Family Law." *Conciliation Courts Review* 16(3), December 1978.

Folberg, H. Jay, and Graham, Marva. "Joint Custody of Children Following Divorce." *U.C.D. Law Review* 12(2), Summer 1979.

Foster, Henry H., and Freed, Doris. "Joint Custody—A Viable Alternative." *New York Law Journal,* November 9, 1978; November 24, 1978; December 22, 1978.

Galper, Miriam. *Co-Parenting: A Source Book for the Separated or Divorced Family.* Philadelphia: Running Press, 1978, p. 155.

Gettleman, S., and Markowitz, J. *The Courage to Divorce.* New York: Simon and Schuster, 1974.

Goldstein, Joseph; Freud, Anna; and Solnit, Albert J. *Beyond the Best Interest of the Child.* New York: Free Press, 1973.

Grote, Douglas F., and Weinstein, Jeffrey P. "Joint Custody: A Viable and Ideal Alternative." *Journal of Divorce,* Fall 1977, pp. 43–53.

Heatherington, Elizabeth M. "Divorced Fathers." *The Family Coordinator* 25: 417–428, 1976.

Hess, Robert D., and Camara, Kathleen A. *Family Relationships After Divorce and Their Effects Upon the Behavior of Preadolescent Children.* Stanford University, School of Education, April 1979.

Jacobson, Doris. "The Impact of Marital Separation/Divorce on Children: Parent-Child Separation and Child Adjustment." *Journal of Divorce* 4: 341, 1978.

Joint Custody: A Handbook for Judges, Lawyers and Counselors. Published by Association of Family Conciliation Courts, May 1979.

Jones, Nolan F. "The Impact of Divorce on Children." *Conciliation Courts Review* 15(2) December 1977.

Kelly, J. B., and Wallerstein, J. S. "Four years later: Children and adolescents reflect on their parents who are divorced." Paper read at the biennial meeting of the Society for Research in Child Development, San Francisco, 1979.

Keshet, H. F., and Rosenthal, K. M. Fathering after marital separation. *Social Work* 23(1): 11–18, 1978.

Knight, Lucy. "Who Has Access to School Records." *American Education,* United States Department of Health, Education and Welfare, Office of Education, June 1977.

Krantzler, Mel. *Creative Divorce.* New York: M. Evans, 1973.

Levine, Marcia W. "New Family Structures: Challenges to Family Casework." *Journal of Jewish Communal Service* 1(3), Spring 1974.

McQuade, Walter, and Aikman, Ann. *Stress.* New York: E. P. Dutton and Company, 1974.

Meehan, Susan. "Children and Divorce: Contested Custody and the Courts." Paper presented at the annual meeting of the American Educational Research Association in Boston, Massachusetts, April 1980.

Metcalf, Ann. "Family Reunion: Networks and Treatment in a Native American Community." *Group Psychotherapy, Psychodrama and Sociometry* 32: 179–189, 1979.

Metcalf, Ann, *With A Little Help from My Friends: Social Networks in Single Mother Families.* San Francisco: Scientific Analysis Corporation, 1980.

Mnookin, Robert, and Kornhauser, Lewis. "Private Bargaining in the Shadow of the Law: A Framework for the Analysis of the Impact of Rules and Procedures on the Distributional Consequences of Separation and Divorce." *The Yale Law Journal* 88: 950, 1979.

Ricci-Firstman, Isolina; Lane, Ralph, Jr.; Sanchez, Lorraine P.; and Westland, Ronald A. *A Study on Catholic Marriage in the United States.* San Francisco: Marriage and Family Research Project, Urban Life Institute, University of San Francisco, 1968.

266   BIBLIOGRAPHY

Ricci, Isolina. "Primary Communities Among Middle Class Americans: Towards an Analysis of an Emerging Phenomenon." *Marriage and Family Counselors Quarterly* 9: 1–11, 1974. Presented at Pacific Sociological Association Meetings, San Jose, March 1974, and based on a Master's Thesis, Pacific Oaks College, 1973.

Ricci, Isolina, "Dispelling the Stereotype of the 'Broken Home.' " *Conciliation Courts Review*, 12: 7–14, 1976.

Ricci, Isolina. Series of Articles on Language and the Single Parent. *Single Parent News*, 1975, 1976, 1977.

Ricci, Isolina. "Divorce, Remarriage and the Schools." *Kappan*, March 1979, 509–511.

Ricci, Isolina. "Child Custody, Right of Privacy and Educational Policy." Presented at American Educational Research Association Meetings, Boston, April 1980.

Roman, Mel, and Haddad, William. *The Disposable Parent*. New York: Holt, Rinehart & Winston, 1978.

Rosenbaum, C. Peter, and Beebe, John E. *Psychiatric Treatment: Crisis/Clinic/Consultation*. New York: McGraw-Hill, 1975.

Schlesinger, B. "Children and Divorce: A Selected Review." *Conciliation Courts Review*, September 1977.

Stack, M. "Who Owns the Child?" *Social Problems* 23: 505, 506, 1976.

Visher, Emily B., and John S. *Stepfamilies: A Guide to Working with Stepfamilies and Stepchildren*. New York: Brunner/Mazel, 1979.

Wallerstein, Judith S., and Kelly, J. B. "The Effects of Parental Influence: Experiences of the Child in Later Latency." *American Journal of Orthopsychiatry* 46: 256–269, 1976.

Weiss, R. S., *Marital Separation*. New York: Basic Books, 1975.

Wiseman, Reva S. "Crisis Theory and the Process of Divorce." *Social Casework*, April 1975.

Wooley, Persia. *The Custody Handbook*. New York: Summit Books, 1979.

Index